Jesus and Human Conflict

JESUS
AND
HUMAN CONFLICT

HENRY A. FAST

HERALD PRESS
SCOTTDALE, PENNSYLVANIA

*Copyright © 1959 by Herald Press, Scottdale, Pennsylvania
Library of Congress Catalogue Card Number: 58-10305
Printed in the United States of America*

Contents

I. INTRODUCTION	1
II. RESIST NOT . . . TURN THE OTHER CHEEK	5
Context in the Sermon on the Mount	5
Exegesis of the Passage	6
The Formula: "Ye have heard"	7
The Antithesis: "An eye for an eye"	7
A Case of Violent Insult	14
Let Him Have the Cloak	18
Go the Second Mile	24
Give to Him That Asks	28
The Meaning of the Passage as a Unit	33
III. INSIGHTS FROM THE OLD TESTAMENT AND CONTEMPORARY JEWISH LITERATURE	39
Relevant Teachings in the Old Testament	39
Illustrations from Contemporary Jewish Literature	43
The Apocrypha	43
Rabbinical Literature	45
Summary	50
IV. JESUS AND THE REVOLUTIONARY MOVEMENT OF HIS TIME	53
The Revolutionary Movement	53
The "Fourth Philosophy"	56
The Zealot Movement	58
Summary	61
Possible Points of Contact with the Revolutionary Movement in the Gospels	63

Simon the Zealot	63
The Arrest and Execution of John the Baptist	63
The Insurrection Under Barabbas	66
The Massacre of the Galileans by Pilate	68
The Two Swords Among the Disciples	69
"The Kingdom of Heaven Suffereth Violence . . ."	73
Summary	74
Jesus' Connection with the Revolutionary Movement	75
Jesus and Herod	76
Jesus and Roman Rule	77
Possible Political Relations of Jesus' Conception of the Kingdom	78
Summary	90
V. PASSAGES APPARENTLY JUSTIFYING THE USE OF FORCE	93
Following Jesus Brings Dissension	93
Not Peace but a Sword	93
Hate Father and Mother	94
Woes Against the Pharisees and Scribes	95
Jesus Expected Wars	96
Sayings Emphasizing the Value of Being Prepared	102
Buy a Sword	102
The Strong Man Fully Armed	105
Not Allow the Thief to Break into the House	106
The King Going to War and Taking Counsel	107
Passages Implying That Violence Is Justified Under Certain Circumstances	108
Jesus Commended a Roman Army Officer	110
Jesus Advocated Obedience to Authority	111
Jesus Demanded Self-Sacrifice in Defense of Values More Important Than Life	114
God Uses Force in Punishment	116

The Cleansing of the Temple	119
Summary	120
VI. PASSAGES EMPHASIZING LOVE AND NONRESISTANCE	124
Jesus Rejected the Principles of Compromise with Evil	124
Jesus Praised the Nonviolent Spirit	125
He Mourns	127
He Is Meek	127
He Hungers and Thirsts After Righteousness	128
He Is Merciful	128
He Is Pure in Heart	129
He Is a Peacemaker	130
He Is Persecuted	132
Jesus Exhorted Men to Live Peaceful Lives	133
Men to Love Their Neighbors as Themselves	137
Love Your Enemies	144
Other Sayings Presupposing This Spirit of Love	150
Jesus Forbade What Was Inconsistent with the Principle of Love	159
Jesus Forbade a Spirit of Faultfinding	159
Jesus Disallowed the Taking of Human Life	161
Jesus Forbade Anger and Scorn	163
Jesus Forbade Attempted Killing of Another	166
Jesus Disallowed Reprisals	170
Jesus Warned Against Covetousness	170
Jesus Called for Conciliation in Disputes	174
Jesus' Own Example Offers Reinforcement	176
Jesus Disregarding the Barriers of Racial and National Prejudice	176
Jesus Treated Outcast Groups with Respect and Regard	176
Jesus' Triumphal Entry Was a Peaceful Gesture	178

Jesus Went to the Cross Nonresisting	180
Jesus Accepted the Cross from Choice	181
Jesus Forgave His Enemies	183
Jesus' Conception of God as Father the Ultimate Basis for His Teaching on Love and Nonresistance	183
VII. SUMMARY AND CONCLUSION	191
The Nonresistance Passage	191
Teachings Supplementing the Passage	196
Teachings Qualifying the Passage	198
The Place of the Principle of Nonresistance in the Teaching of Jesus	202
Bibliography	207

1

Introduction

Few sayings of Jesus have been as perplexing to Christian people through the centuries as those dealing with the principle of nonresistance. The demand of Jesus appears so absolute and unqualified. It does not seem to take into account many important problems of practical ethics.

It is not surprising under these circumstances that interpretations of these passages vary greatly. Occasionally someone questions whether these are genuine sayings of Jesus, but that isn't the real source of controversy. The real controversy centers primarily in the question whether this teaching is practical in a world like ours, whether Jesus really meant what He said, whether in this instance He didn't go too far, and whether in the interest of "realism" and in the light of other Biblical teachings His words must not be qualified.

Christian thinkers and leaders, believing in the trustworthiness of Jesus and His words, who are striving to be true to His teaching and spirit, have offered various explanations which they believe take account of the practical difficulties of obedience to this particular teaching.

Some people simply insist that Jesus meant these words to be taken literally and that settles all questions for them.

Others again claim these sayings are little more than "prudential maxims," i.e., shrewd observations about human relations similar in character and purpose to the wise counsel of the Book of Proverbs and similarly to be interpreted and applied.

Still others have called them "counsels of perfection" applicable in an ideal society but not intended for literal application in an imperfect society.

Some scholars have grouped these sayings with others whose character they claim was determined by Jesus' expectation of the imminent overthrow of the present world order and the early establishment of the kingdom. They were intended to serve only as an interim ethic. These scholars claim Jesus made such extreme and unqualified demands because of the urgency of the shortness of time until the kingdom would burst upon man. Had Jesus expected a long interim, these sayings would certainly have been qualified to suit the requirements of the longer period of history.

Another group of people with a somewhat different approach assert that teachings like these and others, particularly in the Sermon on the Mount, do not concern us but were meant for another dispensation. They were meant for the millennium when in a perfect society these sayings would find perfect and literal application.

Christian peace groups generally insist that these sayings clearly forbid all participation in military training and war. Other Christian groups maintain that Jesus nowhere concerns Himself with the institution of war or with the attitude of His followers in the event of an international conflict. They hold that Jesus concerns Himself only with the proper attitude and conduct of men in their personal relationships. Some, like Tolstoy, have made this the very center of Jesus' ethic; others have relegated it to the outer periphery of His teaching.

To discover, if possible, where in all this controversial area lies the real truth of the position of Jesus as portrayed in the Gospels and what was the real purpose and the full scope, meaning, and implication of the principle proclaimed is the main purpose of this book.

This investigation begins with a study of the primary passage from which the term "nonresistance" gets its name, namely, Matthew 5:38-42 and the parallels in Luke 6:29, 30. Ultimately, however, the study must include the whole of the life and teaching of Jesus in order that one may get a clear understanding of this principle by seeing it in its true perspective. After all, the Gospels do not give merely a collection of sayings and maxims. They present the picture of a matchless personality as He lived with men, served them, and taught them. He was Son of God and Saviour of men. He is the key to His teaching. We may not separate the message of Jesus from His life, death, and resurrection if it is to be understood truly. They form an organic whole in the Gospels; hence to separate His teaching from His person is to devitalize both and to fail to understand either. His life is the natural expression of His message, and His message is needed to reveal the deeper movings of His Spirit. His attitude and teaching on nonresistance can therefore not be understood correctly or fully except against the background of the whole of His own life and spirit. Our basic task therefore is to understand Jesus.

In this attempt to understand Jesus it is well to remember at the outset that Jesus was more than a teacher of ethics. His primary purpose was not to give men a new code of conduct—better, more perfect, and more complete—and urge them to a more perfect obedience to this new code. His primary call to men was a call to a great surrender. "The kingdom of God is at hand: repent ye, and believe the gospel" (Mark 1:15). This was the first message of His ministry according to Mark and this always remained His primary call to men and His great central concern. Men were to respond in love with all the resources of their being to the abounding goodness and love of God the Father. Out of this dynamic personal relation to God would flow God-pleasing life and conduct, needed guidance, right relations of justice and love to fellow men. Through this dynamic personal relationship to God there would also become available to man the power that would make realization of the good life possible. We are here stating somewhat in advance what we hope will become more clear and be recognized as valid in the discussion that follows.

The term "nonresistance," used frequently throughout the book, is not altogether satisfactory. It seems to imply in advance what is really first to be investigated. Nor is it a true reflection of the meaning of the Scripture passage commonly designated by this term. It is retained in this discussion chiefly because it indicates more clearly than any other term the controversial area which we propose to investigate; and because in some circles through long use it has come to stand for a certain way of life deeply rooted in great moral-religious convictions.

In this study we shall begin with a careful analysis and explanation of the primary passage in Matthew and Luke and then supplement it by referring to some of the higher ethical teachings of the Old Testament, and of later Judaism. In the chapters following we shall carefully examine the revolutionary activity prevalent in the time of Jesus together with such portions of the Gospels as appear to have a political reference for the purpose of discovering, if possible, what relation Jesus had with the political situation of the time.

We shall likewise study a large number of related passages, some of which appear to justify resistance and the use of force, and some that appear to reinforce the teaching of Matthew 5:38-42 and its parallel in Luke. The concluding chapter is an attempt to give a comprehensive summary of our findings.

2

Resist Not ... Turn the Other Cheek*

(Integrated as the problem of Retaliation)

CONTEXT IN THE SERMON ON THE MOUNT

The term "nonresistance" is derived from Matthew 5:38-42, in particular the words "resist not him that is evil." It is therefore important that our study begin with an examination of this primary passage together with its Lucan parallel.

In Matthew this passage is found in the Sermon on the Mount, while in Luke it is found in a much shorter Sermon on the Plain. The central theme running through this "Sermon" as recorded in Matthew is the kingdom of God, the character of its citizens and its higher righteousness. (Matthew uses the term "kingdom of heaven" perhaps out of a sensitive regard for the feelings of his Jewish Christian readers.)

It is not without significance that Jesus begins this discourse by calling blessed the poor in spirit and assuring them that the kingdom of heaven is theirs. Goodspeed translates: "Blessed are those who feel their spiritual need...."[1] They are blessed because they know how dependent they are on God for everything needful and good and so they earnestly seek God's presence in their lives. They open their hearts to the rule of God and all the blessings of that rule become available to them.

Jesus in the words that follow now proceeds to describe in illustration after illustration the spirit of these people in whom the rule of God has become a living, working reality as they meet various problems of human life and relationship in a God-pleasing and helpful manner. In the Beati-

* Matt. 5:38-42; Luke 6:29, 30.
1 American Translation.

5

tudes and the teachings that follow, Jesus is not describing separate, unrelated virtues which men are to add to their present stock of virtues. He is portraying the manner with which the person with the kingdom spirit faces the problem of human existence and of human conflict. The teaching on nonresistance is one of the illustrations Jesus used to make clear this spirit. To be correctly understood, this passage must therefore be interpreted in the light of its larger setting in the Sermon on the Mount and of the whole of Jesus' life and teaching.

In Matthew this teaching is one of the six sayings that are contrasted with the things that were "said to them of old." Nonresistance is specifically contrasted with the old law, "an eye for an eye."

In Luke this contrast with the old law is absent and the saying, in somewhat shorter form, is found as a seemingly integral part of the teaching on loving one's enemy. The context in Luke emphasizes the close spiritual kinship between nonresistance and love of enemies.

EXEGESIS OF THE PASSAGE

The Antithesis: "Ye have heard that it was said, An eye for an eye, and a tooth for a tooth: but I say urto you . . ." (Matthew 5:38-42)

The Formula: "Ye have heard"

A formula similar to this was also used in rabbinic circles. Their usual formula ran as follows: "The text says so and so, or, I hear from it so and so; but there is another text. . . .[2] Then followed a Scripture quotation intended to correct the former view. The formula in Matthew begins in a similar way, but it concludes with the words: "but I say. . . ."

One notes at once that the usual rabbinic dependence on the authority of Scripture and the teaching of the elders to

---

2 Harvie B. Branscomb, *Jesus and the Law of Moses*, p. 239 f.; cf. Midrash Rabba on Lev. 23:11 quoted in Schechter, *Some Aspects of Rabbinic Theology*, p. 213 f.; other quotations in Fiebig, *Jesu Bergpredigt*, p. 32 f.

validate a pronouncement is completely absent in this Matthaean passage. Jesus' authority for teaching is not the tradition of the elders or even of Scripture as such but rather His own conviction of truth. This independence of Jesus from the text of the Scriptures and from the tradition of the elders is revealed in other passages, such as those dealing with the laws regarding the Sabbath, fasting, washings, etc.[3] Jesus speaks with the authority of one who knows Himself to be the Son of God and uniquely the spokesman for God. Here He sets the convictions of His mature judgment over against the words that were "said to them of old," about the law of retaliation.

The Antithesis: "An eye for an eye" (Matthew 5:38)

The standard, "an eye for an eye, and a tooth for a tooth," is unquestionably taught in the Old Testament. The exact words quoted are found in a more elaborated form in Exodus 21:23-25; Leviticus 24:17-21; and Deuteronomy 19:16-21.

Exodus 21:23-25: But if any harm follow, then thou shalt give life for life, eye for eye, tooth for tooth, hand for hand, foot for foot, burning for burning, wound for wound, stripe for stripe.

Leviticus 24:19-21: And if a man cause a blemish in his neighbor; as he hath done, so shall it be done to him: breach for breach, eye for eye, tooth for tooth; as he hath caused a blemish in a man, so shall it be rendered unto him. And he that killeth a beast shall make it good: and he that killeth a man shall be put to death.

Deuteronomy 19:21: And thine eyes shall not pity; life shall go for life, eye for eye, tooth for tooth, hand for hand, foot for foot.

It is, however, wrong to assume that these passages correctly represent the general spirit and teaching of the Old Testament. Passages like Leviticus 19:17, 18 and Proverbs 25:21, 22 clearly show the presence of a higher ethical idealism, one that urged merciful, forgiving, and magnanimous

---

[3] Cf. Mark 2:23-28; 2:18-22; 7:1-23.

treatment of the evildoer and forbade hatred and revenge and the bearing of a grudge.[4]

Leviticus 19:17, 18: Thou shalt not hate thy brother in thy heart: thou shalt surely rebuke thy neighbor, and not bear sin because of him. Thou shalt not take vengeance, nor bear any grudge against the children of thy people; but thou shalt love thy neighbor as thyself: I am Jehovah.

The vindictive, vengeful spirit is also present in the writings of the Apocrypha and the pseudepigrapha.[5] For instance, the apocalyptic writers of this period as a whole express the hope not only of a glorious future for Israel but of an equal measure of destruction on her enemies; and there is an evident feeling of keen satisfaction in the latter prospect. Again, in the Book of Jubilees and in II Maccabees stories of the death of notable evildoers evidently were rewritten "so as to furnish examples of this law of retribution" (i.e., the above law, "an eye for an eye").[6]

But side by side with these passages we find Gad 6:3-7:

Love ye, therefore, one another from the heart; and if a man sin against thee, cast forth the poison of hate and speak peaceably to him, and in thy soul hold not guile; and if he confess and repent, forgive him. But if he deny it, do not get into a passion with him, lest catching the poison from thee he take to swearing and so thou sin doubly. . . . And though he deny it and yet have a sense of shame when reproved, give over reproving him. For he who denieth may repent so as not again to wrong thee; yea, he may also honor thee, and [fear and] be at peace with thee. But if he be shameless and persist in his wrongdoing, even so forgive him from the heart, and leave to God the avenging.[7]

---

4 For fuller treatment of Old Testament passages see chapter III.

5 Jewish writings, generally of hidden or assumed authorship, that flourished during the period from 250 B.C. onward and into the Christian era. They exercised a wide influence on Jewish thinking but were not accepted into the collection of sacred writings known as the Old Testament.

6 R. H. Charles, *Religious Development Between the Old and the New Testaments*, p. 135. Note the description of the terrible death of Antiochus Epiphanes (II Macc. 9:1-29) and of Adam and Cain (Jubilees 4:29-32).

7 R. H. Charles, *The Testaments of the Twelve Patriarchs*, Vol. II, p. 341 f.

TURN THE OTHER CHEEK

Here men are urged to rid themselves of hate and to forgive the wrongdoer from the heart in order that the old relationship of trust and good will may be restored.

In the teaching of Judaism contemporary with Jesus as far as that can be determined from extant literature, there is evident a growing humanitarian emphasis and an increasing insistence on forgiveness and nonretaliation in relation to the wrongdoer. The ancient personal prayers of Berachoth IV, 2, 7d illustrate this emphasis.

> May it be Thy will, O Lord my God and God of my fathers, that hatred and envy of us enter not into the heart of man, nor hatred and envy of any man enter into our heart.

In another passage he says:

> May it be Thy will, that I be not angered against my fellows, nor they against me.

And still in another:

> Bring us near to what Thou lovest, keep us far from what Thou hatest.[8]

The old law of retaliation by the time of Jesus, largely because of the substitution of money equivalents for exact retaliation, had ceased to be primarily a law regulating revenge and had become more a principle regulating and defining restitution in case of damage or injury.

Yet there are not a few passages that allow and even condone hatred and revenge, especially if the wrongdoer is an idolater, i.e., a Gentile, or an Am-ha-aretz ("People of the land," i.e., the unlearned masses, peasants), or somebody from one of the other despised classes. Thus one rabbi quotes Leviticus 19:18: "Thou shalt not take vengeance, nor bear any grudge against the children of thy people," and then adds: "but you may take vengeance and bear a grudge against others."[9] Strack-Billerbeck cite similar teachings.

---

8. Claude G. Montefiore, *Rabbinic Literature and the Gospel Teachings*, p. 90.

9 H. L. Strack, *et al.*, *Kommentar zum Neuen Testament aus Talmud und Midrasch*, Vol. I, p. 366. Other citations on p. 365 f.

The original purpose of the law of revenge undoubtedly was to curb and regulate unlimited revenge. In a primitive society a man would often follow without restraint his natural desire for revenge and his crude ideas of justice and he would inflict terrible vengeance on the one who had harmed or wronged him. Thus a comparatively slight injury might be avenged by killing the offender, perhaps even by killing his whole family as in the case of Achan (Joshua 7) or as in the difficulty between Abner and Joab (II Samuel 3:28, 29). The harm that would be inflicted in revenge was measured not so much by a given standard of justice as by a man's rage and his ability to give expression to it.

To curb such unlimited revenge either by the injured person or by his relatives and friends was no doubt the purpose of the original law. It limited the penalty inflicted to the measure of harm done and in so far was an expression of an elemental sense of justice.

Evidently this penalty originally was paid back in kind, "life for life," "breach for breach, eye for eye, tooth for tooth." By the time of Jesus the penalty had very probably largely been reduced to money equivalents. But the law as such could do little to curb the spirit of revenge. It merely emphasized that a man was to consider his injury or wrong requited when the penalty inflicted was the equivalent of his own injury or insult.

Apparently there were many people in Jesus' day (as there are now) whose idea of justice moved on the level of "an eye for an eye," the level of exact justice. Doubtless there were also many others (then as now) who found it hard to live up to this level of "an eye for an eye." But there were likewise present noble spirits who protested vigorously against this prevalent spirit of revenge.

It is obvious from these various citations that "an eye for an eye" is not a true reflection of the total teaching on the subject of retaliation, either in the Old Testament or in the Apocrypha and the pseudepigrapha or in contemporary Judaism. It does, however, reflect an emphasis and an attitude that unquestionably existed in these writings and in the life of the times.

"*Resist not him that is evil*" (*Matthew 5:39*)

It is necessary to say a word here about the variant way in which this clause is rendered in our English versions because that has important bearing on our interpretation of the statement. On the basis of the original Greek it is impossible to determine whether one should translate "Resist not evil" (Authorized Version), "an injury" (Goodspeed and Moffatt) or "him that is evil" (American Standard Version), "one who is evil" (Revised Standard Version, 1946). It is therefore necessary to turn to the context of this passage and to the larger considerations of Jesus' life and teaching for help in clearing up this difficulty.

If the correct reading is "Resist not evil," it might refer to evil in general. But such a statement is inconceivable on the lips of Jesus because stories could be multiplied to show how unalterably He was opposed to evil. A case could perhaps be made for the assertion that Jesus meant: "Do not resist evil with evil," i.e., do not oppose evil with the methods of evil. Jesus would doubtless agree with that position, but to interpret the clause in this way is to put a restriction on this saying that is not there. But finally such an exhortation about "evil in general" does not appear characteristic of Jesus. He did not think of such problems of human conduct and human relationship in the abstract. He was not concerned about ill will in general, but He was tremendously concerned about people in whom ill will had, even for a moment, become a determining and disturbing factor. He wanted people of ill will to become people of good will, but He apparently expended little energy combating evil in general.

The phrase could more plausibly mean "the evil deed," but the transition from a clause where the emphasis is on the evil deed to the following clauses where the emphasis is consistently on persons would be awkward. Furthermore a study of the Jesus of the Gospels makes it clear that He was not so much interested in giving a man help in his relation to an evil deed as in helping him in his relation to a wicked man.

If the correct reading is "Resist not him that is evil," then this might have reference either to the evil one, i.e., the devil (cf. Matthew 13:19, where the same Greek phrase is clearly so used), or to the one committing the evil deed. It is hardly conceivable that Jesus would anywhere suggest that one is not to resist the devil. All the stories of the exorcising of demons refute that idea. So also do sayings like the one in which Jesus criticizes the man who left his house unguarded against the entrance of evil spirits. Matthew 12:43-45; Luke 11:24-26.

The clause might conceivably mean: "Do not resist the 'evil one' with his own weapons," namely, the methods of evil and violence. But one could not possibly carry that idea through consistently in this teaching unit. Neither Jesus nor the early Christian community would say: "If Satan impresses you to go one mile, go with him two," or "Give to Satan what or when he asks."

The only solution that satisfies the requirements not only of this clause but of the whole of this teaching unit as well, and that is at the same time in harmony with the rest of the picture of Jesus in the Gospels, is to regard this phrase as referring to the "evildoer." It is a human relation with which Jesus deals here, the relation of a kingdom citizen to the man who insults, coerces, and imposes on him.

The Goodspeed and Moffatt rendering of this phrase as "an injury" is essentially in harmony with this viewpoint. The expression "an injury" immediately lifts the whole clause out of the realm of the abstract and into the realm of the personal. "An injury" presupposes one who injured.

The next question that confronts us is this: What is the wrongdoing that would bring a man into the classification of "the evildoer" of this passage? The word "evildoer," like the word "neighbor" in Luke 10:29, is left undefined, perhaps

TURN THE OTHER CHEEK

because it is intended to be inclusive. It includes here all that selfish, greedy, or perverted people might do to others. In other words, it includes every kind of wrongdoing. The wide variety of illustrations cited in the passage would seem to bear this out.

The natural reaction to the wrong done is to try to return evil for evil, i.e., to resent and to refuse the unjust or overbearing demand, or to protect oneself with vigor, and with violence if necessary, against the injustice or the wickedness perpetrated, and if possible to see that the wrongdoer gets his due for the injury intended or inflicted. The feelings that are aroused and that largely control the attitude and action in the situation are anger, outrage, and a desire to get even. They are the same feelings which the old law "an eye for an eye" sought to curb.

This natural impulse to retaliate this first clause, "Resist not," completely and uncompromisingly disallows. The verb used here does not admit of much softening or smoothing down. It means to "withstand, resist, oppose."[10] The "Do not resist" is unqualified. There is no indication that resistance to the wrongdoer is ever thought justified, and there is not the slightest suggestion that some kinds of resistance might be less odious than others. This clause has the same absolute quality that some of the other sayings of Jesus have.[11] It is a form of utterance often employed by the prophet in his attempt to rouse his people to repentance and to a new way of life. He does not always stop to qualify his statements in the interest of immediate application, for he is more interested in throwing out a challenge that shall reach not only the ear but also the heart. The new principle or spirit of life to which the challenge calls men can be trusted, he thinks, to make its own adaptation to differing life situa-

---

10 G. Abbott-Smith, *Manual of a Greek Lexicon of the New Testament;* Erwin Preuschen, *Griechisch-Deutsches Woerterbuch zu den Schriften des Neuen Testaments.*

11 Cf. "If any man cometh unto me, and hateth not his own father . . ." (Luke 14:26); "Verily . . . the publicans and the harlots go into the kingdom of God before you" (Matt. 21:31); "Ye . . . shall be perfect . . ." (Matt. 5:48).

tions. Perhaps absolute statements of Jesus like the one above should be read in this light.

In trying to understand this demand of Jesus it must be borne in mind that Jesus is not trying to lay down laws intended to regulate the conduct of a secular community or a secular government; and the early church did not so regard this teaching. The legitimacy of the use of the sword by the government against wrongdoers apparently was not seriously questioned by the early church. (Cf. Romans 13:1-7; I Peter 2:13 f.) It should be obvious, however, that this is not equivalent to saying that Jesus sanctioned the use of the sword by the secular state or that Jesus would have accepted the view that this principle was not applicable and could not be applied to secular society. The secular state probably did not here come into the focus of His attention. He was giving counsel to those who had made the great surrender, but He was not prescribing rules to govern unregenerate man and society. His call to them would doubtless have been, "Repent and put yourself under the rule of God."

But Jesus was not legislating conduct even for His followers although in certain Christian circles there evidently was a tendency to look on His teachings as a new law fulfilling and supplanting the old Torah. Jesus did not intend to supplant the old law, which He regarded as inadequate, merely with a new law. His emphasis was not on a new law but on a new principle, a new spirit that was to possess His followers as sharers of the kingdom life. This new spirit He does not describe by means of abstract terms but by the use of graphic illustrations.

Yet, to say that Jesus' emphasis is on the spirit rather than on the literal statement is not to suggest that Jesus did not mean the saying literally. Certain of His teachings, together with His own example, would tend to show that He must have meant the saying literally. Just how literally He meant it and how far-reaching He thought its application to be is one of the main problems of this study. For the present, it is sufficient to say that the statement is all-inclusive.

TURN THE OTHER CHEEK

The statement is wholly negative. It merely disallows retaliation. It suggests nothing to take its place. It suggests no reason for refraining from opposing the evildoer. Is one to refrain because violence is so utterly futile in solving difficulties and often serves only to aggravate the wrong? Or is one to refrain because it is better to suffer wrong than to do wrong? One might even refrain from resisting the wrongdoer because one believed that he could gain his ends more effectively by passive resistance or non-co-operation. The clause taken by itself seems to suggest nothing beyond passive submission to wrong. It suggests no way of dealing with the desire for revenge.

In the light of these facts it becomes increasingly evident that this statement was not intended to be complete in itself. It was a negative statement that needed the positive counterpart of the verses following for its complete understanding.

"But . . . turn . . . the other [cheek]" (Matthew 5:39)

The original Greek here uses its strongest term of contrast apparently to indicate that the preceding statement is incomplete and needs correction. Paraphrasing for a moment, the force of this "but" would be somewhat as follows: "Do not resist the evildoer, 'but so far from merely doing nothing, this is what you ought to do' "; or "but you are not to be content with that"; or "but you are to go much further than that." Then follow the sayings graphically illustrating this more positive, active course that the disciple is to pursue.

A Case of Violent Insult

The first illustration Jesus uses is a case of violent insult. To strike a man on the right cheek, whereby the use of the right hand was presupposed, meant that he was struck with the back of the hand, and that was regarded in Jewish law as adding to the seriousness of the offense. Thus Rabbi Jehuda (A.D. 150) speaking for Rabbi Jose (A.D. 110) declared a fine of two minas for a slap on the cheek. If done with the back of the hand, thereby striking the right cheek in added insult, he was to pay four minas.[12]

It is obvious that this saying is not intended to prescribe by a legal rule how a man is to react invariably in the specific instance where he receives a blow on the right cheek. The saying merely pictures a common form of physical abuse or insult of the kind that invites quick and violent retaliation, blow for blow. The use of a strong Greek verb and the reference to the right cheek merely serve to accentuate the graveness of the insult and of the spirit of contempt that prompted the act. The illustration in Luke 6:29a is milder but not essentially different.

The clause is wholly unqualified and the supposition is that the person wronged is entirely innocent of provoking in any way the violence inflicted on him by the wrongdoer. The situation pictured is one in which the sympathy is wholly on the side of the one insulted, one in which quick retaliation in kind is commonly condoned. It is an insult which very few people would not thoroughly resent even if they refrained from every form of retaliation.

What is the remedy Jesus proposed for this situation? (1) The words of counsel are directed entirely to the person wronged. It is his attitude and reaction that is the object of Jesus' concern. He is not told to psychoanalyze the wrongdoer to see whether he can find a way of curing him of his mean disposition. Instead, he is given direction as to how he may make his own attitude and conduct right in the given situation. The words by themselves give no suggestion what possible effect this turning of the other cheek may have on the wrongdoer, whether it may convert him to a better state of mind or strengthen him in his overbearing attitude, or whether it will affect him at all. The words taken by themselves show concern only for the person wronged and his proper reaction and conduct. (2) The use of violence in resisting the evildoer or in retaliating is completely disallowed by the previous demand: "Resist not."

12 Baba Kama 8, 6.

TURN THE OTHER CHEEK

This statement, unqualified, appears to sweep all resistance aside. (3) The person wronged is to turn ("offer" in Luke) the other cheek. This statement, like the previous one, is wholly unqualified. No motive is suggested why one is to turn the other cheek, nor is any suggestion made of any beneficent purpose that is to be achieved by this course of action, not even in the person wronged.

It is obvious that it is not a mere passive, stoic submitting to a repetition of the insult or the violence that is suggested here. The verbs "turn" and "offer" indicate something more active. They suggest an actual, even though silent, invitation to repeat the act of violence. Of course one could turn the other cheek in a spirit of bravado or in a spirit of legalistic, literalistic obedience to commandment, but that falls far below the spirit of the man who uttered the words. They rather suggest the presence of a spirit of such large perspective and such inner strength and purity that it is above all thought of resentment and revenge and strong enough to invite further insult and violence. One is not to retaliate or to resist with violence of any kind. More than that, one is to be so far above even the thought of revenge that one can with perfect poise of spirit invite a repetition of the insult.

But why does Jesus suggest such an extraordinary course of action? There is no suggestion in the saying itself that love for the wrongdoer and concern for him is to incite one to turn the other cheek. Neither is there any suggestion that it is the motive of *Reinheit*,[13] the desire to maintain one's inner purity and integrity, that is back of this turning of the other cheek. And there is no suggestion that one is to pursue this course of action as a matter of prudence.[14] It is puzzling to know wherein the prudence would lie. It would, after all, appear to be rather doubtful sagacity to turn the other cheek to one whose ill will had already asserted itself once in this low form of contempt. None of the motives sug-

---

[13] H. Weinel, *Biblische Theologie*, p. 91.
[14] E. F. Scott (*The Ethical Teachings of Jesus*) states that this saying "may possibly be explained as little more than a prudential maxim" (p. 73).

gested appear adequate to explain this invitation to repeat the act of violence and contempt.

Jesus' demand does not at all appear like a studied effort to figure out what would be the best possible and the most permanently helpful solution to the critical problem created by the insulting act of the offender and how He could provide adequate motivation for the desired conduct. He did not approach such human problems in the manner of the rabbi, the scribe, or the moralist arguing his way through a moral problem, carefully weighing the facts and balancing passages of Scripture and then arriving at a reasoned conclusion. Neither did He project some idealistic code of ethics and then try to solve individual moral problems on the basis of this code. He seemed to have a "way of piercing by prophetic insight to the heart of any moral problem."[15]

Jesus simply speaks here with the directness of the prophet boldly proclaiming the will of God. The will of God was His supreme concern. Man's right response to God was an obedience of trust and love. It was not for man to argue or to bargain with God but to accept Him without fear or hesitation. The idea of suggesting a motive for the prescribed course probably did not even enter Jesus' mind. It was the will of the Father, and obedience to His will needed no other motivation. For this reason no motives are assigned nor explanations given like those found in Romans 12:19-21, "Avenge not yourselves, beloved, but give place unto the wrath of God: for it is written, Vengeance belongeth unto me; I will recompense, saith the Lord. But if thine enemy hunger, feed him; if he thirst, give him to drink: for in so doing thou shalt heap coals of fire upon his head. Be not overcome of evil, but overcome evil with good."

"Let him have thy cloak"

Matthew 5:40: And if any man would go to law with thee, and take away thy coat, let him have thy cloak also.

Luke 6:29b: and from him that taketh away thy cloak withhold not thy coat also.

15 T. W. Manson, *The Teaching of Jesus*, p. 292.

TURN THE OTHER CHEEK

Matthew 5:40 gives an instance of a quarrel in court where one man endeavors wrongfully (at least presumably so) to take the inner garment from his fellow man; and the latter is exhorted to let him have the outer garment as well.

The saying as recorded in Luke presents the picture of a robbery in which the offender snatches[16] the outer garment from his victim; and the latter is exhorted not to restrain him from taking the inner garment as well. In the situation that Luke pictures, the order of the outer garment (cloak) and the inner garment (coat) is necessarily reversed from the order it has in Matthew, for the robber would obviously snatch the outer and more valuable garment first.

The illustration in Luke presents an act of direct violence and in this respect is similar to the previous one on turning the other cheek. In Matthew it is not an instance of direct personal violence. Here the wrong is attempted or committed through the instrumentality of the court.

The exhortation on how to meet the wrong is essentially the same, namely, permit the evildoer to take the other garment as well. Matthew uses a somewhat milder verb, "let" (or "permit," "allow"). Luke's verb, "withhold" (or "hinder," "restrain"), evidently suggests that the deprived person is to offer no resistance to any effort to take the inner garment as well.

This saying in Luke cites an offense against one's property rights. The offense is prompted by selfishness and greed, as robberies usually are. The offender, disregarding all considerations of justice and of the rights and needs of another, takes by force or by threat the coat he wants. Such an act normally excites in the person robbed feelings of rage and resentment, and calls forth the impulse to resist the robbery.

But the exhortation leaves no room for any resistance by force. The wrongdoer is not to be restrained in his attempt to take the outer coat. He is not to be restrained even if he

---

16 The Greek verb commonly translated "take away" here has the added meaning of taking "by force and contrary to all right," *widerrechtlich* (Preuschen, *Woerterbuch*).

should attempt to take the inner coat as well. There is no suggestion that either the outer or the inner coat is to be *offered* to him upon his attempt to take it. The implication of the exhortation evidently is that the person wronged is to possess such a reserve of inner strength that he can with perfect calm submit to a double robbery.

The situation in Matthew is not altogether clear. Does it picture a creditor who goes to court to recover a debt and there demands the inner garment of the debtor as pledge of its payment, after the analogy of Exodus 22:26, 27?

If thou at all take thy neighbor's garment to pledge, thou shalt restore it unto him before the sun goeth down: for that is his only covering, it is his garment for his skin: wherein shall he sleep? and it shall come to pass, when he crieth unto me, that I will hear; for I am gracious.

That this ancient practice had led to some abuses on the part of grasping people is suggested in Proverbs 20:16 and Amos 2:8.

Proverbs 20:16: Take a man's garment if he becomes surety for a stranger; hold him to account for the other.
Amos 2:8a: And they lay themselves down beside every altar upon clothes taken in pledge.

But the statement about going to law and taking away the coat does not in itself indicate that the taking of the coat is the exaction of a pledge.[17]

It seems more in harmony with the facts in the case to regard this as simply a quarrel over the possession of a tunic, perhaps somewhat analogous to the situation pictured in Sifre 16 cited by Kittel:

A man is clothed in his garment; another says: This is mine! One man is plowing with his ox; another says: It is mine! One man lives in his house; another says: It is mine! One man is in

[17] The coat referred to in Ex. 22:26, 27 is the outer not the inner garment. Wilhelm Gesenius, *Handwoerterbuch*.

possession of his field; another says: It is mine! . . . If the righteous man is in the right with his demand, he brings proof.[18]

The plaintiff in the Matthaean passage brings no proofs. One gets the impression that the offender, as in the citation above, sees someone clad in a garment that excites his selfish desires and he speaks up: "This is mine!" Being unable or unwilling to take it by force, he desires to take the matter to court and get the coat in that way, i.e., under the guise of legality.

His desire to get possession of the coat is prompted, as in Luke, primarily by selfishness and greed. The normal response of the victim to the offender in a situation like this is essentially the same as denoted by Luke, a feeling of rage and resentment against the man who, in complete disregard of the needs and rights of his fellow man, would wrest from him his coat. The fact that the offender does not resort to violence to obtain the coat but uses the more respectable and approved instrumentality of the court to achieve his evil purpose does not lessen the feeling of resentment nor the desire to resist the attempted robbery.

The suggested way of meeting this (Matthaean) situation is in a measure the same as the one given in Luke. The person wronged is to be ready to let the offender have the other garment as well. But the Matthaean statement is positive, whereas the one in Luke is entirely negative. The Greek verb in Matthew has a positive meaning. In this connection it is used in the sense of "give up" or "hand over."[19] That would make this clause read: "Hand over to him also the outer garment."

The Matthaean clause therefore goes beyond its parallel in Luke, which simply means: "Do not withhold the inner

---

18 Der eine ist in sein Gewand gehuellt; der andere sagt: Es ist mein! Der eine pfluegt mit seiner Kuh; der andere sagt: Sie ist mein! Der eine wohnt in seinem Haus; der andere sagt: Es ist mein! Der eine ist im Besitz seines Feldes; der andere sagt: Es ist mein! . . . Ist der Gerechte mit seiner Forderung im Recht, so bringt er Beweise. Gerhard Kittel, *Die Probleme des palaestinischen Spaetjudentums und das Urchristentum*, p. 32.

19 Preuschen, *Woerterbuch*, p. 190. Liddell and Scott, *Greek-English Lexicon* (New Edition, 1926), p. 290.

garment if he wants it." The Matthaean clause implies a measure of co-operation with the offender. The latter demands the inner garment for himself, and the victim willingly, it seems, at least without protest or resentment, accedes. Then, as if to make the robbery complete, he leaves him also the outer and more valuable garment as well, fully aware that this garment is uncontested and so freely his own.

How radical Jesus' demand was, the Jewish readers would understand more fully than Gentile readers because they knew that it was a maxim of Jewish law that a plaintiff could not come forward in court and merely say, "This is mine!" He must bring proof, and until he presented valid proof the defendant was in the right. Jesus demanded not only that the defendant waive this well-recognized safeguard of legal right but actually exceed it.

Why should a man go to that length in meeting a situation like the one pictured when the offender, presumably, had no fair claim on the garment in the first place? No reason is given or motive suggested. The motive, "Rather suffer wrong than do wrong" (cf. I Corinthians 6:7), would hardly lead a man much further than an unprotesting surrender of the garment unjustly claimed. And the disgrace of allowing a quarrel to be taken to court instead of settling it peacefully,[20] to which Paul refers in the same passage, would hardly lead to anything beyond an "agreement" or at most to a surrender of the object of contention but not to the giving up of the other garment. Votaw declares that one is to be willing to "sacrifice his feelings and his possessions in order to avoid trouble with others,"[21] but that motive is not suggested in the saying. Neither is the mere avoiding of trouble with others in itself sufficient to explain the leaving of the other coat as well.

What motive is to lead men to this course of action? What

---

[20] Cf. Matt. 5:23-26.
[21] James Hastings, *A Dictionary of the Bible*, Extra Vol., "Sermon on the Mount," C. W. Votaw, p. 29.

TURN THE OTHER CHEEK

influence is it to have on the offender? Would not this course of action all too often encourage greed in him? All such considerations are passed by because the offender is not Jesus' primary concern. The question of the possible effect of the general adoption of this principle on organized society is also passed by, partly for the same reason and partly because Jesus is not interested in laying down a code of ethics for society or for wicked men. To these His call would be to repent (cf. Mark 1:15 and parallels) and to yield themselves to the will of God.

In this saying, as in the other sayings of this group, Jesus is directing His words to His followers and is concerning Himself wholly with their proper response in an unpleasant situation. He omits consideration of possible ill effects which the adoption and consistent following of the suggested course of action might have on the person wronged, such as the possible impoverishment of the victim, or the unfavorable mental attitude this ready acquiescence to the unjust demand might create in a person as he faces a world that seems to demand aggressiveness and self-assertion as the price of success. If Jesus thought of these and other problems, they remained a matter of sublime disregard. His prophetic insight convinced Him this was God's will and way for the man wronged. That was sufficient for Him and He thought it should be sufficient for His followers. The consequences of following the will of God need not concern one. The Father's will was bound to be for the good of men. (Cf. Matthew 7:11 and parallel.)

The passage as recorded in Luke is also wholly unqualified, suggesting neither motive nor purpose for the action. Taken by themselves, the words in Luke do not necessarily imply a motive much beyond the stoic ideal of self-mastery. The words in this passage would imply such moral reserves of self-mastery that the victim stood ready to submit to a double robbery without losing his mental and emotional poise. Weinel, commenting on the whole of this Matthaean and Lucan teaching on nonresistance, exclaims: "Here Jesus approaches the stoic ideal."[22] Is that all that is implied in this saying?

The final answer must be reserved until later, but early Christian circles apparently felt that the action would serve in some way the best interests of the wrongdoer. They may have shared Paul's view that it would cause a sense of shame in the evildoer and perhaps convert him.[23] The saying in itself suggests no such purpose or motive.

Again it needs to be said that Jesus, speaking in the manner and spirit of the prophets, addresses Himself wholly to the victim and describes for him without qualification or explanation the God-pleasing spirit and manner for meeting a critical situation. It is clear that this saying, like the previous one, presupposes the presence of a spirit of good will so deep and ever-present that it far outruns the other's unjust demand.

Go the Second Mile

Matthew 5:41: And whosoever shall compel thee to go one mile, go with him two.

This saying on going the second mile is not found in Luke.

There are two questions that arise at once. (1) What was the meaning of the Greek word here translated simply as "compel"? Was it a technical term referring to compulsory services demanded by the government or to conscription by military forces? (2) Did the clause "compel thee to go one mile" necessarily refer to military or governmental compulsion? Would people in the time of Jesus inevitably think of such conscripted services?

The Greek verb used here is of Persian origin and meant "to press into service as royal courier.[24] "The word, originally applied only to a Persian institution, had gained a

---

22 H. Weinel, *Biblische Theologie des Neuen Testaments*, p. 91. ("Hier steht Jesus dem stoischen Ideal nahe.")
23 Cf. Rom. 12:20, 21.
24 Liddell and Scott, *Greek-English Lexicon*.

TURN THE OTHER CHEEK

more general sense as early as the third century B.C.[25] This sense, of course, was itself a technical one at first—but the word must have become so familiar that the Evangelist could use it quite generally for 'to compel.' "[26] The great Greek lexicons all agree in giving the word this general meaning of "compel."[27]

In view of this fact it seems to strain a point when Cadoux claims that Jesus was here using "the technical term for state-conscription of forced labor" and that "probably the words refer actually to the practice of the Roman administration."[28]

That the Roman government, its army, or its police force occasionally conscripted men and beasts to perform some service is readily conceded. The compelling of Simon of Cyrene to carry the cross of Jesus (Mark 15:21) is one evidence of this fact. That this Greek term was used to indicate such conscription of service its use in Mark and Matthew above and its use by Josephus (Ant. 13:2, 3) would suggest. It may even be that it was the term commonly used when referring to state conscription but, according to the testimony of the eminent linguists referred to above, it was far from being confined to this usage. It seems, therefore, unwarranted to conclude that this term necessarily has a military reference.

Does the clause "compel thee to go one mile" necessarily refer to governmental or military compulsion?

The answer to this question lies in the realm of probabilities and hence the question cannot be answered with finality.

What reason could there be for compelling a man to accompany another a mile? There might be a variety of reasons, but the most obvious one would be to carry a burden or perform a task.

---

[25] The earliest known use of the word in Greek is found in the Comedian Menander (Sicyon IV), d. 290 B.C. (Deissmann, *Bibelstudien*, p. 288 footnote).
[26] Deissmann, *ibid.*, p. 87.
[27] Preuschen, Abbott-Smith, Liddell and Scott.
[28] C. J. Cadoux, *The Early Church and the World*, p. 38.

JESUS AND HUMAN CONFLICT

Who would be most likely to make such a demand? Business interests might on occasion coerce a man into some service; robber bands might have reasons to force someone to accompany them; and patriotic groups might compel others to serve their supposedly patriotic purposes. But perhaps those most likely to compel a man's service would be military detachments, police forces, or other governmental agencies.

Did the words of this saying specifically refer to this latter kind of compulsion? The use of the term "whosoever" would seem to indicate that it was intended to include all such cases of compulsion by force.[29] At the same time it is more than likely that Jesus was not unaware of the fact that the popular mind on hearing these words would think first of all of compulsory services forced upon them by their foreign rulers. Their intense hatred of foreign domination would make this almost inevitable. But the use of the general term "whosoever" would indicate that the question of who was guilty of the coercion did not concern Jesus. It was not political advice He intended to give but advice for a personal problem. It was advice intended for any disciple who was compelled to go any mile of service.[30]

It may be well to try to reconstruct the picture Jesus presented. The victim is confronted with the demand that he accompany the offender a mile for the purpose of rendering some service. The demand comes to him in such a form that he can ignore or disobey it only at the peril of life or limb. The idea of being forced into a task wholly against his will awakens in him feelings of resentment and bitterness and the desire to get even. If the victim happens to be a zealous Jewish patriot and the oppressor a representative of the hated Roman rule, this feeling is greatly intensified but not

---

29 A. T. Robertson, *A Grammar of the Greek New Testament*, p. 727.

30 The question of the possible relationship of these words to the political situation of the time comes up for fuller discussion later. Obviously a demand to do positive evil was not to be obeyed. Cf. such uncompromising teachings as that about God and mammon (Matt. 6:24) and about hating father and mother (Luke 14:26).

essentially altered. To the man thus outraged Jesus turns with the charge to go not only the one mile of forced labor but to go two.

It is worth noting that the illustration given is not another case of insult or of robbery. It is an instance of a violent invasion of a man's freedom and his right of self-determination. But the offender does not rob the man of merely some of his time and freedom. He coerces the whole man (steals him, as it were) and makes him serve his own ends. He uses the victim as a means, a tool. He commandeers him as a slave or a beast of burden whose feelings and will do not need to be considered and whose personality does not need to be respected.

The Exhortation: "Go with him two [miles]"

The man thus outraged, who discovers feelings of bitterness and resentment rising within him, who would refuse the demand if he dared, and who can hardly bring himself to go the mile required, is told to go two miles with the offender.

There is something in this demand of Jesus that seems to go beyond the demands in the other sayings in this group. (1) It goes directly counter to man's natural impulse, as do the demands in the other sayings in this group, but it is more exacting. It seems to require a higher quality of spirit. The turning of the other cheek, or the giving of the other garment, these acts can be performed under the impetus of a sudden impulse. They are single acts that can be quickly done, and once accomplished almost as quickly forgotten, the cause of irritation being removed. But in this instance the victim is to subject himself willingly, for the distance of not only one mile but of two, to the immediate company and domination and possible abuse of the offender.

(2) The demand appears more definitely positive in nature than the two preceding ones. Turning the other cheek is to invite further insult; letting a man have the other garment is to let him have more than he demanded. But to

go two miles instead of one is to do more than to allow the man to double his wrongdoing. The victim is not told: "Allow him to coerce you two miles." The element of submission to wrongdoing seems to be crowded entirely into the background in this saying. The suggestion here seems to be that the victim rise at once above the level of resentment and submission and accept the demand as an opportunity for service. As such he is willing to give double the service that a galling force might ask. Jesus suggests that the reply to the hard, insolent demand of the offender be a willing service that far exceeds the unjust demand. This saying, therefore, seems to imply that the victim render good for evil. (Cf. I Peter 3:9; Romans 12:17-21.)

No reason is given why he should go two miles. Is he to go the second mile merely with the idea of making the best of a bad situation? At best that would only help to make the first mile bearable, but it would not lead a man to go two miles instead of one. Is he to do it out of an overflowing kindness or concern for the offender? The saying in itself does not suggest this, but it is difficult to think of giving willingly two miles of service under such circumstances without thinking of its effect on the offender. The words themselves give no suggestion of the possible good results of this action on the wrongdoer, or of similar action on evildoers generally, or on organized society as a whole. Jesus does not stop to explain why one should offer to go two miles. He speaks forth with the intuitive insight of the prophet and boldly declares the will of God in the situation.

"Give to him that asketh thee . . ."

Matthew 5:42: Give to him that asketh thee, and from him that would borrow of thee turn not thou away.

Luke 6:30: Give to every one that asketh thee; and of him that taketh away thy goods ask them not again.

It is not easy to see what relation this saying has to the main idea of retaliation underlying this teaching unit. However, a little closer examination indicates that this is an

TURN THE OTHER CHEEK 29

offense against the charitable impulse. It tries to meet a situation which may easily, though not necessarily, cause annoyance, resentment, and certain acts of a retaliatory character.

Verse 42 of Matthew and verse 30 of Luke are almost identical except that in Luke the addition of "every one" makes the statement very inclusive.

The second halves of these verses (Matthew 5:42b; Luke 6:30b) are quite dissimilar. The saying in Matthew deals with the request for a loan, while in Luke it deals with an illegal appropriation of property.

First we shall examine the meaning of the saying in Matthew: "Give to him that asketh."

The illustration here involves no use of violence or coercion. It is a simple request for help. We are not told exactly what is requested, but the character of the saying implies that perhaps it is a request for money, or for food or clothing.

What is the nature of the "asking"? Are we to think of the petitioner as of the beggar type? Today oriental countries are sometimes almost overrun with people who beg on the streets or go begging from house to house. That there were such beggars in Jesus' day is more than likely, and references in rabbinical literature would tend to corroborate this fact.[31] Such beggars can at times become very annoying by their brazenness and persistence.

If Jesus thought of an offensive form of begging, it is not indicated in these words. The simple and unqualified "asketh thee" would suggest that the saying was intended to include any request for aid or relief, the brazen begging of the professional mendicant as well as the simple cry for help.

To such requests for help (the implication seems to be that there will be repeated requests) there are basically two kinds of responses. (1) The person asked may be moved to

---

[31] Tosefta Peah 4:8 points to such begging and emphasizes that it is the business of organized charity to take care of such cases.

pity because of the petitioner's need and may try to do what he can and what seems best under the circumstances. (2) He may be moved to resentment because the request disturbs his complacency and interferes with his selfish interests. In this case he either ignores the petitioner's request, rudely turns him away, or grudgingly tosses him a coin.

Jesus' exhortation in this situation is a wholly unqualified "give." Whether to give what is asked or as much as is asked, these and other questions about the wisdom of such seemingly indiscriminate giving remain unanswered. The exhortation seems to be quite all-inclusive. "Give to him that asketh" is to say in effect: "Give to every one that asketh," as Luke has it.

Several things should be noted in this exhortation. (1) The advice, as in the previous illustrations, is not analytical. It does not aim to give detailed directions for meeting every circumstance. Instead, it aims to reveal the spirit with which God wants men to meet the petitions of their fellow men. (2) The exhortation, as in the previous cases, is directed toward the one who is inclined to feel resentment at the approach of his fellow man. He is told that the proper response to the situation is to accede to the wish of the petitioner. The unqualified "give" of this saying seems to imply a *glad,* not a grudging or resentful giving. (3) The person approached is not told why he is to honor the request of his fellow man. There is no suggestion that he is to be moved by the thought of the need or the welfare of the petitioner. Perhaps that is taken for granted, but the idea is not expressed. (4) The exhortation does not require that double the request be granted. Why is it that the simple meeting of the request of the petitioner is sufficient for this situation while in the previous cases the exhortation demands double of what was asked? Is it because in such a case as this where no coercion is used "the spontaneity of the compliance is sufficiently shown by a simple granting of the request"?[32] Perhaps. But it is interesting to note that the exhortation

[32] H. H. Wendt, *Teachings of Jesus,* p. 133 footnote.

does not even specify that one is to grant the full request. Quite obviously the emphasis here is not on what or how much to give but on the fact that such requests for help should be met with a spontaneous willingness to help. Compared to this spontaneous willingness the amount given was of decidedly secondary importance and so is not mentioned.

In the second part of this saying in Matthew we deal not with a request for a gift but for a loan.

The reaction to a request for a loan was sometimes annoyance and resentment, followed by a cold refusal of the request. Such an unfavorable reaction is the only type that concerns us in this saying. The unfavorable reaction was probably caused largely by the fear that the one requesting the loan would be unable to pay back the principal and perhaps even default on the interest. The consequent refusal of the request aroused embarrassment, annoyance, and resentment. Sometimes unwillingness to grant a loan was caused by the nearness of the sabbatical year when all loans were to be remitted.[33]

Jesus' exhortation is that one is not to turn away from the person requesting a loan. The Greek word for "turn away" signifies more than a mere refusal of the loan. It has a passive reflexive meaning here: "To turn oneself away from."[34] The reference is therefore to a psychological turning rather than to mere mechanical turning away. The saying might well be paraphrased: "Do not turn inwardly away from the would-be borrower through motives of resentment or ill will." The advice is stated negatively, but its implication is positive. Not to turn away from the borrower really means, by inversion, to show oneself willing to meet the request for a loan. The implication of the words would seem to be that this willingness is to be a spontaneous rather than a forced willingness.

The exhortation is wholly unqualified. No reason is given

---

[33] Cf. Ex. 21:2-4; Deut. 15:12-15; Strack and Billerbeck, *op. cit.*, p. 347, Deut. 15:7 ff. (116-18), 98a.
[34] Abbott-Smith, *op. cit.*, p. 55.

why one is to meet the request for a loan. Neither is there any indication that one is to grant the exact sum asked. No attempt is made to arouse sympathy for the need of the borrower, or to awaken a sense of responsibility for his welfare, or to have one gauge the amount of the loan by the need of the borrower. The words are directed wholly to the person approached and to his proper response to the request. In a straightforward, even though negative, way he is told what is the God-pleasing way of meeting the situation. He is not to close his heart against the appeal of the needy brother. We are not told specifically that this is the God-pleasing way, but that is the inescapable conviction back of the saying.

Next we turn to the meaning of the saying in Luke 6:30: "Give to every one that asketh thee; and of him that taketh away thy goods ask them not again."

The first part of the saying in Luke is practically identical with the saying in Matthew and need not detain us. The "every one" in Luke does not go much further than the saying in Matthew except that it removes all possibility of a cunning evasion of the exhortation.

In the second part of this Lucan saying the robbery idea of the previous verse reappears. There (verse 29b) the robber snatches the outer garment. Here he wrongfully, and perhaps forcibly, seizes the man's goods. Such seizure of property is always resented, and one's first impulse is to demand its return at once.

In the exhortation of Jesus the following points are to be noted: (1) The demand for the return of the stolen goods is completely disallowed. Not only is the victim not to attempt to *take* them back by force but he is not even to *ask* them back. (2) The exhortation is directed wholly to the person deprived and what is for him the right attitude in such a situation. The question whether the suggested course of action might not give too much encouragement to the evildoer to persist in his wrongdoing does not receive consideration. Its omission is no indication that it is not to be consid-

TURN THE OTHER CHEEK 33

ered in deciding on the proper course of action in the given case. It merely indicates that this aspect of the case did not enter into the focus of Jesus' purpose. (3) The saying is unmotivated and unexplained. It suggests no motive for the course of action, and no purpose that it is to accomplish.

In a straightforward way the victim is told what to do under the circumstances, the presumption being that this expresses the will of God in the matter. (4) The emphasis obviously is not on the specific action but on the activating spirit. The implication seems to be that the person robbed is to be possessed of such resources of inner strength and goodness, resources that are divinely conditioned, that he can without resentment, bitterness, or vindictiveness give up all claim to the property stolen. Whether any concern for the welfare of the evildoer enters into the command will have to be taken up later, but it is difficult to see how any decision can leave out entirely consideration for the evildoer. (5) on the surface of things this exhortation seems like a retreat from the position taken in verse 29b. The victim is not urged to let the offender take more if he wants to. He is merely urged not to demand return of what was stolen in the first place. But the situations are not altogether analogous. In verse 29b the robber is in the act of snatching the outer garment and the victim is told not to hinder him from taking the inner garment as well, if he should be disposed to do so. Here the robbery seems to be a completed act and the robber has taken all he wants. The exhortation of verse 29b would therefore hardly be applicable here. Under the circumstances given, the exhortation in verse 30b moves perhaps on as high a plane as the one in verse 29b.

The Meaning of the Passage as a Unit

In our attempt to understand the meaning of this passage as a unit it is well to summarize briefly the main conclusions reached thus far.

This saying is best understood as a prophetic type of utterance. Its interest is not primarily ethical or legal but religious. It seeks to make known the will and purpose of God, not to reconstruct society or improve and perfect an ethical or a legal code. No attempt is made to justify the course suggested by citing reasons, or by indicating purposes, or by setting forth motives for it. Neither does it introduce qualifications or safeguards to commend its practicality and prevent its misunderstanding. The will and purpose of God in the mind of Jesus needs no justification or qualification. It is motive enough in itself, and its purpose is bound to be for the good of men.

The saying is prophetic also in that the insight is gained intuitively rather than through the careful weighing of facts and possibilities. For this reason we must not expect to find a carefully balanced and full-rounded statement covering all aspects of the problem. These often are a matter of sublime unconcern to the prophet because he believes that the principle announced is sufficient to work out a satisfactory solution to all related problems. Something like that seems to be true of this saying of Jesus on the question of retaliation. We must be careful, therefore, lest we expect this saying to cover more than was intended. Nevertheless, it is legitimate and even necessary that we try to probe through to possible deeper meanings and larger principles back of it which are perhaps not obvious on the surface but which become evident through a study of the passage in relation to the larger record of the life and teachings of Jesus.

The advice given is personal rather than political. There is no inevitable military or political reference in any of the sayings in this group. In fact, the situation pictured in no case seems to be the point of focus. It is the personal response to the situation that is the object of concern, and the situations pictured seem to have been selected primarily for their value in illustrating the personal response. A variety of illustrations were used, no doubt, to add clarity and emphasis to the statement, but they were also used very likely to emphasize that the principle announced could and should be applied in all similar cases of provocation. As

TURN THE OTHER CHEEK 35

such, they would, of course, include cases of military and political coercion. Whether the saying as a unit, especially in view of the reference to the case of impressment, was uttered with a possible side reference to the tense political situation of the time must be discussed later.

Jesus does not deal with this problem in the abstract. He is not declaring His mind on the legitimacy of the use of force or on the place of retaliation or exact justice in human society. His interest lies in people who are provoked to revenge, ill will, and the use of violence, and His desire is to help them face their situation with a spirit that lives above the plane of resentment, anger, and malice.

The advice is not intended for general application by secular society or secular governments. Jesus seems to have had no desire to legislate for secular society. His words were directed to would-be kingdom members to whom He tries to show the quality of spirit with which they are to face all such situations that incite resentment and the desire for retaliation.

The saying is opposed to the law and the spirit of revenge. It disallows all use of violence, all desire for revenge, and all resentment and ill will. All the sayings in this teaching unit are one in emphasizing this fact.

The words are directed wholly at the person wronged and to his right attitude in the matter. There is no word directing attention to the wrongdoer or to the disturbed relationship caused by the wrong. Neither is there any reference to the good the suggested action is to accomplish in the wrongdoer. The attention of the person wronged is focused entirely on himself and how he is and is not to react in the situation.

This teaching unit demands of the person wronged more than a mere stoic endurance of wrong, although a certain amount of that would be required to fulfill the demands of the different sayings in the group. It demands more than a suffering of wrong in preference to doing wrong, though doubtless Jesus would agree to that. It demands of him also

36   JESUS AND HUMAN CONFLICT

more than just ordinary prudence, although experience undoubtedly proves that it is often wiser not to resist the evildoer but rather to turn the other cheek. It also demands more of him than the exercise of the principle of nonviolence or non-co-operation in the situation, although that thought is certainly expressed, particularly in the first clause. Finally, it demands more than keeping oneself free from all taint of hatred, although Jesus would undoubtedly agree that one should by all means strive to maintain one's inner purity and integrity by avoiding all traces of resentment and ill will. But none of these principles suggested seem big enough singly to account for the exacting demands of this sayings unit. These words demand the presence of a spirit of such inner strength and poise that the person can with perfect equanimity suffer twice the indignity and twice the robbery, exceed by twofold the unjust demand, and meet with spontaneous willingness the request for a gift or a loan.

But the saying seems to demand of the person wronged even more than that. It seems to require a spirit so superior to insult and revenge that it can meet the situation with a measure of creativity. Turning the other cheek, going the second mile, and so on, instead of retaliating, is to show a certain resourcefulness in meeting the situation.[35]

It is obvious that Jesus did not here give specific directions which He expected men to follow literally in all similar situations. He wanted men to be possessed of a spirit that could under varying circumstances resort to so surprising and creative a method as turning the other cheek instead of responding with the usual retaliatory measures. Turning the other cheek in the situation Jesus pictured was indeed a creative act. It transformed the whole situation. The old wrong with its blow on the cheek and its appeal to thoughts of bitterness and vengeance has now passed wholly out of the focus of attention and a new situation has arisen whose

[35] The suggestion that one endure *twice* the indignity, etc., seems to me to be more than a mere objective standard by which one may test the completeness of one's freedom from the spirit of hatred and revenge.

TURN THE OTHER CHEEK

impetus is in the direction of reconciliation and a constructive solution of the problem. It is now no longer the person wronged who is on the defensive but the wrongdoer, and the appeal of the new situation is not toward an aggravation but toward a righting of the wrong. The aim of this passage appears to be not so much to give a technique for meeting such situations as to describe a spirit that could meet them resourcefully creatively.

This summary still leaves certain questions unanswered. Granted that the object of Jesus' concern in this teaching unit is the person wronged and his right attitude in the matter, could anyone possibly follow the suggestions of this teaching, i.e., turn the other cheek, go the second mile, etc., without thinking of its possible effect on the wrongdoer and the solution of the problem of the disturbed relation between the offender and his victim? Could Jesus, who had shown such special concern for the sinner,[36] commend to His followers and would-be followers a course of action that was devoid of all concern for the sinner? Having taught that there is "joy in heaven over one sinner that repenteth, more than over ninety and nine righteous persons, who need no repentance,"[37] could Jesus turn and proclaim as the will of God a course that showed no interest in saving this sinner from his malice and ill will to a better state of mind? Is it possible to isolate one person in a problem that involves two and prescribe for him a right attitude or a course that does not include at least in the background of the mind a thought for the welfare of the other? Did Paul perhaps catch its true spirit when he speaks of overcoming evil with good and heaping coals of fire on the evildoer's head?[38] Is a true appraisal of the full reach and meaning of this passage possible without taking account of the spirit of the man who uttered these words and without taking note of the other

---

[36] Cf. Mark 2:17 and parallels, "I came not to call the righteous, but sinners. . . ."

[37] Luke 15:7; cf. also Matt. 18:12-14; Luke 15:8-32.

[38] Rom. 12:20, 21.

sayings and incidents that reveal His attitude to wrongdoers?

A second question that is unanswered and that needs further study is this: What is the spirit that is to possess a man, a spirit so superior to insult and revenge that a man can with perfect poise and even resourcefulness meet in the suggested way situations such as Jesus pictured?

To answer these and other questions we must inquire further into the larger record of the life and teaching of Jesus and also into the Jewish background of His thought. It is only thus that we may hope to discover the real thought of Jesus in the matter of one's relation to the wrongdoer.

3

Insights from the Old Testament and Contemporary Jewish Literature

This chapter will make no attempt to give an exhaustive analysis of Jewish thought in regard to retaliation and the right attitude to the evildoer. Its aim is rather to select from Jewish literature such of the higher ethical teachings as may throw light on the thought and emphasis of Jesus.

Relevant Teachings in the Old Testament

First, there are accounts of great national heroes which give illustrations not only of the generous treatment of evildoers but also of the favorable results flowing from such noble dealing. The wrongdoer, filled with a sense of shame, leaves off doing the evil he intended. There is, for instance, the story of how Joseph returned good for evil to his brethren, who had sold him into slavery, and of the deep repentance to which his act gave rise. The action of Joseph in this story is singularly free from the spirit of vengeance.[1] There is also the story of David who in his flight from Saul on one occasion found himself in a position where he could have killed Saul and avenged himself on the latter for all the suffering Saul had caused him. David refused, however, to take advantage of the occasion. Saul, discovering the next morning that his life had been in the hand of his enemy but that David had refused to take vengeance, cried out: "Thou art more righteous than I; for thou hast rendered unto me good, whereas I have rendered unto thee evil."[2] We are told how Saul was moved to tears by this magnanimity and left off pursuing him for the time being.

[1] Gen. 42—45.
[2] I Sam. 24:1-22.

Then there is the story of Elisha and the invading Syrians. In this story the king of Israel was not allowed to take vengeance on the invading enemy who had so strangely been delivered into his hands. He was urged instead to set food before them. The result of this noble gesture was that the "bands of Syria" departed quietly and "came no more into the land of Israel."[3]

Two things about these stories are significant. (1) Magnanimous treatment of evildoers, returning good for evil, evidently was regarded as adding to the greatness and esteem of national heroes. (2) This largehearted treatment of the evildoer served to convert the latter to a better course of action.

Secondly, there are teachings that urge a lofty standard of conduct toward the evildoer. The Old Testament ethic on this subject reaches perhaps its highest point in the words of Leviticus 19:17, 18: "Thou shalt not hate thy brother in thy heart: thou shalt surely rebuke thy neighbor, and not bear sin because of him. Thou shalt not take vengeance, nor bear any grudge against the children of thy people; but thou shalt love thy neighbor as thyself: I am Jehovah." In verse 34 the following words are added: "The stranger that sojourneth with you shall be unto you as the home-born among you, and thou shalt love him as thyself."

The emphasis in this passage is not on the outward conduct but on the inward spirit that should prevail. One is not to hate a fellow Jew. Even where one has good cause for hatred, one is urged to use the method of rebuke rather than a method that would involve sinning against him. And in case of personal insult one is not to take vengeance, not even to bear a grudge. One is to love one's neighbor as himself. These words cut at the very root not only of the law of revenge but of the spirit of revenge as well. They forbid not only the act but also the spirit of retaliation by substituting for it the positive spirit of love.

This conduct is urged not from a calculating spirit that

[3] II Kings 6:21-23.

expects some benefit from the right conduct, nor is it urged from mere considerations of prudence. It is religiously motivated: "I am Jehovah." Because of the character of God, and because of their relation to Him as His people, men are to refrain from hating and bearing a grudge, and are to love their neighbor as themselves. The conduct that is envisaged in this passage does not go beyond possible relation with fellow Jews, and even verse 34 does not include more than the *Ger,* the sojourner; but the principle proclaimed is universal in character.

In the Book of Proverbs there are a number of passages which deal with the question of retaliation. Some of these virtually set aside the old principle of retaliation. "Say not thou, I will recompense evil [i.e., 'I will take vengeance for wrong'[4]]: wait [i.e., 'trust'[5]] for Jehovah, and he will save thee."[6] A similar couplet occurs in 24:29: "Say not, I will do so to him as he hath done to me; I will render to the man according to his work." Verse 17 of the same chapter, "Rejoice not when thine enemy falleth, and let not thy heart be glad when he is overthrown," even goes so far as to prohibit rejoicing at the fall or punishment of the enemy. (Cf. Job 31:29, 30.) The fine spirit of this verse is somewhat marred by the words that follow: "Lest Jehovah see it, and it displease him, and he turn away his wrath from him."[7] There is a difference of opinion among scholars as to whether the verse expresses fear that God will turn His wrath away from the enemy to *you* or whether it merely means that God will turn His wrath away from the enemy and leave him unpunished. Whether we adopt the one view or the other, the essential fact remains that it is a selfish consideration that keeps one from rejoicing at the punishment of the enemy. However, the significant thing about this passage is not the negative side of the words but the fact that God is repre-

---

4 Oesterley, *Book of Proverbs,* p. 172.
5 *Ibid.*
6 Prov. 20:22.
7 Prov. 24:18.

sented as being displeased with any gloating over the punishment of an evildoer.

But there is a passage in Proverbs that goes even further than this. Chapter 25:21, 22 suggests that the best way of dealing with an enemy is to return good for evil. "If thine enemy be hungry, give him bread to eat; and if he be thirsty, give him water to drink: for thou wilt heap coals of fire upon his head, and Jehovah will reward thee." The goal of this course of action, "[heaping] coals of fire upon his head," is not the shame of the evildoer but his sincere repentance. We have here, therefore, a real approach to the interpretation Paul puts on these words in Romans 12:21: "Overcome evil with good." The mind is to be turned away from one's own insult and desire for revenge. It is to turn instead to the evildoer and the means of bringing him to a better state of mind. The method suggested is generous dealing.

The high idealism the Hebrew sages seem to have reached in these words is somewhat marred by the last phrase, "and Jehovah will reward thee," which introduces a touch of the mercenary spirit that is frequently present in these sayings of the wise. A man is not asked to do the good deed for its own sake but for the sake of the reward God will give him. But in spite of this mercenary touch it is significant that this returning of good for evil is regarded as pleasing to God and an object of his reward as over against the method of revenge.

Exodus 23:4, 5 urges a magnanimous attitude toward one's enemy in the case of lost property. "If thou meet thine enemy's ox or his ass going astray, thou shalt surely bring it back to him again. If thou see the ass of him that hateth thee lying under his burden, thou shall forbear to leave him, thou shalt surely release it with him." Deuteronomy 22:1-4, covering essentially the same idea, speaks only of the lost property of a brother, perhaps not with the idea of restricting the application of Exodus 23:4 f. only to a brother Jew but with the idea of extending it definitely to include the brother Jew. The question arises whether the primary intention of Exodus 23:4 f. is to urge that one's interest in restoring the lost property to a friend be equally extended to the enemy or whether the primary interest lies in the sacredness of property. The emphasis in Deuteronomy would lead one to conclude the latter, but in either case the lost property is to be restored. And in either case it is significant that a man's natural feeling of revenge is to be restrained in the interest of the common good.

ILLUSTRATIONS FROM CONTEMPORARY JEWISH LITERATURE

The Apocrypha

There are numerous sayings in Jewish Apocryphal writings urging men not to avenge themselves. Three quotations will be sufficient for our purpose of illustration.

1. The "Secrets of Enoch" (50:4) urges men not to avenge themselves, because God will do it for them (perhaps with the thought in the background of their minds that God would do it much better than they could do it themselves and with no unpleasant consequences to their own person). "If ill-requitals befall you, return them not either to neighbor or enemy, because the Lord will return them for you and be your avenger on the day of great judgment, that there be no avenging here among men."[8]

2. A nobler passage is found in Sirach 27:30—28:7: "Wrath and anger, these also are abominations, and a sinful man clingeth to them. He that taketh vengeance shall find vengeance from the Lord, and his sins God will surely keep in memory. Forgive thy neighbor the injury done to thee, and then, when thou prayest, thy sins will be forgiven. . . . Remember thy last end, and cease from enmity; . . . and be not wroth with thy neighbor . . . and overlook ignorance." The demand to refrain from "wrath and anger" and "enmity" and from taking "vengeance," and instead to exercise forgiveness, is a high one; but the motive urged is in the main

[8] R. H. Charles, *The Apocrypha*, Vol. II, p. 460.

a prudential one. "On a man like himself he hath no mercy; and doth he make supplication for his own sins?"[9]

3. The "Testaments of the Twelve Patriarchs" contain a passage that far transcends either of these. It is all the more remarkable because it does not stand as an isolated oasis in a desert but is in full harmony with the high ethical emphasis in that book. Gad 6:3 ff.:

> Love ye, therefore, one another from the heart; and if a man sin against thee, cast forth the poison of hate and speak peaceably to him, and in thy soul hold not guile; and if he confess and repent, forgive him. But if he deny it, do not get into a passion with him, lest catching the poison from thee he take to swearing and so thou sin doubly. . . . And though he deny it and yet have a sense of shame when reproved, give over reproving him. For he who denieth may repent so as not again to wrong thee; yea, he may also honor thee and be at peace with thee. And if he be shameless and persist in his wrongdoing, even so forgive him from the heart, and leave to God the avenging.[10]

This passage is especially remarkable because it reveals a true understanding of the psychological basis for any real solution of the difficulty between the offender and the offended. The solution lies in the restoring of the relationship of trust and love and fellowship which has been marred by the wrongdoing. Even when the offender fails to respond, or responds imperfectly to the attempted reconciliation, the offended person is yet to give evidence of the same reconciling spirit of forgiveness, first of all by ridding himself of the feeling of personal resentment, and second by showing a sympathetic attitude to the offender.

The passage urges, first of all, that there be present in every person a constant and genuine love for the other. Presumably this attitude of love is regarded as the necessary basis for, and perhaps the necessary agent in, the fulfillment of what follows. In case a man wrongs you, the first thing you must do is to get rid of the feeling of personal resent-

9 *Ibid.*, p. 408.
10 R. H. Charles, *Pseudepigrapha*, Vol. II, p. 341; Gad 6:3 ff.

ment, and then speak to him in words whose sincere intent is the restoring of peace and harmony. If he confesses and repents, you are to forgive him. If he denies the guilt or the charge, the one thing you must not do is to lose your temper, for you may make him angry and cause him to curse, and you will thus become responsible for a double wrong on his part. If he denies the fault and yet under reproof (presumably of a gentle sort) reveals a sense of shame, you must give up any further reproof. Although he may outwardly deny his fault, his sense of shame may yet cause him to repent so that he be at ease with you, perhaps even honor you, and refrain from any further repetition of the wrong. But if he shows no sense of shame and persists in his wrongdoing, he must in that case be left to God, but your forgiveness is, nevertheless, to be extended to him sincerely and wholeheartedly.

Rabbinical Literature

A great variety of sayings in rabbinical literature cover the general subject of one's relation and attitude to the wrongdoer. We quote only a few of the higher ethical teachings in order to indicate various aspects of the teaching. Passages protesting against hatred, anger, and the vengeful spirit, and urging forgiveness are many.

"The evil eye, the evil *yeser* (desire), and hatred of his fellow creatures drive a man out of the world" (Rabbi Joshua, A.D. 90; Aboth 2:11; SB, p. 364). Montefiore maintains that the "driving out of the world" is meant in a psychological rather than in a literal sense. The punishment a man receives is what he has made for himself by his selfish nature. It is the selfish man that hates, and it is only selfish people who hate him in return.[11] In other words, hatred isolates a man from the society of his fellow men. The violent temper of Rabbi Shammai (30 B.C.) for instance, is contrasted with the *Sanftmut* (mildness, gentleness) of Hillel. The attitude of the former would have driven men out of

11 Montefiore, *Rabbinic Literature*, p. 89.

the world, while the latter had brought them under the wings of the Shekinah, i.e., permitted them to become proselytes.[12]

Another passage graphically illustrates this same idea. "If A says to B: 'Lend me your scythe,' and B refuses, and the following day B says to A: 'Lend me your spade (or axe),' and A replies: 'I will not lend it to you even as you refused to lend me your scythe,' that is revenge which is forbidden in the law. But if A says to B: "Lend me your spade (or axe),' and he refuses, and if the following day B says to A: 'Lend me your scythe,' and A replies: 'Here it is. I am not like you who refused to lend me your spade,' that is bearing a grudge which is also forbidden."[13]

The Jerusalem Talmud has preserved a number of ancient personal prayers that reveal a spirit of marked nobility. "May it be Thy will, O Lord and God of my fathers, that hatred and envy of us enter not into the heart of men, nor hatred and envy of any man enter into our heart." A student's prayer read as follows: "May it be Thy will, that I be not angered against my fellows, nor they against me." Another prayer read: "Bring us near to what Thou lovest, and keep us far from what Thou hatest." And of Rabbi Mar Zutra it was said that every night on retiring he would implore: "Forgiveness be to all who have troubled me." Another rabbi said at the close of his life: "I never went to bed with the curse of my fellow" (Megillah 28a).[14]

The principles upon which men are urged to act in case of insult or violence or wrong are various. Sometimes they represent stoic endurance of wrong. "He who listens to his malediction in silence shall be called a saint" (Midrash Psalm 16; 62a—SB, p. 370).

Sometimes men are urged "not to stand upon their rights." To be yielding means "to go beyond one's nature or natural

---

12 Strack and Billerbeck, *op. cit.*, Vol. I, p. 276.
13 Montefiore, *Rabbinic Literature*, p. 89 (in Strack and Billerbeck, Vol. I, p. 277).
14 Montefiore, *Rabbinic Literature*, p. 90 (in Strack and Billerbeck, Vol. I, p. 277).

inclinations," i.e., not to insist on one's own will and desire. Related to this is another rabbinic expression: "Act within the line of legal right" ("i.e., not perchance to demand more even than the strict letter of the law allows, not even to insist on the letter of the law but to keep on this side of the line of legal right, to be satisfied with less than one could by right demand").

Men are also at times urged that it is better to suffer wrong than to do wrong. "Let a man always belong to the persecuted rather than to persecuting."[15] "This is what people used to say: Let a man sooner be cursed than cursing."[16] One of the noblest passages urges: "Of them who are oppressed and do not oppress, who are reviled and do not [in reply] revile, who act only from love [to God], and rejoice in their sufferings, the Scripture says: They who love Him are like the sun when it rises in its might."[17]

Sometimes men are urged to endure wrong not only in silence and with complete self-mastery but even with a sense of humor. There was a proverb which said: "If men call you an ass, go and put on a saddle."[18] A variant of the above in the Palestinian tradition ran like this: "If a man says to you: *Deine Ohren sind Eselsohren* (your ears are the ears of an ass), do not pay any attention to it. But if two men should say it to you, then go and get a halter."[19]

Sometimes men are told that their action should be controlled by the principle of regard for the wrongdoer. Illustrations are given to show that this action has resulted in the conversion of the evildoer. Baba Mezia 32b states that if there are two cases of need, to unload a friend's ass and to unload an enemy's ass, the enemy is to take precedence. If you ask why, the answer is, to crush the evil desire.[20] Here

---

15 R. Yehuda (269).
16 Strack and Billerbeck, *op. cit.*, Vol. I, p. 370.
17 Montefiore, *Rabbinic Literature*, p. 54.
18 Baba Kamma 92b (Raba 352), Strack and Billerbeck, *op. cit.*, Vol. I, p. 341.
19 Genesis Rabba 28b, *ibid.*, p. 341.
20 *Rabbinic Literature*, p. 93.

it is clearly the evil desire of the man who is tempted to leave the enemy and his ass unaided, while he goes to the assistance of the friend, that is, to be crushed. But in T. Baba Mezia 2, 26 (375) it is clearly stated that the object is to "crush (i.e., change) the heart of the enemy." That is the reason why one is to help the enemy unload before helping the friend to load his ass.[21]

An interesting and pertinent story is told by Rabbi Alexander (270): Two donkey drivers who were enemies were on their way when the ass of one fell under his burden. The other saw it but passed on. Remembering the law of Exodus 23:5 f.: 'If thou see the ass of him that hateth thee lying under his burden, . . . thou shalt surely release it with him,' he promptly turned around and helped him. The other one said: "So much did B love me and I knew it not." The two of them then went to an inn and ate and drank and came to love one another. If you ask what brought about the peace and reconciliation between the two, the answer is, the knowledge of the law which one of them possessed. The same story with additions is found in Tanchuma Mishpatim 91a and Midrash Psalm 99, 4 (212a).[22]

Whatever method one finally uses toward the evildoer, one must show a proper regard for the other's feelings. "Whoever makes his neighbor's face blanch (from shame) before others, is as if he shed blood, . . . for the red disappears and the white comes."[23] Moore adds: "To put one's fellow to an open shame is counted one of the gravest sins."[24] It is classed by the rabbis with the sins that shut out from the world to come.

Various motives are suggested why one is to be magnanimous rather than vindictive toward the offender. Besides the motives indicated above there are also the following:

The duty of forgiveness toward the offender. This is emphasized in the strongest terms. "Sins that are between a

---

21 *Rabbinic Literature*, p. 93; Strack and Billerbeck, *op. cit.*, Vol. I, p. 369.
22 *Ibid.*
23 Baba Mezia 58b, George F. Moore, *Judaism*, Vol. II, p. 147.
24 *Ibid.*

man and his fellow, the Day of Atonement does not expiate until he has conciliated his fellow."[25] Tosefta Baba Kamma 9, 29 has this statement: "If a man has received an injury, and if the wrongdoer has not asked his forgiveness, he must nevertheless ask (God) to show him pity." Rabbi Gamaliel, quoting Deuteronomy 13:17, "That the Lord may show thee mercy and have compassion upon thee," adds: "Let this be a sign in thy hand that whenever thou art compassionate, the Compassionate One will have compassion upon thee."[26] Another passage declares: "Raba said, He who is forgiving, him they forgive all his transgressions. Whom does God forgive? Him who overlooks the transgression (of others)."[27] Rabbi Meier (150), we are told, was led by his wife to change his prayer for the death of certain ruffians who had annoyed him greatly, into a prayer for their repentance. The prayer was heard and they repented.[28]

If the wrongdoer asks forgiveness and makes his amends, it is the duty of the person wronged to forgive him. "When thou hast mercy upon thy fellow, thou hast One to have mercy on thee; but if thou hast not mercy upon thy fellow, thou hast none to have mercy on thee."[29]

Men are urged repeatedly to imitate God, especially in His attitude of forgiveness to the wrongdoer. "As God is called merciful and gracious, so do thou be merciful and gracious, offering gifts gratis to all; as the Lord is called righteous and loving, so be thou righteous and loving."[30]

Men are also urged to give fair treatment to hated or despised classes because of "the sanctification of the Name." One passage emphasizes this strongly: "To rob (defraud) a Gentile is worse than to rob an Israelite on account of the profanation of the Name."[31] Moore comments: "That is, no doubt, the prevailing motive. One must do what is just to

25 M. Yoma 8, 9, in Moore, *Judaism*, Vol. II, p. 154.
26 Montefiore, *Rabbinic Literature*, p. 54.
27 *Ibid.*, p. 135.
28 Strack and Billerbeck, *op. cit.*, Vol. I, p. 370.
29 Tanchuma B. Wayyera 30, 52a, in Moore, *Judaism*, Vol. II, p. 154.
30 Sifra 85a, in *Rabbinic Literature*, p. 105.
31 Moore, *Judaism, op. cit.*, p. 109.

the *goi*, not for his sake but for God's sake. The glorification of Israel's God is the greatest duty of the Israelite's life."[32]

Abrahams suggests that the example of Joseph was frequently set up as an ideal of one's attitude to the wrongdoer. "The example of Joseph so very deeply impressed Jewish thought that it is set up as an exemplar for God Himself."[33] He cites as "an oft-repeated idea" a passage from Pesikta Rabbathi (138a):

> Comfort ye, comfort ye my people, saith your God (Isa. 40:1). This is what the Scripture hath: O that thou wert as my brother (Cant. 8:1). What kind of brother? . . . Such a brother as Joseph to his brethren. After all the evils they wrought unto him Joseph said, Now therefore fear ye not: I will nourish you, and your little ones. And he comforted them, and spake kindly unto them (Gen. 50:21). . . . Israel said unto God: Master of the world, come regard Joseph. After all the evils wrought by his brothers he comforted them and spake to their heart; and we, on our part, are conscious that we caused Thy house to be laid waste through our iniquities, we slew Thy prophets, and transgressed all the precepts of the law, yet, O that Thou wert as a brother unto me! Then the Lord answered: Verily, I will be unto you as Joseph. He comforted his people and spake to their heart.[34]

Summary

In summarizing the main emphases in this higher ethical teaching in Jewish literature we point out the following:

1. It attempts to deal with the springs of action rather than with mere outward conduct, to correct a wrong spirit rather than merely wrong action.

2. It strongly and insistently condemns hatred and anger, the evil desire and the vengeful spirit out of which acts of revenge and violence spring.

3. It insistently emphasizes the duty of forgiveness, and it strongly commends love and magnanimity in dealing with the offender.

---

32 Moore, *Judaism*, Vol. II, p. 105.
33 Israel Abrahams, *Studies in Pharisaism*, I, p. 155.
34 *Ibid.*

4. The basis for a forgiving, largehearted attitude to the evildoer is found in the will and the character of God. God is merciful, compassionate, and forgiving toward men, and therefore men are to be merciful, compassionate, and forgiving to one another, even to enemies. As He requites good for evil, so men are to return good for evil. As He has been gracious and loving toward Israel, so the Israelites are to be loving in their relation to one another. They are to love their neighbor as themselves. In their relations with others they are to refrain from all acts that may reflect discredit on Israel's God. His will for men is regarded as a sufficient motive for conduct.

5. The words are generally directed at the aggrieved person, but they do not concern themselves exclusively with the correction of his state of mind. For the Hebrew writers the fear lest the person wronged be led into acts and attitudes that would rob him of his inner purity and his integrity is not the matter of chief concern. They recognize the fact that there are other factors, besides those of the person wronged and his right attitude in the matter, that need to be considered in the solution of the problem. They seem to sense the fact that the real tragedy in the wrongdoing lies not in the act itself but in the marred relationship of trust and love. For this reason their solution of the problem does not lie in an attempt to patch up the difficulty by a delicate balancing of fines and penalties but rather in the attempt to re-establish normal and free relations of fellowship.

6. For this reason the conversion of the wrongdoer is, to these Hebrew thinkers, of primary importance. Fellowship, they realized, was possible only where there was mutual good will. Consequently the conversion of the wrongdoer's ill will into good will became a matter of primary concern to them. The power to effect this change in the wrongdoer and to restore him to the plane of fellowship, they believed, lay peculiarly in the hands of the one who had been wronged. His refusal to become bitter, resentful, and vengeful in the face of the wrong or to allow the wrong to destroy or even

to diminish the spirit of good will and fellowship he had for the other, this together with the unmistakable assertion of his good will and forgiveness by the returning of good for evil, they believed, would have a powerful effect in changing the ill will of the wrongdoer.

In their best thought both the Old Testament and contemporary Jewish literature urge charity toward the wrongdoer and in the matter of retaliation. The spirit of resentment and revenge is to be displaced by an attitude that attempts to recall the offender to his better self and restore him to a relation of true fellowship.

4

Jesus and the Revolutionary Movement of His Time

The Revolutionary Movement

In recent years great stress has been laid on the intense national feeling and the widespread revolutionary activity among the Jews during the time of Jesus. Simkhovitch[1] and Klausner[2] among others have painted an impressive and detailed picture of this political situation in an effort to show how it affected Jesus' life and message. It does not appear necessary to review again the story they have so well told of the origin and development of this revolutionary movement; but it is necessary to evaluate the possible influence of this movement on the teachings of Jesus. For this reason we call attention to certain aspects of the general problem.

For information about this movement we are dependent almost wholly on the works of Josephus, well-known Jewish historian (A.D. 37-95), principally *The Antiquities of the Jews* and *The Jewish War*.

Estimates of the strength and energy of the movement during the time of Jesus are based very largely on the disorders and the violence immediately preceding the time of Jesus, specifically those following the misrule of Herod the Great (died 4 B.C.), and of his successor Archelaus (banished A.D. 6), and on the later fierce fanaticism and violence which followed the reign of Herod Agrippa I (A.D. 44) and culminated in the disastrous war of A.D. 66-70. It is easy but unwarranted to conclude that the revolutionary

[1] V. G. Simkhovitch, *Toward the Understanding of Jesus.*

[2] Joseph Klausner, *Jesus of Nazareth*, Second Book, Chapter I, "Political Conditions." p. 135.

spirit that arose during and immediately following the reign of Herod the Great continued unabated and increased in a steadily ascending scale to the height of the violence and fanaticism manifested during the period of the great war. The impression one gets from a reading of Josephus is rather that there was a comparative lull in revolutionary activity during the years A.D. 6-44.

Josephus devotes very little space to the events of this period. In *The Jewish War* he covers this interim in three short paragraphs, not including the difficulty under Petronius, governor of Syria (A.D. 40-41). In *Antiquities* this period, including a few events not recorded in *The Jewish War*, is covered in six paragraphs.

From A.D. 6 to 44, i.e., after the disturbance caused by the census under Quirinius in A.D. 6, Josephus lists only the following events as of sufficiently provocative nature to stir up the spirit of revolt:

The building of the city of Tiberias by Herod Antipas on the site of an old burial ground in complete disregard of Jewish sensibilities.[3] Josephus suggests that this continued to be a source of offense to pious Jews, but there is no indication that it ever caused any violent disturbance.

The frequent changes in the office of high priest by Valerius Gratus, procurator from A.D. 14 to 26.[4] That the Jews should resent such tampering with the office of the high priest by the political power, especially if that power were Gentile, was almost inevitable, but Josephus does not indicate that such was the case on this occasion.

Herod's marriage to Herodias and the murder of John the Baptist.[5] The marriage to Herodias was a source of offense to pious Jews, who regarded it as an adulterous union. About the murder of John the Baptist Josephus remarks that

---

[3] *Life and Works of Flavius Josephus*, tr. by Wm. Whiston. "Antiquities" XVIII, 2, 3; "Wars" II, 9, 1. (This work is divided into two parts, "Antiquities" with XX parts, and "Wars" in VII parts. The numbers given refer to the numbering system of the work instead of pages.)
[4] *Ibid.*, "Antiquities" XVIII, 2, 2.
[5] *Ibid.*, XVIII, 5, 2.

THE REVOLUTIONARY MOVEMENT

"some of the Jews thought that the destruction of Herod's army (by Aretas, King of Arabia) came from God, and that very justly, as a punishment of what he did against John, who is called the Baptist."[6]

The bringing of the Roman standards into Jerusalem by Pilate upon his assuming the office of procurator in A.D. 26.[7] Josephus relates how this caused a popular protest. Multitudes of Jews came to Caesarea unarmed and for days petitioned for the removal of the standards from the city. There was no display of violence on the part of the Jews, not even after Pilate's threat of the use of force.

Pilate's use of the money from the temple treasury to pay for the construction of an aqueduct into Jerusalem sometime during the latter part of his procuratorship. This act caused "many ten thousands"[8] to get together and make "a clamor against him [Pilate]" and insist "that he should leave off the design."[9] There were those who heaped a measure of abuse on Pilate, but there was no mob violence or armed resistance. Pilate met this protest by setting his soldiers upon the multitude, killing "a great number of them"[10] and wounding others.

Pilate's attack on the Samaritans at Mt. Gerizim (A.D. 36-37). This was the immediate cause for Pilate's removal from office, but it really had little direct relation to the attitude of the Jews to Rome.

The demand of Caligula through Petronius that his statue be set up in the temple (A.D. 40-41). This demand was met with a similar unarmed protest on the part of "many ten thousands"[11] of Jews who prostrated themselves before Petronius for forty days.

None of the protests, as recorded by Josephus, give the impression of being instigated by a highly inflamed or

6 *Ibid.*
7 *Ibid.*, XVIII, 3, 1; "Wars" II, 9, 2.
8 *Ibid.*, XVIII, 3, 2; "Wars" II, 9, 4.
9 *Ibid.*
10 *Ibid.*
11 *Ibid.*, XVIII, 8, 3.

highly inflammable public opinion. They appear rather as the natural popular reaction to the provocations that called them forth.

Considering, then, the limited discussion given them, the events cited above evidently did not appear, to Josephus, to be important factors in the developments leading to the Great Jewish War. In *The Jewish War*, for instance, the disturbances incident to the bringing in of the Roman standards and the building of the Jerusalem aqueduct by Pilate are covered in three short paragraphs while the building of the city of Tiberias is given no more than mere mention. The frequent changes in the high priesthood by Valerius Gratus and the killing of John the Baptist by Herod are not mentioned at all. And neither in the *Antiquities* nor in *The Jewish War* is there any attempt made to connect these disturbances in any way with subsequent revolutionary activity.

These observations are not intended to suggest that there was no revolutionary spirit or rebellious activity during the time of Jesus. That the revolutionary spirit and activity was not absent during this period will be pointed out later. Here it is necessary only to show that it is quite possible to exaggerate the intensity and the extent of the spirit of revolt during the time of Jesus.

The "Fourth Philosophy"

A word needs to be said about Judas of Galilee and his connection with the disturbance created by the taking of the census under Quirinius (A.D. 6) and with the subsequent founding of the so-called "Fourth Philosophy" of the Jews. Judas of Galilee is often identified with Judas, the son of Hezekiah, who was the leader of the Galilean "robber" bands which Herod the Great so ruthlessly crushed in the beginning of his reign.[12] But Josephus seemingly takes pains to keep them separate. He calls the latter

---

[12] So Joseph Klausner, *Jesus of Nazareth*, p. 162; Simkhovitch, *Toward the Understanding of Jesus*, p. 7; Emil Schuerer, *Geschichte des Juedischen Volkes*, Vol. I, p. 486.

THE REVOLUTIONARY MOVEMENT 57

definitely, "Son of Hezekiah."[13] The former he calls "Judas, a Gaulonite, of a city whose name was Gamala."[14] He never calls him a robber.[15] He refers to him several times as a philosopher.[16] In other words, Judas of Galilee was a philosopher, a teacher of revolutionary doctrines, not the leader of a robber band. He charged his countrymen that "they were cowards, if they would endure to pay a tax to the Romans, and would, after God, submit to mortal men as their lords. This man was a teacher of a peculiar sect of his own and was not at all like the rest of those their leaders.[17] In what respect he differed from other revolutionary leaders Josephus does not explain, unless it be that he was a "philosopher" rather than a "robber."

Judas and his co-worker Sadduc, a Pharisee, had tried to induce the people to revolt during the time of the census. In this they failed because of the efforts of the high priest, Joazar, son of Boethus, who persuaded the people to submit. But they succeeded in forming a so-called "Fourth Sect" whose members differed from those of the sect of the Pharisees chiefly because of their "inviolable attachment to liberty"[18] and their willingness to suffer anything rather than surrender this liberty.

In *Antiquities* 20, 5, 2 Josephus states that he has elsewhere related how Judas "caused the people to revolt against Rome." "But his words may only imply that some of the people were persuaded to withdraw their allegiance."[19] The sons of Judas became leaders of violent revolutionary bands,[20] but Judas himself was likely nothing

13 "Antiquities" XVII, 10, 5.
14 *Ibid.*, XVIII, 1, 1.
15 Josephus uses the term "robber" loosely. At times the term refers simply to a highway robber. At other times he uses this term to refer to individuals active in the Jewish underground. These men lived in hiding places and got their sustenance by robbery if necessary, doubtless justifying their action on patriotic grounds. It was obviously often difficult to distinguish between "patriotic robbery" and highway robbery.
16 "Wars" II, 8, 1; 2, 17, 8.
17 "Wars" II, 8, 1.
18 "Antiquities" XVIII, 1, 6.
19 F. J. Foakes-Jackson, *Josephus and the Jews*, p. 264.
20 "Antiquities" XX, 5, 2; "Wars" II, 17, 8-10.

more than "one of those dangerous persons who use their position as teachers to incite discontent and revolution"[21] and who in this position "preached a dangerous nationalism which led to rebellion long after his death."[22]

The Zealot Movement

It is commonly assumed that this movement was identical with the so-called "Fourth Philosophy" founded by Judas the Gaulonite, and likewise with the "Sicarii." Closely associated with this idea is the assumption that an unbroken line of leadership spearheaded this movement, beginning not only with Judas of Galilee but with his supposed predecessor, Hezekiah, head of the Galilean robber band crushed by Herod the Great.

In answer to this Jackson and Lake declare that "hardly any of these assumptions is well founded."[23] They point to the following evidence:

Josephus states in *The Jewish War* that the Sicarii arose during the time of Felix (A.D. 52-60). They were called Sicarii because they wore concealed daggers under their garments. On festival days they would mingle with the crowds and, using these concealed daggers, would assassinate their victims.[24] Their first victim, according to Josephus, was Jonathan, the high priest. After that they assassinated men on such frequent occasions that a reign of terror ensued. Later these Sicarii became an organized band with headquarters in the fortress of Masada. Here under the leadership of Eleazar, a descendant of Judas, they maintained themselves until after the fall of Jerusalem. During the siege of Masada that followed, the whole company of Sicarii within the walls engaged in a wholesale mutual self-slaughter rather than fall into the hands of the Romans. Only two women and five children were left in the fortress

---

21 *Ibid.*
22 Foakes-Jackson, *op. cit.*, p. 264.
23 Jackson and Lake, *Beginnings of Christianity*, Vol. I, "The Zealots," p. 421.
24 Josephus, "Wars" II, 13, 3.

THE REVOLUTIONARY MOVEMENT

when the Romans finally took it.[25] Some of the Sicarii fled to Alexandria in Egypt and some to Cyrene, so that the organization in Judea was completely broken up.

The first use of the word "Zealot," Jackson and Lake point out, is found in *The Jewish War* 4, 3, 9.[26] After that the term is used frequently and always with the same meaning. Josephus presents it as the name the followers of John of Gischala had seized for themselves. John was the leader of the group that defended Gischala, the last city of Galilee to surrender to the Roman armies under Titus. Finally, being forced to flee, John and his followers escaped to Jerusalem. Here they started a popular movement against the high priestly families and their supporters, which resulted in considerable bloodshed. Eventually he became a powerful leader of one of the rival factions that fought each other, both before and during the siege of Jerusalem. But Josephus always clearly distinguishes the Zealots from the other factions, for he always uses the word in this specific and exclusive sense to designate the followers of John of Gischala. He pictures them as equally opposed to the Sicarii, the priestly faction, and the followers of Simon ben Giora.

Jackson and Lake further point to the fact that "in the New Testament (i.e., Acts 22:3), in the Greek Apocrypha (i.e., II Maccabees 4:2), and in Josephus in passages earlier than the rise of John of Gischala (i.e., *Antiquities* 12, 6, 1) the term used always means 'zealous.' It is the equivalent of the Hebrew *Canah*, a title of God and of men who are 'jealous' for God's honor, such as Elijah."[27]

Referring to the name "Simon the Zealot" appearing in Luke 6:15 and Acts 1:13 they declare that he "appears to be identical with Simon the Cananaean in Matthew 10:4 and Mark 3:18. But it is obvious that Simon can scarcely have

---

25 "Wars" VII, 8, 1-7; VII, 9, 1-2.
26 There is a previous use of the term in "Wars" II, 22, 1, but it occurs in a paragraph where previous reference is made to events that are taken up in their proper historical sequence in 4, 3, 9. The contention of the authors is therefore essentially correct.
27 Jackson and Lake, *op. cit.*, Vol. I, p. 425.

been called a Zealot in the sense of belonging to the party of John of Gischala, and therefore the theory has arisen that there was a party called Cananaeans in Aramaic and Zealots in Greek before the last days of Jerusalem, identical with the 'Fourth Philosophy' described by Josephus."[28] In the end the authors conclude: "It is possible that we have all been wrong in translating the Greek of Luke, or explaining the transliterated Aramaic of Matthew, as 'Simon the Zealot,' and that it should be 'Simon the zealous'; or in other words that there is no reference at all to any political party but merely to the personal character of Simon.[29]

These deductions of Jackson and Lake appear, on the whole, to be sound even though, as in the case of Simon the Zealot, they are perhaps not altogether conclusive. But in the light of the facts presented by Josephus, it appears to be unwarranted to speak of the revolutionary movement in Jesus' day as the "Zealot" movement.

It is therefore not very clear just what this revolutionary movement in Jesus' day was and how it was active. Josephus reports that Judas the Gaulonite and Sadduc taught that "this taxation (under Quirinius) was no better than an introduction to slavery, and exhorted the nation to assert their liberty. . . . They also said that God would not otherwise be assisting to them than upon their joining with one another in such counsels as might be successful, and for their own advantage; and this especially, if they would set about great exploits, and not grow weary in executing the same."[30] According to *The Jewish War*[31] he told his countrymen that "they were cowards, if they would endure to pay a tax to the Romans, and would, after God, submit to mortal men as their lords."

In *Antiquities* 18, 1, 6 Josephus says the adherents of the "Fourth Philosophy" have "an inviolable attachment to liberty, and say that God is to be their only Ruler and Lord.

28 *Ibid.*
29 *Ibid.*
30 "Antiquities" XVIII, 1, 1.
31 "Wars" II, 8, 1.

They also do not value dying any kinds of death, nor indeed do they heed the death of their relations and friends, nor can any such fear make them call any man lord."

On the basis of such summary statements it is impossible to construct a clear and satisfactory picture of this movement during the time of Jesus, especially when Josephus fails to give any clear and concrete evidences of the activity of the movement between the time of Judas' attempted revolt in A.D. 6 and the reign of Agrippa I (A.D. 44). On the basis of the facts available we are not even sure whether this movement was a definite party. Josephus' classification of it as a fourth "philosophy" or "sect" by the side of the three other well-known Jewish parties, the Sadducees, the Pharisees, and Essenes, would suggest that he regarded it as a definite party. But Josephus' failure to mention a specific name for this "Fourth Philosophy" might indicate that the movement or party was not very clearly defined or very compactly organized. The suggestion that this revolutionary movement was known as the party of the "Cananaeans"[32] Jackson and Lake describe as "merely a guess, though a probable one, based on a retranslation of 'zelotes,' in Josephus, combined with an imperfect appreciation of its usage."[33] (The reference here is to the statement made above that "zelotes" is to be translated as "zealous" rather than "Zealot.")

Summary

The following conclusions emerge out of the preceding discussions on the revolutionary movement during the time of Jesus:

It is impossible to give any clear picture of the revolutionary movement during the time of Jesus, either as regards its organization, its activity, or its energy.

Its activity likely consisted more in spreading revolution-

---

[32] On the basis of the reference to "Simon the Cananaean" in Matt. 10:4 and Mark 3:18 where Luke, seemingly referring to the same disciple, has "Simon the Zealot" (Luke 6:15; Acts 1:13).

[33] Jackson and Lake, *op. cit.*, Vol. I, p. 425.

ary teaching and discontent than in fomenting actual riots and armed resistance.

It seems to have been most prominent in Judea. That is where Judas the Gaulonite and his sons were active. "Conditions elsewhere in Palestine were better since the government was in the hands of a Jew, even though he was not altogether independent."[34]

Even in Judea this period (A.D. 6-44) was a time of comparative peace. "The silence of Josephus surely allows us to infer that for a considerable time, after some vigorous measures taken by Gratus against some insurgents, there was not much to disturb the peace of Palestine."[35] Jackson and Lake state that "never in its long history had Jerusalem experienced such unbroken peace and progress as in the century preceding the outbreak of the Jewish war: the riots and petty rebellions were but symptoms of troubles to come."[36]

Josephus' silence is not conclusive. It may merely mean either that his sources did not supply him with definite information or that he did not think it essential to record all the riots and petty rebellions that broke out from time to time. That there were riots and petty rebellions inspired by this revolutionary movement Josephus' summary statement, that "all sorts of misfortunes also sprang from these men" (i.e., the followers of Judas the Gaulonite) and that "one violent war came upon us after another."[37] would seem to suggest. How frequent and how serious these disturbances were it is impossible to determine on the basis of Josephus. The Gospels refer to certain incidents, some of which are not mentioned in his writings, that cast light on the revolutionary movement in the time of Jesus, but these references are so meager that they fail to throw much additional light on the record of Josephus.

34 Klausner, *op. cit.*, p. 164.
35 Foakes-Jackson, *op. cit.*, p. 162.
36 Jackson and Lake, *op. cit.*, Vol. I, p. 12.
37 "Antiquities" XVIII, 1, 1.

POSSIBLE POINTS OF CONTACT WITH THE REVOLUTIONARY
MOVEMENT IN THE GOSPELS

Simon the Zealot

The references to Simon the Zealot[38] and to Simon the Cananaean[39] have already been discussed. The facts available indicate that these references offer but doubtful evidence for the presence of a definite revolutionary party during the time of Jesus.

The Arrest and Execution of John the Baptist

The arrest and murder of John the Baptist have also been referred to above. Josephus definitely attributes the capture and subsequent death of John to Herod's fear of an uprising. John is not mentioned in *The Jewish War*, but in *Antiquities*[40] the relevant passage runs as follows:

> Now when others came in crowds about him, for they were greatly moved by hearing his words, Herod, who feared lest the great influence John had over the people might put it into his power and inclination to raise a rebellion (for they seemed ready to do anything he should advise), thought it best by putting him to death to prevent any mischief he might cause, and not bring himself into difficulties, by sparing a man who might make him repent of it when it should be too late. Accordingly he was sent a prisoner, out of Herod's suspicious temper, to Machaerus . . . and was there put to death.

In the Synoptic Gospels John's arrest and execution appears to be a retaliatory measure intended to avenge his criticism of the marriage of Herod and Herodias as "unlawful,"[41] i.e., as adulterous. There is nothing in the Synoptic record to suggest that there was anything politically dangerous in the activity of John; neither is there any hint that Herod feared that political disturbances would result from John's preaching, unless the mere presence of soldiers among

38 Luke 6:15; Acts 1:13.
39 Mark 3:18; Matt. 10:4.
40 "Antiquities" XVIII, 5, 2.
41 Cf. Mark 6:14-29; Matt. 14:1-12; Luke 9:7-9. Also Mark 1:14; Matt. 4:12.

the groups of inquirers[42] constitutes such a hint. To Luke the presence of these soldiers is nothing but additional evidence of the great power of John's appeal. Under the influence of John's powerful preaching the multitudes and the publicans and even the soldiers are led to come forward and ask: "What then must we do?"[43]

But the question arises: How did these soldiers happen to be among the crowd of listeners? Were they drawn there merely by their curiosity to see and to hear this popular preacher, or had they been sent by Herod to keep an eye on the crowds and to be on hand to check any incipient revolutionary demonstrations that might develop? We do not know, but in view of Josephus' story the latter supposition does not seem impossible. This supposition is further strengthened by the report in Luke that Herod was evidently keeping a watchful eye on Jesus and His followers and that he "would fain kill" Jesus. Luke 13:31. Herod's reason for wanting to kill Jesus could hardly be any other than political. So it is not impossible that these soldier inquirers among John's listeners were sent by Herod to watch the crowds. The account by itself gives not the slightest indication that their presence had any such basis in fact. But the failure of the Synoptic Gospels to mention the political reason for the arrest and execution of John may be due in part to the desire to show that Christianity was, and from its very beginning had been, politically harmless.

Whatever reason there may have been for Herod's suspicions in regard to this popular movement John himself seems not to have been the cause of it. He appears, even in Josephus, to have been completely innocent of any revolutionary intention. Josephus describes him as "a good man" who "commanded the Jews to exercise virtue, both as to righteousness toward one another, and piety toward God, and so to come to baptism: for that the washing (with water) would be acceptable to him, if they made use of it,

---

[42] Luke 3:10-14.
[43] Luke 3:10-14.

not in order to the putting away (or remission) of some sins (only), but for the purification of the body: supposing still that the soul was thoroughly purified beforehand by righteousness."[44]

According to the Synoptic record[45] the arrest of John was the occasion that started Jesus upon the work of His ministry. But there is little, if anything, to confirm the idea that this arrest caused Jesus to use caution in beginning His ministry. If there had been any fear of Herod, He would hardly have started His ministry in Galilee, which was part of Herod's dominion, where any subsequent popular movement would almost certainly be watched with suspicion.

Plummer sees evidence of caution in Jesus' manner in the words of Matthew 4:12: "Now when he [i.e., Jesus] heard that John was delivered up, he withdrew into Galilee." He states that "*withdrew* into Galilee" "does not mean that He *returned* thither after the temptation; . . . perhaps Matthew means that He retired to a part of the dominions of Antipas where He would be less likely to be molested by him than in the region where the Baptist had been working."[46] The word "to withdraw (frequently in the sense of avoiding danger)"[47] by itself would allow this interpretation of the words in Matthew. But the meaning of the verb is not sufficiently specific to make the above interpretation inescapable. The words that follow this statement ("and leaving Nazareth, he came and dwelt in Capernaum")[48] serve to make the meaning of the verb even more uncertain. A withdrawal to centers like Nazareth and thence to Capernaum does not seem like retiring from danger or molestation. Then it must also further be noted that neither Mark nor Luke gives the slightest support to the meaning given to the Matthaean pas-

---

44 "Antiquities" XVIII, 5, 2.

45 Mark 1:14; Luke 4:14.

46 Plummer, *An Exegetical Commentary on the Gospel According to St. Matthew*, p. 47.

47 Abbott-Smith, *op. cit.*, p. 35; Preuschen says, "sich zurueckziehen, entweichen."

48 Matt. 4:13.

sage by Plummer. Nevertheless, it is possible that this interpretation may be correct and that Matthew may reflect the true historical situation, namely, that Jesus withdrew for a time to a more quiet part of Galilee until He could start His work without involving it at once in political danger.

The Insurrection Under Barabbas

Josephus makes no mention of Barabbas or of any insurrection in which he might have taken part, and so our information about this sedition is limited entirely to the Gospels. The references here are very brief. Mark states: "And there was one called Barabbas, lying bound with them that had made insurrection, men who in the insurrection had committed murder."[49] Luke's statement is a little more specific when he speaks of him as "one who for a certain insurrection made in the city, and for murder, was cast into prison."[50] Matthew simply calls him "a notable [notorious][51] prisoner."

Mark appears to take for granted that his readers would know who this "one called Barabbas" was and that they would know about the "insurrection" and the insurgents. How serious this sedition was we have no way of knowing. Josephus' silence would suggest that it was not a very serious disturbance from the political point of view. The words in Mark do not necessarily imply anything more than a semi-political riot in which blood was shed. If the insurrection had been of serious proportions, we would hardly expect Pilate to listen to any plea for his release. The Gospel account suggests that the choice between Barabbas and Jesus was not between a great patriot and Jesus but between a dangerous criminal, perhaps an irresponsible leader of radical insurgents, and a perfectly innocent man. Whether Barabbas and the other rebels were identified with any organized revolutionary group it is impossible to determine.

49 Mark 15:7.
50 Luke 23:18, 19.
51 Matt. 27:16.

THE REVOLUTIONARY MOVEMENT

The Gospels make no attempt to connect them in any way with any large revolutionary group. They are not classed either as Zealots or as Cananaeans. They are merely classified as rebels who had stirred up sedition and violence.

While the Gospels picture Barabbas as an irresponsible rebel, dangerous to the common good, for whose release the mob could only be prevailed upon to ask by the clever strategy of the leaders, it is possible that the mob in reality thought of him as a champion of national rights and that their clamor for his release in preference to Jesus was really an expression of their secret sympathy with him.

Jackson and Lake[52] characterize this Paschal season as "to all appearance an anxious time. Pilate had come to Jerusalem, and Herod Antipas, according to Luke, was there with an armed force, so that evidently the Roman and the Galilean authorities feared a serious disturbance. The sedition of Barabbas and the tumultuous reception of Jesus increased their apprehensions, and it was impossible to trust the temper of the people; so Barabbas was seized and arrangements were made to arrest Jesus as quickly as possible and execute Him, contrary to Jewish law, before the celebration of the festival.... Pilate, who felt that at any cost the people must be quieted before the feast day, consented to condemn Jesus, and hurried Him to His death."

The facts in the case hardly warrant such strong assertions. It is very doubtful whether one is warranted reading in this Lucan passage (23:11) "Herod with his 'armed forces.'" "His soldiers" does not necessarily indicate anything more than that Herod in Jerusalem was surrounded by the ordinary bodyguard that he considered necessary for his safe journey. The "soldiers" in this passage are mentioned quite casually when Luke reports that "Herod with his soldiers set him [Jesus] at nought."[53] There is no emphasis on Herod's coming to Jerusalem with his soldiers.

Furthermore, Herod could hardly come to Jerusalem with

---

[52] Jackson and Lake, *op. cit.*, Vol. I, p. 8.
[53] Luke 23:11.

an "armed force" without inviting the suspicion of the Roman authorities unless he came by their direct invitation. And Pilate would hardly invite Herod to come to his assistance unless the situation appeared so grave that he doubted his ability to cope with it. If so grave a situation had confronted Pilate, it would have received mention in Josephus and it would also be reflected in the Gospel story.

Pilate's presence in Jerusalem on the occasion of this feast in itself indicates no unusual anxiety on the part of the Roman authorities. The well-known Roman suspicion of crowds would almost inevitably have insured Pilate's presence in the city at such an outstanding feast as the Passover. The Gospels give no hint that the Roman authorities watched with any unusual diligence for stirrings of a revolutionary nature. Of course, the silence of the Gospels cannot be used as evidence to prove the absence of any unusual watchfulness. The fact that there had been a recent riot in which Barabbas and some other rebels had been captured would inevitably lead the Roman officials to a more careful scrutiny of the movements of the festival crowds.

The Barabbas insurrection may serve to explain the hesitancy of the Jewish leaders to proceed against Jesus "during the feast, lest a tumult arise among the people."[54] But in itself this precaution against giving occasion for "tumults" during feast days is no evidence of any unusual anxiety. Knowing that such riots, or gatherings that could be so interpreted, only resulted in more restrictions of their freedom, the Jewish leaders tried to avoid as far as possible all occasions for stirring up the multitude.

The Massacre of the Galileans by Pilate

Luke 13:1 refers to "the Galilaeans whose blood Pilate had mingled with their sacrifices." In verse four, there follows a reference to "those eighteen upon whom the tower in Siloam fell." Josephus makes no mention of the latter incident, and for the former he has no unmistakable parallel.

54 Matt. 26:5.

THE REVOLUTIONARY MOVEMENT

The incident about the falling of the tower of Siloam is intimately associated by Eisler with the above-mentioned massacre of the Galileans. Rejecting various types of structures as descriptions of this tower, he states that it "must have been a fortress tower"[55] on the city wall. He points out how improbable it would be for the Romans to allow a fortress tower to fall into such a state of disrepair that it would tumble over either by accident or by earthquake. It must therefore have been pulled down in the course of a siege, the occasion for which he finds in the revolt during which Pilate massacred the Galileans. At this time Jerusalem sympathizers took possession of the tower of Siloam and Pilate laid siege to the tower and overthrew it "with battering-ram and 'testitudo.'"

The possibility of the tower's having been overthrown in the course of some siege operations against rebels who had taken their stand in that structure cannot be denied. But there is no proof that this structure necessarily was a fortress tower. Luke 13:4, 5 gives not the slightest support to Eisler's supposition. In the mind of the evangelist, the fall of the tower was wholly an accident, an act of God.

The Two Swords Among the Disciples. Luke 22:35-38

And he said unto them, When I sent you forth without purse, and wallet, and shoes, lacked ye anything? And they said, Nothing. And he said unto them, But now, he that hath a purse, let him take it, and likewise a wallet; and he that hath none, let him sell his cloak, and buy a sword. . . . And they said, Lord, behold, here are two swords. And he said unto them, It is enough (verses 35, 36, 38).

The problem of verses 35, 36 will come up for discussion later. Here we are concerned only with the question: How did two of the followers of Jesus happen to carry swords?[56]

---

55 Robert Eisler, *The Messiah Jesus and John the Baptist*, p. 507. The massacre of the Galileans and its relation to the fall of the tower of Siloam is covered in pp. 500-10.

56 Eisler's suggestion (*The Messiah Jesus*, p. 369) that each of the dis-

No positive answer can be given. The passage seems to have been puzzling from the earliest days of the church. The Greek term used here can mean "a large knife or dirk" (used for sacrificial purposes) or a "short sword or dagger."[57] Chrysostom, to whom this passage proved puzzling, suggested that the two swords were sacrificial knives. Other similar explanations have been offered repeatedly since that time, but all such "explanations" appear to be evasions of the obvious import of the passage. The passage refers to swords, not knives.

Goguel suggests the possibility that the swords may have been found in the upper room[58] and subsequently carried along, perhaps partly because of a misunderstanding of the saying about buying a sword and partly perhaps because of the gravity of the impending crisis. He further calls attention to the fact that according to Josephus[59] "the country was so unsafe that the peaceful Essenes did not travel without weapons."[60] But what Josephus actually says is that they carried weapons "on account of the robbers."[61] He speaks of robbers here as a class rather than as a particular group of "robbers" engaged in political brigandage.

In this passage, "on account of the robbers" appears to suggest nothing more than that the country was unsafe because it was inadequately policed. There were frequent robberies and the Essenes as a matter of self-protection carried a short sword with them. That may give a possible explanation for the two swords among the disciples. It is possible, however, that the number of robberies may have been increased considerably by the activity of members of rebellious groups who were often guilty of brigandage. The public at large would hardly be able to distinguish between

ciples carried two swords is an attempt to read into the Greek something that obviously is not there.
57 Abbott-Smith, *Lexicon*.
58 Maurice Goguel, *Life of Jesus*, p. 453.
59 "Wars" II, 8, 4.
60 Goguel, *op. cit.*, p. 453 footnote.
61 "Wars" II, 8, 4.

THE REVOLUTIONARY MOVEMENT 71

the robberies that sprang from personal greed and those that sprang from so-called patriotic motives. The motives frequently were not unmixed. In any case it is impossible to determine at this late date what percentage of robberies were perpetrated by members of insurgent groups and how much of this carrying of weapons was intended as a protection against lawless elements in the country.

Easton[62] suggests that "it was in accordance with His [Jesus'] commands that forcible resistance in Gethsemane occurred." But what did Jesus hope to accomplish by such forcible resistance? Why then did He not arrange definitely for the arming of all the disciples? Easton leaves these questions unanswered.

Pfleiderer[63] thinks that what Jesus feared was the weapon of an assassin. He did not expect a formal arrest. Two swords would be "enough" to protect Himself from the hand of hired murderers. As soon as Jesus recognized that it was a formal arrest that He had to face, He restrained His disciples from forcible resistance with a "Hold, no more" (Luke 22:51).

All of these statements suggest possible explanations of the two swords among the disciples, but they are at best little more than guesses. The situation is admittedly difficult to explain, especially in view of Eisler's claim that the Jews, in common with other provincials, were not allowed to carry arms.[64] The story as told in Luke portrays the possession of the two swords by the disciples as a matter of surprise. That would tend to give support to the idea that the disciples had picked up the swords under the stress of impending crisis. The possession of the weapons would likely be unknown to all except the two who carried them. The answer of Jesus: "It is enough," i.e., "Enough of this," would

---

62 *Christ in the Gospels*, p. 194 and footnote.
63 *Primitive Christianity*, Vol. II, p. 181 ff.
64 *The Messiah Jesus*, pp. 507 and 616 ff. Eisler makes no attempt to explain the discrepancy between the law forbidding the ordinary citizen to carry arms and Essenes carrying weapons regularly.

be a sufficient answer for that kind of situation. The two swords were not evidence of revolutionary intention so much as an attempt to guarantee the personal safety of Jesus. But perhaps no entirely satisfactory solution is possible.

The clause, "It is enough," is obscure. Two swords very obviously were not "enough" to offer effective resistance to arrest or to attacks from His enemies. They might prove an effective protection against assassins, but the idea that Jesus feared assassination and sought to safeguard Himself against it by making sure the disciples were provided with some swords is a mere supposition. And that Jesus should have had nothing but an ironical reply to the situation created by the swords in the disciple group is not wholly satisfactory either. "It is enough" can also mean "Enough of this." Jesus, discovering the two swords among His disciples and sensing how far they still were from understanding the true character of the kingdom and how badly they had misunderstood His saying about the sword, dismisses further discussion of the subject with an almost weary and impatient "Enough of this." The stress of the impending crisis and the urgency of the rapidly dwindling time were weighing heavily upon Him. This was a singularly inopportune time to correct their wrong conceptions and discuss adequately the ethics of the use of the sword in the protection and promotion of that which is ultimately good in the mind and purpose of God. Events would all too soon demonstrate what He had meant by His reference to buying a sword and how dangerous and self-defeating was the use of the sword.

But in the final analysis it is not a matter of great moment whether we are able to establish the exact meaning of Jesus' reply in this instance. His best answer to the situation is given when He disallows Peter the use of his sword in the critical moment of His arrest.[65] Jesus does not charge His disciples to cast away at once the two swords, but He for-

65 Luke 22:51; Matt. 26:52.

THE REVOLUTIONARY MOVEMENT

bids their use in His behalf or in behalf of His cause, the cause of the kingdom of God. Fuller discussion follows.

"The kingdom of heaven suffereth violence . . ." (Matthew 11:12; Luke 16:16)

This saying is reported differently in Matthew and in Luke. Matthew reads: "And from the days of John the Baptist until now the kingdom of heaven suffereth violence, and the violent take it by force." In Luke we read: "The law and the prophets were until John: since that time the kingdom of God is preached, and every man presseth into it." The Greek of Matthew can be translated either as "The kingdom of God arrives with force"[66] or "It is forced violently, one tries hard to make it come by violent means."[67] In the latter case, the saying would appear to be a protest against the activity of revolutionary groups who would force the coming of the kingdom by the use of violence and armed aggression.

The meaning of the passage varies also with the interpretation one places on the concluding statement about the violent taking the kingdom by force—whether one regards it as uttered with approval or disapproval. If Jesus regarded the taking by force with approval, then the sense of the saying might correspond with Harnack's suggestion: "Since the kingdom is now breaking in with might and main, one must also with might and main lay hold on it to possess it lest it escape one's grasp. There is something military in the illustration, but not in the actual fact."[68] If Jesus regarded it with disapproval, then the saying might, as suggested above, be a protest against attempts of revolutionary groups to force the coming of the kingdom by military aggression.

---

66 Goguel's translation and comment, p. 277 ff., footnote. Preuschen renders the middle form: "bricht sich mit Gewalt Bahn," and the passive form: "das Himmelreich wird vergewaltigt."

67 *Ibid.*

68 Harnack, *Militia Christi*, p. 4 footnote. "Weil das Himmelreich jetzt mit Gewalt, d.h. stuermisch eindringt, so muss man gewaltsam zugreifen, um es nicht vorübergehen zu lassen, sondern um es fuer sich zu gewinnen. Etwas Kriegerisches liegt nur im Bilde, nicht in der Sache."

74   JESUS AND HUMAN CONFLICT

The context appears to be of no help either in Matthew, where the words are uttered as part of Jesus' comment on the work of John the Baptist,[69] or in Luke, where the words seem to be directed at the "Pharisees who were lovers of money."[70] The passage thus remains somewhat obscure. It does, however, seem possible that the activity of representatives of revolutionary groups on various occasions may have proved embarrassing and disappointing to Jesus in His work and preaching. In their zeal they may have tried in various ways to push Him into leading a revolutionary movement that would throw off the Roman yoke, restore freedom, independence, and empire to the Jews, and set up the kingdom. This passage might then voice Jesus' disappointment with these groups, who would force the coming of the kingdom, and His protest against their activity.

Summary

From the preceding study of possible references to the revolutionary movement in the Gospels, there emerge the following conclusions:

1. The references are few and of the barest kind.

2. They offer at best but very doubtful evidence for the presence of a definite revolutionary party during the time of Jesus.

3. They point to the presence of a seething revolutionary ferment that kept alive the spirit of revolt and the feeling of resentment against foreign domination and that burst out now and then, under provocation, in riots and violence.

4. The spirit of revolt and the revolutionary activity do not appear to be so widespread or so intense and clear-cut and energetic, or so well organized that involvement for Jesus was unavoidable. National resentment against Roman domination, and impatience with its yoke there was indeed, but feeling did not run as high nor was the national crisis as

69 Matt. 11:2-30.
70 Luke 16:14.

immediate as during the period following the reign of Herod Agrippa in A.D. 44. Hence Jesus could concern Himself with the basic relations of human life and with the teaching of the kingdom without first having to remove of necessity from the minds of the people certain immediate critical national problems that shut out consideration of all else.

JESUS' CONNECTION WITH THE REVOLUTIONARY MOVEMENT

What was Jesus' attitude to the revolutionary movement of His day? Did He identify Himself with it? Did He ignore it? Or did He take care not to be entangled in it? Were any of His teachings given with the intention of guiding or frustrating it directly or indirectly? What was Jesus' attitude to the governments against whom ardent nationalist groups were preaching violent resistance? These and other related questions must come up for discussion now.

Jesus and Herod

What was Jesus' attitude to Herod Antipas and his rule?

The evidence is meager, but the following incidents throw some light on the question.

Jesus evidently tried to avoid falling into the hands of Herod, as John the Baptist had, and perhaps experiencing a like fate. He appears to have been aware of the political danger threatening Him from the side of Herod, a danger reflected in passages like Mark 3:6 where the Pharisees and Herodians "[take] counsel against him, how they might destroy him," and Luke 13:31 where "certain Pharisees" warn Jesus that "Herod would fain kill thee." The withdrawal of Jesus from Galilee into the regions of Tyre and Sidon and of Caesarea Philippi, together with His rapid movement from city to city subsequent to the period known as the "Galilean Crisis,"[71] is generally regarded as evidence of His attempt to avoid the threatening political danger.

71 Cf. John 6:60-71.

76 JESUS AND HUMAN CONFLICT

Jesus on one occasion warned the disciples to "beware of the leaven of the Pharisees and the leaven of Herod."[72] The "leaven" of this passage is commonly interpreted as having reference to the evil tendencies of teachings of the Pharisees and of Herod. The leaven of Herod is thus said to refer to the worldliness characteristic of the man and his court.

It is interesting to note that neither Matthew nor Luke makes this reference to the leaven of Herod. Matthew warns against the leaven of the Sadducees and Luke omits it entirely. Goguel suggests "the (Marcan) saying about the leaven was originally a warning of Jesus to His disciples about the dangers which threatened Him, dangers which possibly threatened them as much as Himself. These words belong to a period when the hostility of Herod had not yet been declared openly, but when Jesus had already foreseen it."[73]

In other words, Jesus in this saying was not urging active opposition and revolt against Herod. He was merely urging His disciples to be on their guard against the dangers, whether political or moral, which threatened them from the side of Herod.

Jesus on one occasion, when He had been warned of Herod's desire to kill Him, referred to this ruler as "that fox."[74] Whether Herod actually intended to kill Jesus or merely wished to intimidate Him cannot be determined, but Jesus evidently saw through the craftiness of Herod's scheme, for He requested His informants to tell "that fox" that He would not be intimidated, but would finish the work which He was called to perform.

On the one and only occasion that Jesus and Herod met, namely, at the time of the trial,[75] Jesus refused to answer any of Herod's questions. The evangelist suggests that He was unwilling to satisfy the tetrarch's idle curiosity "to see some miracle."[76]

72 Mark 8:15. Cf. Matt. 16:6; Luke 12:1.
73 Goguel, *Life of Jesus*, p. 349.   75 Luke 23:6-12.
74 Luke 13:32.   76 Luke 23:8.

The above incidents reveal on the part of Jesus no spirit of revolt against, nor any political disapproval of, Herodian rule as such. Jesus appears to avoid, as far as is consistent with His mission, arousing Herod's political suspicions and hostility. He evidently withdraws from the threatening danger when it develops; but He neither preaches nor embodies a spirit of revolt against Herodian rule and its complete subserviency to Rome. Whatever opposition to or disapproval of Herod there is in His word or action is a disapproval of Herod's character. He warns against Herod because he is a "fox" and a timeserver, and He "answered him nothing"[77] because He recognized the insincerity and superficiality of the man.

Jesus and Roman Rule

What was Jesus' attitude toward the Roman government whose rule was so bitterly resented by patriotic groups?

The fact one notices at once is that the Gospels record no clear instance of any criticism of Roman rule. Such immediate occasions for critism of Rome as the report about the Galileans whose blood Pilate had mingled with their sacrifices, or that of the perishing of the eighteen upon whom the tower of Siloam fell (if a political event)[78] Jesus passes by without an open or direct remonstrance. Of course the absence of such remonstrance in the Gospels cannot be used as conclusive evidence that Jesus did not on occasion criticize Roman rule. Such criticism if it occurred might have been omitted by the evangelists. Nevertheless, it is quite possible that to Jesus, to whom personal rightness with God was the primary concern, the question of outward rule was a secondary matter and He consequently expended little or no effort on the problem of improving the conditions of government.

On the occasion of His trial Jesus seems to treat Pilate, the representative of the Roman government, with more respect

[77] Luke 23:9.
[78] Luke 13:1-3.

than Herod. He answers Pilate's question, "Art thou the King of the Jews?" with a frank and honest, "Thou sayest,"[79] but Herod He had "answered nothing." It is true that Mark reports that during the remainder of the trial He "no more answered anything; insomuch that Pilate marvelled,"[80] but Jesus' refusal to answer is not a reflection on the Roman court but rather on the charges of His accusers. To the indignities connected with the trial, brutal and wholly unwarranted though they were, and to the sentence inflicted He submitted without protest or resistance. And all through the trial there is no evidence of any resentment that He as a Jew should be tried before a *Roman* tribunal. There certainly is no evidence, either in His words or His demeanor, of any spirit of bitterness, revolt, or resentment such as one might expect if He were sympathetic with the aims of the national revolutionists.

The classical passage dealing with the subject of Jesus' attitude to Rome is found in Mark 12:13-17:

And they send unto him certain of the Pharisees and of the Herodians, that they might catch him in talk. And when they were come, they say unto him, Teacher, we know that thou art true, and carest not for any one; for thou regardest not the person of men, but of a truth teachest the way of God: Is it lawful to give tribute unto Caesar, or not? Shall we give, or shall we not give? But he, knowing their hypocrisy, said unto them, Why make ye trial of me? bring me a denarius, that I may see it. And they brought it. And he saith unto them, Whose is this image and superscription? And they said unto him, Caesar's. And Jesus said unto them, Render unto Caesar the things that are Caesar's, and unto God the things that are God's. And they marvelled greatly at him. (Parallel passages in Matthew 22:15-22; Luke 20:20-26.)

It is interesting to note that the question is so phrased in the Greek as to suggest that the inquirers thought the paying of the tax was entirely optional. It was not a matter of moral

---

[79] Mark 15:1-20; Matt. 27:1-31; Luke 23:1-25.
[80] Mark 15:5; Matt. 27:14.

THE REVOLUTIONARY MOVEMENT

obligation. It was simply a question of giving or not giving according as the law permitted it or not. The form of Jesus' reply suggests that in His mind the paying of the tax was more than a matter of giving or not giving. It was paying back of something justly owed. It was, therefore, a matter of moral obligation.

The real reply of Jesus is not phrased in the form of an argument but in the form of a counter question, a form not infrequently used in so-called *Streitgespraeche* (controversy discourses). In this counter question, Jesus draws the attention away from the controversial issues of the moment and makes His questioners face the realities of the situation. "Bring me a denarius, that I may see it," He requests.

Evidently those leaders had little difficulty in producing this coin. It was found in more or less common circulation in the country. Taking the coin, Jesus asks further: "Whose is this image and superscription?" The reply is inescapable and they answer: "Caesar's." Jesus thereupon promptly drives home the logic of the situation which His question has created and replies: "Render unto Caesar the things that are Caesar's. . . ."

According to rabbinic teaching, the rule of a king was regarded as being coextensive with the region in which money of his coinage was accepted as a medium of exchange.[81] When, therefore, these Jewish leaders produced the Roman denarius out of their midst, they were proving in effect that they had accepted Caesar's rule over their nation. If they accepted Caesar's rule and shared in the benefits that accrued therefrom, then they were under moral obligation to pay the taxes necessary to maintain that rule. They would be paying only what they rightfully owed.

Whether Jesus went through any such process of reasoning in arriving at His conclusion is doubtful. He appears rather to have arrived at it by quick intuitive insight on the

---

[81] Cf. Sanhedrin 2, 20b, 17 where Abigail (I Sam. 25:23) refuses to accept David's jurisdiction because Saul's mintage was still accepted as legal tender. Cf. also Meg. 14b. in Strack and Billerbeck, *op. cit.*, Vol. I, p. 884.

basis of what was right and proper in the situation. It is also very doubtful whether Jesus intended to give any clear-cut generalized statement of a man's obligation to government. It does appear, however, that the logic of the situation created by His question, especially in view of rabbinic teaching on the subject, would drive home some such conclusion.

Mark and Matthew state that the questioners were "certain of the Pharisees and of the *Herodians*." Just who the Herodians were is uncertain. They did not constitute a religious party and apparently were not a definite political party either. They may have been Jews who favored Herodian rule and who desired the restoration of the former Herodian kingdom. They may also have been officials of Herod.[82] Goguel, who points out evidences of Herod's hostility to Jesus and stresses its possible influence on Jesus' ministry, sees in the approach of these "Herodians" an attempt on the part of the tetrarch to discover Jesus' attitude toward the political authorities.

In any case, the question asked was not merely a theoretical one intended to test the astuteness of Jesus. It was a question that was agitating the minds not only of the Herodians but of many patriotic Jews as well. Ever since the revolt of Judas the Gaulonite in A.D. 6, the payment of this Roman poll tax had been regarded with resentment as peculiarly the badge of their national servitude to Rome.[83] The tax was further abhorrent to them because the Roman coins in which the tax had to be paid bore the image of Caesar, and appeared as a transgression of the second commandment.[84]

When, therefore, these leaders asked: "Is it lawful [i.e., is it permitted to a pious Jew] to give tribute unto Caesar?" they were asking the question of national revolution. For this reason Jesus' answer to the query was of truly critical importance. In the minds of these leaders, Jesus had either

---

[82] Goguel, *Life of Jesus*, p. 347 and footnote.

[83] Cf. Josephus, "Antiquities" XVIII, 1, 1; "Wars" II, 8, 1.

[84] Ex. 20:4. In A.D. 35, Pilate struck coins decorated only with the laurel wreath and the augur's wand evidently for the purpose of trying to satisfy Jewish sensibilities. (Abrahams, *Studies in Pharisaism*, I, p. 64.)

THE REVOLUTIONARY MOVEMENT 81

to defend Roman rule and thereby estrange all loyal pious Jews or else to take an active stand against it by advocating refusal to pay the tax and thus risk possible arrest and execution by government authorities as a dangerous radical.

Dibelius states the dilemma of Jesus in the following way:

The issue here lies between the political opposites of military occupation and patriotic religion. Jesus does not accept these alternatives but instead formulates another; namely, God and the world. As surely as the coin carries the image of Caesar, so surely does it represent "the world" and so surely does it belong to the lord of this world, Caesar. The religious patriots think only of the worldly alternative of patriotic nationalism (country) and military occupation instead of the other all-overarching one, above all the world even the nation and its rights—and God. When therefore Jesus says: "Give to Caesar what your eyes tell you obviously belongs to him (not what belongs to him by reason of the divine order!!) and give to God what is His," He obviously uses an ironic parallelism—one surely does not need to argue this point. It never entered Jesus' mind seriously to place the rights of Caesar and the rights of God on the same level. The rights of Caesar stem from the world order and Jesus does not evaluate this. . . . He appears to say: Give to God exactly like you do to Caesar; in reality, however, He means: above all else and perhaps even in conflict with all else give to God what is God's. Those people who from apparently pious interests are asking: "Do you side with the national revolution?" receive no answer. Instead they are being shamed and are being reminded where the truly pious interests lie. The demands of their patriotic nationalism are worldly, perhaps necessary, perhaps harmful. Jesus does not rule on the merits of these any more than He rules on the merits of various social systems. All who discuss this question or think themselves qualified to judge on this matter must first of all hear the question He asks, asks even in that moment when people confront Him with their national problem, namely: Has the demand of God been met? God's demand remains, but Caesar's demand is only for this world where coins with his image are being struck; he is provisional exactly like this metal with the image of Caesar on it.[85]

[85] Martin Dibelius, *Das Soziaille Motiv im Neuen Testament*, p. 13. (Pamphlet.) A free translation.

This statement of Dibelius is illuminating. He points to the following propositions that appear to us as essentially correct:

First, Jesus faces the problem raised from a larger viewpoint than did His questioners, or for that matter, than did national revolutionists generally. For them it was largely a question of legal right. Could a pious Jew, loyal to the law and the national destiny, submit to this tax imposed by a Gentile nation and pay it in a coin whose image of Caesar suggested idolatry? The broader implications of what was truly and morally right in the situation evidently were not ordinarily considered. The Jews were seldom able to view this problem dispassionately and see it detached from national feeling and ambitions. Jesus takes the problem and by a skillful question strips it of these surface feelings and antipathies and makes them see the real moral problem involved. The coin which they handed Him and with which they paid the poll tax belonged to Caesar; they admitted it. It was then nothing more than a matter of ordinary human right and obligation to pay to Caesar what obviously was his due. Paying or not paying the tax, therefore, in no sense implied acceptance or repudiation of Roman rule. It merely meant that one recognized his moral obligation to the government whose rule prevailed.

For this reason those among His questioners who were trying to discover whether He sided with the national revolutionists received no answer. "Render unto Caesar . . ." was in no sense a defense of Roman domination. It was merely stating clearly the logic of their own answer to His question: "Whose is this image and superscription?"

Second, Jesus in this answer is not trying to define one's right relationship to state and church. In the minds of Jesus' questioners and perhaps of Jewish nationalists generally, the present national alternative (clearly suggested in their question) was either submission to foreign Gentile domination or loyalty to pious patriotic national interests. Jesus quite obviously did not agree. The alternative was a larger one, suggested by Him in the terms "Caesar" and "God." But for Him it was not really a problem of "either—or" but one of "both—and." His reply is not: "Render unto Caesar . . . *but*. . . ." It is rather: "Render unto Caesar . . . *and*. . . ." With the detailed issues that arise between the demands of church and state Jesus evidently does not concern Himself. He is trying to lead His questioners to see this problem not in the light of its conflicts but in the light of its moral obligations and thus to challenge them to fulfill their obligations to both, Caesar *and* God.

Whether Jesus proposed an alternative as sweeping as the one Dibelius suggests, namely, "Welt" and "Gott" (world and God), seems doubtful. Such a generalization in answer to a concrete question would make Jesus appear more like an ethical philosopher than a religious teacher. That He looked beyond the mere paying of the tax and even beyond the mere political relations to Rome (perhaps to include the larger obligations to government), and also beyond mere pious patriotic nationalism (perhaps to include the larger obligations to God and His rule) seems obvious. But to declare that Jesus in His reply generalized about "Welt" in His reference to "Caesar" seems too sweeping.

Just what constituted one's moral obligations to government, or to God for that matter, is left undefined. Jesus expects His hearers to "think on these things" and discover for themselves, under divine guidance, what these obligations are in specific situations. Here He does not stop to give detailed definitions of one's comparative obligations to church and state or to set limits to one's obedience to the demands of the state.

The manner in which Jesus' answer is phrased would make it appear as though one were to give to God exactly as one would give to Caesar. That this could not possibly be Jesus' meaning hardly needs emphasis. Dibelius therefore undoubtedly is right when he suggests that Jesus' emphasis is not on the first part at all but on the second, namely, on rendering to God the things that are God's. The demands of Caesar are confined to this earthly existence, but the demands of God are eternal. The obligations to the two are therefore not equal. There are obligations to Caesar that are to be met just as truly as those we owe to God, but the latter, in the mind of Jesus, are immeasurably more important. To meet these obligations to God must consequently be the chief concern of man.

This saying of Jesus thus obviously does not offer the desired counsel on the burning political question of the day except as it suggests a facing of the realities instead of the controversial aspects of the situation, or as it directs attention to moral obligations instead of to the prejudices of religious-national feeling, or as it points out the decidedly secondary importance of political relations and obligations as compared with the all-important obligations to God. Jesus did not commend to His countrymen the expediency of submission, neither did He give a direct or even an implied sanction to Roman domination. His saying offered comfort to neither nationalist nor Hellenist.

Nevertheless Jesus' reply did give an answer to the question of national revolution, but He answered it on a plane higher than that on which it was asked. For His questioners, this was a problem of political, patriotic, pious nationalism. But Jesus indicates that the issue is much more than political; it is theological. It is not merely a question of "Shall we give or shall we not give?"[86] It is much deeper. The problem of a person's relation to Caesar—whether to co-operate, submit, resist, or withhold co-operation—cannot be solved apart from God. It cannot be isolated and solved by itself as if it bore no relation to the supreme obligation which he, and Caesar no less, owes to the sovereign God and His government of the world.

Jesus' questioners had in a greater or less degree thus compartmentalized their thinking on this problem. This was a political, patriotic issue which they tried to think through as a thing by itself. It was not a religious question. Their

86 Mark 12:15.

religious life and activity was too often a thing apart whose connection with the problem of national revolution was only indirect and then by way of tense national feeling. Religion was invited in to provide pious sanction and motivation to passionate nationalism.

Jesus indicates in His answer that such an isolation of a human problem from its relation to the all-pervading purpose of God is impossible. So He at once takes this question of man's obligation to the state out of its compartment of patriotic, self-sufficient nationalism and links it to the all-encompassing obligation man bears to God. He implies that a person who gives God the all-important place in his life and thought that he owes Him will be able to discover what his rightful relation to the government should be—whether and when and how to co-operate, submit, resist, or withhold co-operation. He will know that he must give Caesar what is due him, but remember that this is subject to the supreme allegiance and obedience he owes God. This supreme allegiance to God will serve to right, ennoble, and sanctify the whole relation to the state.

Again it must be emphasized that Jesus almost certainly did not go through any such laborious process of reasoning in order to arrive at His conclusion. Intuitively He saw and boldly proclaimed a divine principle whose far-reaching import we have tried to discover and explain.

Possible Political Relations of Jesus' Conception of the Kingdom

The answer to the problem of Jesus' attitude to the revolutionary movement of His day also involves a discussion of certain aspects of His thought of the kingdom. Did He think of the kingdom as in any sense a political entity? Did His idea of the kingdom include political freedom and autonomy for the nation? Could or would its coming be precipitated or hastened by the use of political measures?

To the national revolutionists the coming of the Messianic kingdom meant complete freedom from foreign domination

86   JESUS AND HUMAN CONFLICT

and the establishment of the nation in a place of supremacy among the countries of the earth. They believed that ultimately this condition of affairs would be established by God, but they also believed "that God would not otherwise be assisting to them than upon their joining with one another in such counsels as might be successful and for their own advantage; and this especially, if they would set about great exploits, and not grow weary in executing the same."[87]

In the thought of Jesus this political hope and this idea that political measures were necessary in order to bring about the establishment of the kingdom appear to be completely absent. For Jesus, the kingdom was not a political order whose realization could be furthered by political manipulation and aggression. Neither was it an idealistic social or economic order which men by their own efforts could evolve or establish. For Him the kingdom was "an exclusively religious entity and value."[88] It was always *God's* kingdom and its character and meaning were determined wholly by what God was and willed. It represented a condition of affairs in which God's will was done on earth as it was done in heaven. Viewed from the Godward side, it represented the consummation of God's great and good purposes for man. From the manward side, it represented the fulfillment of man's highest good, both personally and socially. This great good was not something to be snatched or achieved. It was God's supreme gift to man and its coming was in the Father's own hands.[89] Its consummation would mean the overthrow of the present world order,[90] but the overthrow was not engineered by human effort and intelligence but one that would come to pass through the outworking of the Father's own beneficent purpose.

Since the kingdom represented both man's highest good and the true fulfillment of God's gracious purposes for man,

87 Josephus thus describes, in part, the activity of the followers of Judas the Gaulonite. "Antiquities" XVIII, 1, 1.
88 Bundy, *Religion of Jesus*, p. 110.
89 Luke 13:32.
90 Mark 13; Matt. 24; Luke 21.

since it came not by man's effort but through the power of God's love, and since its coming would be sudden and unexpected, there was nothing more imperative than that man should make certain now that he would be allowed a share in the blessing of the kingdom. The conditions for entrance were necessarily determined by the character of the coming kingdom. Since this realm was above everything else, one in which men gave the same free and glad obedience to the will of God that was given to Him in heaven, entrance into its life and blessing necessarily required from would-be members a wholehearted personal commitment to the will of God.[91] It required repentance,[92] i.e., a will and purpose so changed and transformed as to conform with the will and purpose of God. It required likewise a childlike spirit,[93] a childlike response to the will of the Father. Except a man became as a little child, he could not enter the kingdom.[94] It was only in this way that a man was fit to enter into the family relation that would prevail in the kingdom.

It was to this work of inspiring men to make the necessary preparation for entering the kingdom when in God's own time it should come that Jesus devoted His life and energy. He did not think He had been sent to set the stage for the kingdom nor to precipitate its coming. All that was in the Father's hands. His mission was to preach the message of the kingdom, to declare to men the will and way of God, and to challenge them to repent and surrender their wills and their lives to the will of God. The method He used was consequently not a method of coercion but of persuasion. He did not come to overawe but to serve.[95] He appealed not to the political ambitions and prejudices of the nation but to the consciences of its members. He tried to commend the kingdom to men not by self-assertion and a

---

[91] Matt. 6:24, 33. Cf. also Mark 8:34, 35 and parallels; Luke 14:33; Mark 10:29, 30 and parallels.
[92] Mark 1:15; Matt. 4:17.
[93] Mark 10:15; Matt. 18:3; Luke 18:17.
[94] *Ibid.*
[95] Mark 10:42 ff.; Matt. 20:25 ff.; Luke 22:25 ff.

display of power but by self-giving and by proclaiming in word and life the spirit that would prevail in the kingdom.

The problem of political freedom, either of the individual or of the nation, really had little, if any, relation to the all-important problem of one's relation to the kingdom. Change in political status, either of the individual or of the nation, would neither hinder nor help either the coming of the kingdom or one's entrance into it. Discussion of the political problem was therefore of no help in the work of preparing men for the kingdom.

Discussion of this problem could easily have served, however, to dissipate the force of His message. Specific utterances on the merits of the nationalist cause would almost inevitably have drawn Him and His whole cause into the maelstrom of political discussion and agitation with the result that He would be classed, perhaps now with one and again with another of various partisan viewpoints and prejudices. Now He would be identified with the revolutionary cause and be regarded either as a national champion or as a dangerous agitator, and then again He might be regarded as an apologist for Rome and a traitor to the people. It was therefore part of His divine wisdom to avoid the danger of such identifications which could only serve to weaken His work and the cause of God's kingdom.

It appears, however, that the political situation was likely not so acute nor the national feeling and the revolutionary spirit so bitter and tense and widespread that the avoiding of national issues was impossible. That is to say, the national situation does not appear to have been so immediately critical, either morally or politically, that He had to say something on that issue if He would be heard at all. It is possible therefore that Jesus for good and sufficient reasons may have avoided specific utterances on political issues which were morally indifferent; lest both He and His message be identified with partisan viewpoints and movements.

But to say this is not to suggest that He avoided entirely the question of national revolution. Though He did not face it as an issue by itself, He dealt with it indirectly by emphasizing and exemplifying the spirit that would prevail in the kingdom and that must possess all would-be members, at the same time protesting against motives and attitudes that were out of harmony with the spirit of the kingdom. Inevitably such a protest would include such unworthy motives and attitudes as lay back of and found expression in some of the nationalistic and revolutionary activities.

A discussion of Jesus' possible connection with the revolutionary movement also raises the question whether He included in His messages of the kingdom the idea of social salvation or of group action in the achievement of that goal. That His teaching had social bearings is obvious. Loving one's neighbor as oneself, doing unto him as one would have him do to us, being merciful, forgiving, peace-loving—these and other similar teachings unquestionably had social bearings. Likewise Jesus' idea of the kingdom must have included the vision of a brotherhood in which and through which God's loving purpose would find true and perfect expression.

There is also evidence to show that Jesus gave encouragement to co-operative activity in the work of saving the lost and in preparing men for membership in the kingdom. The sending out of His followers in groups of two on missionary tours is one such evidence. Jesus had no confidence in man's power to save himself, not even when he tried to achieve it through co-operative endeavor. In the mind of Jesus there was no salvation, either personal or social, except through the power of God. Even when He encouraged co-operation in the work of calling men to repent, it was not the group that saved, but God speaking and working through the group. But evidently Jesus thought that a group working together in the doing of God's will offered a larger and a more effective channel through which the Spirit of God could speak to the consciences of men.

It is, therefore, impossible to speak of Jesus teaching the idea of social salvation. The ideal of a perfect society, free from sin and free to rise to its highest possibilities, is embodied and transcended in His idea of the kingdom. But the perfect society of the kingdom is realized not by the efforts of man but by the power of God. It is a perfect society composed of individuals who have made a personal response to the call to repent and surrender.

Jesus' comparative silence on the political issue of His day is sometimes explained as due to His early expectation of the kingdom. It was therefore not important that He concern Himself with a world order that would soon pass away.

Without entering into a discussion of this highly controversial question it should be emphasized that Jesus' teaching about the kingdom was not determined by considerations of the length or shortness of the interim until the kingdom would come. It was determined wholly by the character and will of God. The kingdom was always God's kingdom. This was God's supreme good and men were urged to seek first the kingdom and its righteousness. All other concerns of human existence, hope, and relationship were secondary and these human values would find their realization to the degree in which they related themselves to this highest good, this great call of Jesus. In other words, Jesus' comparative silence on the political question of His day cannot be interpreted as an accommodation to the times.

SUMMARY

Summarizing the conclusions that have emerged from our study of Jesus' possible connection with the revolutionary movement of His day we may point out the following propositions:

1. The revolutionary movement of Jesus' time, both according to the evidence supplied by Josephus and according to that reflected in the Gospels, appears neither to have been sufficiently well defined, sufficiently intense, nor sufficiently widespread to make avoidance of the issue it presented an impossibility to Jesus if He would catch the ear of the nation.

THE REVOLUTIONARY MOVEMENT

2. Nationalistic feeling and the spirit of revolt were sufficiently strong to cause both Herod and Rome to watch with suspicion any popular movement and gathering of crowds. This fact may well have caused Jesus to use caution lest both He and His cause become identified with partisan viewpoints and prejudices, and perhaps become subject to unnecessary political danger.

3. Where Jesus appears to have been brought face to face with nationalistic problems, for instance, in the query about the Galileans slain by Pilate and in the question of tribute money, He lifts the issue out of the political-national plane into the personal-religious plane and challenges men to repent and to make sure at all cost that they are in right relations with God.

4. Direct criticism of Roman rule, if any, is nowhere recorded in our Gospels.

5. Such disapproval as we find is not political, but rather ethical and moral.

6. Jesus' conception of the kingdom was wholly free from current dreams of political freedom and national ascendancy. It was entirely a religious entity whose coming could not be hastened or precipitated by organized or forceful measures of any sort. It would come by the power of God and entrance into it was open only to those who by repentance and childlike trust and surrender made the appropriate response to the appeal of God.

7. The determinative influence molding Jesus' attitude to the problem of national revolution was not the shortness of time before the coming of the kingdom. It was rather the will and character of God, the nature of the life that would prevail in the kingdom. His silence on this question was determined by its relative unimportance compared with the all-importance of the coming of the kingdom and the urgency of meeting the spiritual conditions for entrance into it.

8. Jesus' interest was not in economic, social, or political change, but in personal, moral transformation. The ideal society would be established not by men but by God in His

gift of the kingdom. Man's part was to make sure that he would be allowed to share in the blessings of the kingdom, and hence he was challenged to turn away from present standards of life and accept now the life that would prevail in that realm. From the acceptance of that life there would inevitably flow an interest in trying to win others to repentance and to a surrender of their lives to the will of God, and from it would flow also change in economic, social, and political attitudes and relations.

But in order to get a total picture of the principle of non-resistance in the Gospel, it is necessary to go beyond the material covered and examine a large variety of relevant sections. It is to this relevant material that we turn in the succeeding chapters.

5

Passages Apparently Justifying the Use of Force

There are in the Gospels passages that report sayings, deeds, and attitudes of Jesus or describe God's attitude toward evildoers which apparently imply that resistance of some sort is justified and perhaps even required under certain circumstances. These passages must be examined in order to get a full-rounded picture of Jesus' answer to the problem of human irritation and conflict.

FOLLOWING JESUS BRINGS DISSENSION

Not Peace But a Sword

Matthew 10:34: Think not that I came to send peace on the earth: I came not to send peace, but a sword.

Luke 12:51: Think ye that I am come to give peace in the earth? I tell you, Nay; but rather division.

The meaning of these two passages is essentially the same even though they reveal various verbal dissimilarities. "Sword" in Matthew and "division" in Luke are examples.

This saying belongs to those familiar eschatological utterances in which reference is made to the disorders that would precede the last days before the coming of the kingdom. Similar sayings are found in Mark 13:12, 13; Matthew 10:21, 22; 24:9; Luke 21:16, 17, and also in Micah 7:6 of which Matthew 10:35b, 36 is almost a verbal quotation. The saying evidently tries to warn Jesus' followers that the last days will cause a disruption of the most intimate relations of human life, the relations of the home. In Matthew, who quotes Micah, this disruptive influence appears to proceed from the younger members of the family, but in Luke the disruptive influence may proceed from either the young or the old.

94   JESUS AND HUMAN CONFLICT

The "sword" in Matthew almost certainly has no reference to war. It is merely a graphic expression forcefully picturing the violent dissension that following Jesus might bring. That is borne out by the words that follow, where the reference is not to any war situation of whatever kind but wholly to the far-reaching cleavage that would penetrate even the intimate personal relations of the home.

This saying of Jesus obviously was intended to explain to the emerging Christian fellowship the baffling fact that acceptance of Jesus' message by one or more members of a family would not infrequently break family relations. These words almost give one the impression that Jesus purposely intended to bring discord, perhaps even violence, into family relations. But Jesus' hearers doubtless understood better what He meant than we of today who use different modes of expression. They understood perfectly that He (Jesus) was warning them about baffling experiences they would meet in their preaching of the kingdom and He was explaining to them that even so puzzling and distressing a result as a broken family relation might in the unsearchable wisdom of God fulfill a beneficent purpose. They knew that such disruptions often came as a matter of fact where men are true to the message of Jesus and this frequently in spite of everything they could do.

It is clear, however, that this saying was not intended to encourage the followers of Jesus to foment trouble. It was merely intended to forewarn men and to reassure them when such disruptions occurred. The words that follow suggest no use of strong measures in meeting the situation. They exhort rather to steadfast loyalty and patient endurance..

Hate Father and Mother

Matthew 10:37: He that loveth father or mother more than me is not worthy of me; and he that loveth son or daughter more than me is not worthy of me.

The word "hateth" in Luke can hardly mean hate in the absolute sense. The one who taught men to love their enemies would hardly utter so complete a contradiction as acceptance of "hate" in this literal sense would imply. The expression is evidently used with the intention of stating in the strongest terms possible the absolute devotion required of would-be followers. God's call to men could brook no competing interest, neither mammon[1] nor even the strongest human ties. "The requirement to *hate* father and mother, etc., means that the extremest violence must be offered to one's own affections and inclinations in cases where family ties conflict with personal allegiance to the call of Christ. Natural feelings must in such a case not only be denied but slain."[2]

It is, therefore, not the question of hatred or of the use of force with which Jesus concerns Himself here. He merely emphasizes the absolute character of the demand of God on the allegiance of men. The *hating* of father and mother does not intimate that they are to be opposed or resisted in any way. The utterance of Jesus aims to stress in unmistakable terms the fact that in a case of conflicting loyalties and interests family loyalties must be sacrificed or at least completely subordinated.

WOES AGAINST THE SCRIBES AND PHARISEES

Matthew 23:1-36; Luke 11:37-52; Mark 12:38-40

It is not necessary for the purposes of this investigation to enter into a discussion of the whole problem of the controversy between the Pharisees and Jesus. The question that concerns us primarily is this: "What light does this denunciation of the Pharisees and scribes throw on the problem of nonresistance?"

The Gospels do not picture any immediate, particularly aggravating occasion or act as having provoked the attack on the Pharisees. In Matthew, these severe words were spoken in Jerusalem in a setting where they appear as a

---
[1] Matt. 6:24.
[2] Manson, *The Gospel of Luke*, p. 175.

counteroffensive against opponents who have been trying to ensnare Jesus in cunning controversy. In Mark and in Luke in the parallel Jerusalem setting, Jesus offers only a rather mild protest against "the scribes who desire to walk in long robes, and to have salutations in the marketplaces, and chief seats in the synagogues, and chief places at feasts: they that devour widows' houses, and for a pretence make long prayers; these shall receive greater condemnation" (Mark 12:38-40).

Luke, however, records in chapter eleven a vigorous denunciation that parallels in vehemence the one found in Matthew 23. This attack occurs during the time of the so-called Perean Ministry when His work was rapidly drawing to a close. He is the guest in the home of a Pharisee. The shocked amazement of the host that Jesus "had not first washed before dinner"[3] provides the occasion for His vigorous reproof of the Pharisees and the lawyers. Montefiore, who is much disturbed by the severity of Jesus' denunciation, wonders whether Luke here records the true or the full historical occasion for this outburst because in his judgment such an attack on such an occasion would have been "the height of discourtesy."[4] It should be added here that in the Lucan chronology, Jesus, perhaps not many days previous, had had a very unpleasant experience with "some" who were maliciously charging that He was driving out demons by Beelzebub, the prince of demons.[5] Luke, however, in this story does not identify these opponents as Pharisees.

All this of course emphasizes that the Gospel writers did not find this denunciation to be a problem in their portrayal of Jesus. They take no pains to explain that there was an immediate or an accumulated exasperation that caused Jesus to burst forth. Perhaps they realized it was not irritation, annoyance, and loss of patience that caused these

---

[3] Luke 11:38.
[4] Claude G. Montefiore, *The Synoptic Gospels*, Vol. II, p. 946.
[5] Luke 11:15.

caustic words. Perhaps they sensed a nobler motive and purpose back of these severe words than is obvious on the surface.

The picture which the anti-Pharisaic censure presents is not altogether fair to the Pharisees as a group. That has been adequately pointed out by men like Moore, Montefiore, Herford, Abrahams, and others. The Pharisees as a whole were not "conscious and calculating hypocrites whose ostentatious piety was a cloak for secret villainy.[6] Nevertheless these scholars readily admit that there were many among the Pharisees to whom Jesus' description would with more or less fitness apply.[7]

Whatever the truth may be, an attempt must be made to discover what light the character of this denunciation of opponents throws on Jesus' answer to the problem of human conflict and to the question of "nonresistance."

The denunciation as reported in the Synoptic Gospels does not appear to be an attack against specific persons or even against a specific group of persons. It is not so much the Pharisees against whom Jesus inveighs as the sin which He sees most glaringly illustrated among certain Pharisees. The Pharisees as a whole were the best people Jesus knew. They were the best informed and they were, as a whole, best in the matter of piety and perhaps also best in the matter of moral conduct. But they were, perhaps because of this very fact, peculiarly in danger of the type of hypocrisy which Jesus so severely castigated. Evidently in the judgment of Jesus there were not an inconsiderable number among them who were guilty of this sin. This type of self-deception and hypocrisy was, however, not confined to the Pharisees. There were people everywhere who were saying, "Lord, Lord,"[8] but did not the things which the Lord commanded them.

---

6 George E. Moore, *Judaism*, Vol. II, p. 193.

7 Montefiore, *The Synoptic Gospels*, Vol. II, p. 727; *Rabbinic Literature*, p. 322; Moore, op cit., Vol. II, p. 192 ff.; T. R. Herford, *The Pharisees*, p 210; Israel Abrahams, *Studies in Pharisaism and the Gospels*, II, p. 30.

8 Matt. 7:21; Luke 6:46.

It was, therefore, not a personal enmity that led Jesus to pick out the Pharisees (and scribes) for denunciation. He was not trying to get even with the Jewish leaders for their opposition to and hindrance of His work by means of a public rebuke. There is no evidence of that spirit of revenge. In every one of these sayings Jesus appears to look beyond the Pharisees to the sin which He condemns. Jesus evidently saw in this sin, this self-deception, one of the most serious obstacles to the acceptance of God's call to repentance and to readiness for the coming of the kingdom. That is why He attacks it with such uncompromising vigor. This sin was frustrating the will and purpose of God not only in their own lives but in the lives of others as well.

The Pharisees were indeed the occasion for Jesus' denunciation of hypocrisy. According to the Gospels, they were more or less guilty of the faults with which they were charged. They had been, and were now enjoying privileges and opportunities far beyond those of the common folk and so there was far less excuse for the existence of these evils among them than among the common people. Instead of these privileges leading them to a glad and eager acceptance of the call of God, their position of opportunity had led them to spiritual pride and complacency. It had made them blind to their own sinfulness and had made them strangely impervious to the call for repentance and surrender.

They had proved themselves not only unresponsive to the appeal of Jesus, but also almost equally unresponsive to the appeal of John the Baptist.[9] They appeared to be so sure of themselves that they were inclined to discount any message or work that did not fall within the framework of their own system of thought. It is possible that Jesus felt that if He would save them for the kingdom, He must first save them from themselves and from their self-complacency. He must blast the shell of their self-assurance. So He paints in its starkest nakedness the sin of which many of them were

9 Cf. Mark 11:27-33 and parallels.

PASSAGES APPARENTLY JUSTIFYING FORCE 99

guilty, and from which many others were not entirely free. His purpose was not to embarrass them publicly, but rather to pierce through the obstructing shell in order that He might reach their consciences. In the attempt to win these Jewish leaders to the cause of the kingdom, He used the most potent appeal He could devise, this drastic revelation of their own inner fault.

The severity of the attack, therefore, was not an evidence of the loss of all patience. It was not an admission that in this conflict the way of love and good will was inadequate and could not be relied upon and that, hence, coercion—the coercion of public condemnation—must be resorted to as the final court of appeal. The attack was rather a picture of love asserting itself in the most vigorous fashion—a picture of love resorting to drastic measures in the attempt to save.

The severity of the denunciation undoubtedly was in part called forth by His keen sense of social responsibility. It was an expression of righteous indignation. To these Jewish leaders had been entrusted the religious leadership of the people. Their unresponsiveness to the call of God was a betrayal of that trust. It was not only that they, having the key of knowledge, failed to enter in themselves, and so failed to give the leadership they should, but they prevented others from entering[10] by actively opposing the work of Jesus.

Seeing the disastrous effect of this type of hypocrisy not only on themselves, but on others as well, He burst forth with the passion and the vehemence of the prophet in a fierce indictment of this great obstructing sin. Nowhere is He as severe with sin as here. It appears almost as if He were here passing His moral condemnation not only on hypocrisy, but on sin itself. Its consequences were so disastrous because they cursed not only the doer, but others as well.

It is true that the charges hurled at the Pharisees (and scribes) were not altogether fair to the group as such. But

---

[10] Luke 11:52; Matt. 23:13.

it should be remembered that He was not indicting every Pharisee (or scribe). He cried out: "Woe unto the Pharisees [and scribes] who . . ." do this and that. He was indicting those Pharisees (and scribes), whoever they might be, who were guilty of the sin with which He charged them. But with them He was indicting men everywhere who had allowed, or were allowing, this sin to become incarnate in their lives.

We may now restate some of the conclusions reached for the light they may throw on the problem of coercion.

1. Jesus' rebuke was not prompted by personal animosity or by a desire to strike back at His enemies. Consequently, it offers no encouragement to revenge, say, by resorting to public rebuke.

2. Jesus' denunciation was not a public rebuke of personalities but rather a public rebuke of sin. However, Jesus never thought of sin in the abstract. He always thought in terms of men yielding to sin. So it is not hypocrisy as an abstract evil that He attacks, but rather Pharisees, scribes, and others who were guilty of that sin. His reproof was aimed not so much at the person as at the unregenerate heart and will. He reproved in order that He might save, not in order that He might flay and punish. His was the rebuke of one who knew that it was not the Father's will that one of His children should perish.[11] It was the rebuke of one who shared his Father's concern for those who went astray. It was, therefore, a rebuke of love resorting to drastic measures in order that it might save. Jesus' use of denunciation would, consequently, appear to give a certain relative justification to the use of moral force in dealing with evildoers, provided it sprang from and was controlled by a godlike purpose and spirit.

3. The rebuke was public, but there is no indication that Jesus resorted to public condemnation for the purpose of *coercing* the unregenerate will. He did not believe in trying to save men by "lording it"[12] over them. He tried to save

[11] Matt. 18:12-14; Luke 15:4-7.   [12] Mark 10:42 ff. and parallels.

PASSAGES APPARENTLY JUSTIFYING FORCE 101

them by self-giving and self-forgetful service.[13] The rebuke in this case, therefore, was not intended to coerce men in this unworthy sense but rather to confront them in such a forceful and inescapable way with the fact of their own great obstructing sin that they would turn to God with a cry of true penitence: "Father, I have sinned,"[14] and with a genuine willingness to surrender heart, mind, and soul to the will of God.

4. Evidently righteous indignation against willful unbelief and against people who carelessly or knowingly obstructed the flow of the spirit in the lives of others[15] was, in the mind of Jesus, perfectly consistent with the spirit of love and was perhaps under certain circumstances the inevitable expression of understanding love.

JESUS EXPECTED WARS

Mark 13; Matthew 24; Luke 21; specifically Mark 13:7, 8; Matthew 24:6, 7; Luke 21:9-11

The idea that wars, international conflicts, and other disturbances were to precede the last days was a commonplace in Jewish apocalypses.[16] The fact that Jesus expected wars to precede the coming of the kingdom gives no more sanction to participation in war than His expectation of famine gives sanction to participation in the creation of famine conditions. The purpose of the reference to wars and tumults and distresses is to reassure the Christian community for the time when such conditions might arise. They were not to allow such disorders to disturb their faith. Such conditions were bound to come, but they were not the last word in the matter.

The use of "must needs come to pass" (verse 7)[17] does not

---

13 Mark 10:43-45 and parallels.
14 Luke 15:21.
15 Cf. Mark 9:42 and parallels (question of offenses).
16 So II Es. 5:5; 6:24; Baruch 27:2-4; 48:32, 37; 70:3, 6-8; Enoch 99:4, 6; 100:1-3; Jubilees 23:20-24; and others.
17 Cf. Dan. 2:28 ff., 45.

in itself necessarily mean that wars, etc., are divinely foreordained[18] as precursors of the kingdom. But the reference to these calamities as being "the beginning of travail"[19] would suggest that the disturbances were regarded as having some genetic relation to the coming of the kingdom.

If these wars were regarded as filling a place in the economy of God, there is no suggestion that the followers of Jesus were to try to further that divine economy by taking part in or by promoting such wars. The emphasis is, on the contrary, all on watchful and prayerful waiting and on patient endurance in the face of such distressing experiences.[20]

SAYINGS EMPHASIZING THE VALUE OF BEING PREPARED

Buy a Sword. Luke 22:35-38[21]

When I sent you forth without purse, and wallet, and shoes, lacked ye anything? And they said, Nothing. And he said unto them, But now, he that hath a purse, let him take it, and likewise a wallet; and he that hath none, let him sell his cloak, and buy a sword (verses 35, 36).

The passage obviously is difficult because it appears to be so utterly contrary to the whole tenor of Jesus' life and thought. For instance, did Jesus with the approach of the crisis seriously consider the advisability of armed resistance against His enemies? Did He, who refused to strike a blow in defense, either of Himself or of His cause, and who did not even allow others to strike a blow in His behalf,[22] now exhort His followers to procure swords in order that they might be prepared to defend themselves against an unfriendly and hostile world? Did He who had said: "Whosoever would save his life shall lose it; but whosoever shall lose his life for my sake, the same shall save it,"[23] now turn

18 Preuschen, *Woerterbuch*, p. 267.
19 Mark 13:8.
20 Mark 13:9, 23, 33-37.
21 This passage has been discussed in part in the section of the "Two Swords," pp. 88-91.
22 Matt. 26:52; Luke 22:51.
23 Luke 9:24 and parallels. Cf. also Luke 17:33.

PASSAGES APPARENTLY JUSTIFYING FORCE 103

and urge His disciples by all means to get a sword and strive to save their own lives? Did Jesus now advise His disciples that their lives "must be preserved at any cost, so that in their case violence must be met with violence"?[24] Did Jesus in a moment of real crisis repudiate His earlier teaching not to resist the evildoer by charging His disciples now to be prepared to meet sword with sword? Did He mean to suggest that since He would soon no longer be able to protect them against their enemies they would have to depend on the sword for their needed protection?

To ask these questions is to reveal some of the serious difficulties which confront the view that "sword" in verse 36 is to be taken literally and seriously. Acceptance of that view would demand of Jesus almost a complete reversal of the whole tone and tenor of His life and teaching in the moment of crisis. Such a reversal is inconceivable in a person of the moral strength and perfection of Jesus, the Son of God.

Manson suggests, as one of several possible explanations, that Jesus, knowing the death of the disciples was not required for the fulfillment of the will of God, made an effort to save them by suggesting that they arm themselves "against what might yet prove a murderous attempt upon their lives."[25] This explanation is unconvincing: (1) because such a suggestion on the part of Jesus would appear inconsistent with the emphasis of His whole life and thought; (2) because the sequel of the two swords at the very best gives but doubtful support to this view (cf. page 69 f. above); (3) because the method suggested would not appear to be a very good way to secure the safety of the disciples in the given situation. If Jesus had seriously planned to secure their safety, the obvious way would have been to urge them to scatter and flee rather than to arm and thus take a chance on their ability to cut their way out in a hand-to-hand encounter.

Manson suggests as another possible explanation that

---

[24] B. S. Easton, *The Gospel According to Luke*, p. 329.
[25] Manson, *Gospel of Luke*, p. 247.

104   JESUS AND HUMAN CONFLICT

Jesus may have meant His words literally and ironically. Catching a glimpse of one or the other of His disciples snatching a sacrificial knife and secreting it under his cloak, He cries out: "Yes, provide yourselves with swords, at whatever cost!"[26] That Jesus should have had nothing but playful or sad irony for a situation so charged with serious consequences as the possession of swords by the disciples at a time when He momentarily expected His arrest is strangely unsatisfactory and out of harmony with Jesus' character.

Harnack's explanation,[27] therefore, still appears to be the most satisfactory. He suggests that Jesus meant His words seriously, but metaphorically. Jesus wanted to point out how utterly different would be the situation they would face henceforth from the situation they had faced when He had sent them forth without provisions of any sort.[28] Then they had met a friendly, hospitable world which had gladly received them as representatives of the popular prophet of Galilee. But now He was about to be numbered among the criminals and the manner of their reception would be completely reversed. They would meet an inhospitable, hostile world in which want and hunger and persecution awaited them. "Against it they would have to muster all their resources and the sword would in the future be their most indispensable tool. He had in mind a militant preparedness to defend the Gospel with every resource; they, however, understood Him literally and pointed to the two swords under their garments."[29]

This explanation is not without difficulties, for, as Harnack rightly observes, we are not prepared in the beginning to regard "sword" in a metaphorical sense. But it has the advantage of being consistent with the spirit and the teach-

26 *Ibid.* Cf. also Burkitt, *Gospel History and Its Transmission*, p. 141 f.
27 Harnack, *Militia Christi*, p. 4 footnote.
28 Mark 6:8, 9 and parallels.
29 Harnack, *Militia Christi, op. cit.* "Gegen sie," Harnack remarks, "muessten sie alles aufbieten, und das Schwert werde in Zukunft ihr noetigstes Werkseug sein. Er meinte die kriegerische Bereitschaft, das Evangelium mit allen Mitteln zu verteidigen; sie aber verstanden ihn sinnlich und wiesen auf die zwei Schwerter hin die im Gemache waren."

PASSAGES APPARENTLY JUSTIFYING FORCE 105

ing of Jesus and of fitting in naturally and easily with the reference to the two swords in verse 38.

The word "sword" in this passage, therefore, very probably has no reference whatever to a physical weapon. Consequently this saying cannot be regarded as offering any justification for armed resistance and the use of the sword. The complete absence of any encouraging response by Jesus to the display of the two swords by the disciples together with His subsequent disallowance of the use of the sword at the time of His arrest would appear to reinforce this view.

In fact, it seems quite obvious that Jesus did not intend to give specific directions for meeting the changed situation. He did not suggest that they must never fail to provide themselves with purse and wallet and sword when they went out. He would hardly have encouraged the attitude of fear and worry and concern for one's own safety which such a constant attention to the carrying of sword or purse or wallet would develop. The emphasis on the need for purse and wallet and sword is intended to suggest by a sort of metonymy the privation and persecution which they might be called upon to face.

The Strong Man Fully Armed. Luke 11:21, 22; cf. Mark 3:27; Matthew 12:29

When the strong man fully armed guardeth his own court, his goods are in peace: but when a stronger than he shall come upon him, and overcome him, he taketh from him his whole armor wherein he trusted, and divideth his spoils. (Luke's version is quoted because it appears to be the stronger statement.)

It is not necessary for the purposes of this discussion to go into a detailed analysis of the passage. This saying concerns us only because of the character of the figure used. Did the military figure used in this case imply that Jesus approved of a man's fully arming himself against a possible attack in order to keep his goods in peace? The question opens up the larger problem whether similar implications are to be deduced from other uses of military figures and of figures involving the use of force. Did Jesus' use of such illustrations imply tacit approval of the situation pictured?

Such a conclusion would introduce endless confusion into the message of Jesus. The above saying is clearly a parabolic utterance, and as such it is not intended to give a picture every detail of which is to be regarded as presenting an approved situation. So to interpret Jesus' parables is to do utter violence to them. The parabolic illustration was chosen for its familiarity and its appropriateness to the teaching of a spiritual truth and not for its ethical correctness. That seems to be true of all of Jesus' illustrations.[30] The above illustration evidently was chosen on that basis. It was simply intended to point out clearly that the despoiling of a strong man was everywhere accepted as evidence that he must have met a stronger man. By the same token, the fact that demons were being cast out should be evidence to people that one stronger than the prince of demons had arrived. Nothing further than this should be read into the illustration.

This saying, therefore, has no bearing whatever on the question of armed preparedness. That problem did not come within the range of this utterance, not even by implication.

Not Allow the Thief to Break into the House

Luke 12:39, 40: But know this, that if the master of the house had known in what hour the thief was coming, he would have watched, and not have left his house to be broken through. (Cf. Matthew 24:43, 44.)

The problem in this passage, in so far as it concerns us, is essentially the same as that in the previous passage, namely, are any implications to be drawn from the character of the illustration used? Did this parabolic picture imply approval of forcible resistance as a method of restraining a thief?

The story itself simply suggests that no man, knowing

[30] Cf. Parable of the Unjust Judge (Luke 18:2-7) or that of the Unjust Steward (Luke 16:1-13).

PASSAGES APPARENTLY JUSTIFYING FORCE 107

that his house was about to be entered and robbed of its goods, would allow himself to fall asleep and thus permit the thief to enter unhindered and carry away his possessions. On the contrary, he would watch and not allow himself to be surprised by the thief. He would be waiting for him, prepared to do what he could to prevent the robbery. The sheer spontaneity and inevitableness of this response to the given situation appear to be the point of the illustration. Evidently the story was chosen because cause and effect in the popular mind was so clear and the reaction so natural that the mention of the sudden coming of the Son of Man would suggest just as clearly and naturally the need for an alert, prepared watchfulness.

But does not the suggestion that no man would allow his house to be despoiled without doing all he could to prevent it imply that in Jesus' mind that was the way in which every man should meet such a situation, namely, by resisting the thief and not allowing him to take cloak, or coat, or money? If so, the implication would be a direct contradiction of the saying: "From him that taketh away thy cloak withhold not thy coat also."[31]

Obviously such implications cannot be read into or out of the illustrations of Jesus without confusing His message. His illustrations did not imply a necessary ethical approval of every detail or even of the main action.[32] His attention was focused on the "point" to be illustrated. The ethical standard of the action or the ethical implications of the story itself or of its details were not evaluated by themselves. The implications were beside the point, and the problem they raised would not have occurred to the mind of the unsophisticated hearer. So in the case of this illustration the problem of the proper procedure against the housebreaker does not enter in at all, not even by implication. The ethics of resisting thieves is not evaluated either directly or indirectly.

[31] Luke 6:29.
[32] Cf. Parable of the Unjust Steward (Luke 16:1-13).

108   JESUS AND HUMAN CONFLICT

King Going to War and Taking Counsel. Luke 14:31, 32

Or what king, as he goeth to encounter another king in war, will not sit down first and take counsel whether he is able with ten thousand to meet him that cometh against him with twenty thousand? Or else, while the other is yet a great way off, he sendeth an ambassage, and asketh conditions of peace.

This verse appears to be similar in meaning to verse 28 preceding. "For which of you, desiring to build a tower, doth not first sit down and count the cost, whether he have wherewith to complete it?" The point of verse 28 is manifestly also the point in verse 31 which merely uses a military figure to reinforce the same thought. The two illustrations are taken from well-known facts of experience. They denote merely that following Jesus in the way of the kingdom would involve self-denial and that no man should lightly undertake to follow Him without first calmly and soberly counting the cost. The preparedness urged here is an inner ethical preparedness for the possession of an ethico-religious value and has no reference whatever to preparedness in the event of war.

Passages Implying That Violence Is Justified Under Certain Circumstances

Mark 9:42: And whosoever shall cause one of these little ones that believe on me to stumble, it were better for him if a great millstone were hanged about his neck, and he were cast into the sea. (Cf. Matthew 18:6, 7; Luke 17:1, 2.)

These words were intended to emphasize how terribly serious a matter it was to seduce anyone from his faith. Among the rabbis this sin was classed with the greatest of sins. They stated that if trees were burned because they had caused man to stumble, how much more should that be true of one who caused another to fall into the ways of death.[33] They also said that to cause a "neighbor's face to blanch

[33] Cf. Sanhedrin 55a (quoted in Strack and Billerbeck, *op. cit.*, Vol. I, p. 779).

[from shame] before others" was as if one "shed blood."[34] They classed this sin with those that shut out from the world to come.

Mark 14:21 (cf. Matthew 26:24), speaking of the betrayer, comments: "Good were it for that man if he had not been born." That seems to be also the basic meaning in the above passage on offenses, except that the latter suggests that it were better if the culprit were drowned and so no longer a menace to others. The saying, however, is not to be considered as a literal advice that such a man be actually drowned or killed. It is not to be taken literally any more than the subsequent exhortations that one cut off hand or foot if it causes one to stumble. The utterance is not a charge prescribing specific procedure against offenders. It is rather at once a dramatic presentation of the dreadful seriousness of the sin and a dramatic appeal to men to guard against giving occasion for stumbling.

The question of the justifiability of the use of force in an attempt to restrain or to punish the evildoer does not appear to enter for consideration. The thought of protecting the "little ones" from those who cause them to stumble apparently does not present itself. The attention seems to be focused on the harm the offender is doing to himself rather than on the harm he does to others. "It were better *for him*," we read, not "It were better *for society*," that he be drowned. So blameworthy was this sin that it were better for the offender that he be dead than that he live and continue to cause others to fall and thus continue to pile up blame in the sight of God. The enormity of the crime appears to be measured in terms of its seriousness in the thought of God rather than in terms of its disastrous social consequences.

The passage, therefore, offers no suggestion as to what society ought to do to protect the "little ones" against those who cause them to lose their faith. Instead, it presents an appeal to the individual to use the utmost care lest he prove an offense to others.

---

[34] Baba Mesia 58b (quoted in Moore, *Judaism*, Vol. II, p. 147).

110   JESUS AND HUMAN CONFLICT

JESUS COMMENDED A ROMAN ARMY OFFICER

Matthew 8:5-10; Luke 7:1-10

This passage need not detain us. Jesus obviously commends the centurion for his faith, not for his position. This commendation of his faith can no more be regarded as an approval of his military occupation than the commendation of the faith of the Syrophenician woman[35] can be regarded as an approbation of her occupation, whatever it was.

Of course, this does not explain Jesus' silence about the centurion's occupation. If Jesus did consider war and the whole business of war as evil, why did He not exhort this believing officer to leave his unholy vocation? A completely satisfactory answer does not seem possible where the argument must be built up almost wholly on the silence of Jesus. The following observations may perhaps offer a partial explanation for His silence: (1) Critical remarks to the officer about his occupation at a time when he was pleading for the life of a trusted servant would appear strangely inappropriate. (2) Granted that the occasion offered opportunity for discussion of important problems of life, it is hardly probable that Jesus would have used the occasion to pass judgment on the officer's vocation. It seems more probable that He would have challenged him to surrender his life to God and prepare for the coming of His kingdom. Jesus would hardly have been willing to confuse the primacy of this call by injecting into it a demand for change of occupation. Such a change, if He regarded it as imperative, He likely expected to follow as the result of a transformed life and mind. Inner moral transformation always was more important to Jesus than outward change.

These observations may offer a partial explanation for Jesus' silence on this occasion, but they cast no light on His attitude toward the work of the military profession. They serve, however, to point out how precarious it is to interpret

[35] Matt. 15:28.

Jesus' silence either as approval or disapproval of, or even as indifference to, the centurion's military occupation.

JESUS ADVOCATED OBEDIENCE TO AUTHORITY

"Render unto Caesar . . ." Mark 12:13-17 and parallels

This passage has been discussed at length on earlier pages. There remain for discussion, however, certain additional questions, certain implications which have not been examined previously. For instance, did Jesus deliberately advocate the paying of taxes to Rome, knowing that they would be used to finance military campaigns and operations? Again, did the exhortation to give to Caesar what rightfully was his infer that one owed and should render general obedience to Caesar? And if so, did not that involve tacit approval of the methods of violence employed by the government, including the method of war?

The answer is difficult because it involves an attempt to estimate the reach and penetration of Jesus' mind on a specific occasion and in a specific utterance. That obviously is impossible. All one can hope to do is to suggest probabilities.

Bearing this in mind, we suggest that the problem of taxes financing military campaigns in all probability did not present itself to the mind of Jesus. He did not approach the question of the tribute from the standpoint of an ethical philosopher, nor did He give His answer on the basis of an analytical judgment. In other words, He did not speak as one whose mind took in all possible implications of a situation. He spoke as one whose mind quickly sensed God's will and penetrated to basic facts and meanings. Having sensed God's will and grasped these facts and meanings, He spoke with prophetic disregard of detailed application. For this reason, it appears doubtful whether the above question presented itself to His mind on this occasion.

This does not mean that Jesus was indifferent to or unaware of such practical questions of conscience as the above.

For Him, however, they were secondary issues. The primary task was to know God's will and way in any situation. Knowing this would put a person in contact with needed resources of wisdom and power so that he could respond to such practical issues in a God-pleasing manner.

If the disciples would have asked Jesus for an answer to this question, He probably would have insisted that, subject to their supreme obligation to God, it was still right and God-pleasing that they contribute the tax to the support of orderly government. But He probably would also have repeated for them one of His vigorous stewardship parables strongly emphasizing that men in government and governments are accountable to God for the way they manage this stewardship entrusted to their care. He probably would have told them how the blessing of God rests upon the "faithful and wise servant, whom his lord hath set over his household, to give them their food in due season.[36] This promise would be just as valid if the servant were the government in power. He would also have told them how the judgment of God falls upon that servant[37] (or government) if and when he (or it) begins to misappropriate, use wastefully or selfishly, this stewardship of taxes, man power, and other God-given resources or opportunities. Let a man, therefore, watch and pray that his obligations to government, whatever they may be, are always paid in harmony with his supreme allegiance to God and in accordance with His will. If he does this, he need not charge misrule of government or its misuse of funds from taxes against his conscience. As a kingdom citizen, he, of course, can never be indifferent to any mismanagement in government or to any national sin or failure in stewardship. He will "mourn"[38] over it, but he will be comforted in the confidence that God's will and rule will ultimately prevail and in the knowledge that in his own life His rule is already operative because of his unreserved surrender to Him.[39]

36 Matt. 24:45-51. Cf. also Luke 12:42-46.
37 *Ibid.*
38 Matt. 5:4.
39 Matt. 5:3.

PASSAGES APPARENTLY JUSTIFYING FORCE 113

The second question about the possible larger reference of the saying to include obedience to government has been discussed previously.[40] It was there pointed out that Jesus in His answer probably looked beyond the mere paying of taxes to include, perhaps, even the larger obligations to government. But it was also pointed out that the extent of those obligations was left wholly undefined. Very obviously, however, Jesus' emphasis on the primacy of one's obligation to God would limit one's obedience to government to those acts which did not conflict with the known will and purpose of God.

The principle just stated really answers also the third question about a possible implied approval of the government's use of methods of violence. Obedience to Caesar, in the mind of Jesus, was wholly secondary to obedience to God. One could not, therefore, give approval to any act of government which one conceived to be contrary to the will of God.

That the early followers of Jesus so conceived of their relations to the government is amply proved by the fact that so many of them were willing to endure persecution and death at the hands of government officials rather than disobey the will of God. Their obedience to the government did not make them uncritical of its acts and demands. Even the Pauline conception that governments were ordained of God to be ministers of good to the righteous and avengers of wrath to the wicked[41] did not serve to make them wholly uncritical of the government.[42] The conviction that one must "obey God rather than men"[43] took possession of the Christian community early,[44] and Christians generally apparently held consistently to the belief that their obedience

40 Page 78 ff.
41 Cf. Rom. 13:1-7.
42 Cf. Acts 16:37; 22:25.
43 Acts 5:29; 4:19.
44 The conviction was no new discovery of the Christian community. It was widely current in Jewish circles. Cf. the story of Dan. 3 and the many occasions from the Maccabean time onwards when the Jews would rather suffer all manner of indignities and even death than disobey God.

to human authority must always be subject to their obedience to God. Consequently, it is unwarranted to conclude that Jesus' statement to "render unto Caesar the things that are Caesar's" implied sanction of the methods of violence used by the government. He did not attempt to solve that problem for government.

JESUS DEMANDED SELF-SACRIFICE EVEN TO THE POINT OF DEATH IN DEFENSE OF VALUES MORE IMPORTANT THAN LIFE

Mark 8:34, 35: If any man would come after me, let him deny himself, and take up his cross, and follow me. For whosoever would save his life shall lose it; and whosoever shall lose his life for my sake and the gospel's shall save it. (Parallels in Matthew 16:24, 25; Luke 9:23, 24; cf. also Matthew 10:38, 39; Luke 14:27; 17:33.)

Jesus in this passage is emphasizing that in order to be a true follower of His, a man must renounce himself, i.e., "he is to cease to make himself the object of his life and action."[45] He is to "deny himself and carry out that self-denial even to death."[46] Evidently any disciple who would truly follow Jesus must also follow Him in giving up every selfish interest, if necessary even life itself, for the cause of the kingdom.

Verse 35[47] reinforces this idea except that it states definitely the object for which one is to sacrifice himself. It is a self-sacrifice for the sake of Jesus and naturally also the cause He represents.

A similar idea of sacrifice for others is expressed in Mark 10:43-45: "Whosoever would become great among you, shall be your minister; and whosoever would be first among you, shall be servant of all. For the Son of man also came not to be ministered unto, but to minister, and to give his life a ransom for many."[48]

---

45 Gould, *Gospel of Mark* (ICC), p. 155.
46 *Ibid.*
47 Verse 35 does not directly concern us here.
48 Cf. Matt. 20:26-28; Luke 22:26, 27.

The kind of self-giving enjoined is that which found expression in Jesus Himself. It was a self-sacrifice that drew its passion and power from His love of God and of man; that found its goal in the fulfilled will of God, the highest good of man; that finally was guided in its course by a wholehearted surrender to the will of God. It was a self-sacrifice that found its supreme expression not on the field of battle but on the brow of Calvary.

That kind of self-sacrifice would inevitably put a limit not only on the kind of values for which one would give his life, but also on the manner in which that sacrifice would be made. For instance, Jesus' self-sacrifice on Calvary was not made in behalf of some supposedly great, but illusory, cause which actually had neither an enduring foundation nor an enduring goal. Neither was it a sudden rising to heroic heights under the impetus of a great crisis which threatened a cause He never before had espoused. Neither did Jesus fall while fighting enemies of the cause with their own weapons of violence.

His self-giving on Calvary was made in behalf of the greatest cause on earth, the cause of God for the salvation, the ultimate good, of men. It was not precipitated from without as a result of a great crisis. It was a sacrifice which He gladly and willingly made because He recognized it as unavoidable and necessary for the realization of the divine purpose. His self-giving on Calvary was not a surprise intrusion into the framework of His life. It was of one piece with His whole life in which personal interests, and even life itself, had ever been subservient to the cause of the kingdom.

Even as the course of Jesus' life had always been determined by the will of God, so now the manner of His supreme sacrifice was also determined by what He recognized as the will of God. It was not determined by the strange work of fate or by His own manipulation of events. Both the cause and the manner of His self-giving were determined by what God was and willed.

In the final analysis, however, it was not so much self-sacrifice in *defense* of values more important than life that Jesus demanded. What Jesus required and emphasized in these sayings was such a supreme devotion to the highest, the kingdom of God, that all selfish interests and even life itself would gladly be sacrificed for its promotion and possession.

GOD USES FORCE IN PUNISHMENT

There are a number of passages that picture God as acting with severity toward evildoers under certain circumstances. It is not necessary to go into a detailed analysis of each passage because it is only the general problem of God's use of force that concerns us here. We mention a number of such passages:

The wicked Husbandmen. Mark 12:1-9; Matthew 21:33-41; Luke 20:9-16. The pertinent passage is contained in the last verse. "What therefore will the lord of the vineyard do? he will come and destroy the husbandmen, and will give the vineyard unto others" (Mark 12:9). Matthew adds: "He will *miserably* destroy those *miserable* men. . . ."

The Unmerciful Servant. Matthew 18:32-35. "And his lord was wroth, and delivered him to the tormentors, till he should pay all that was due. So shall also my heavenly Father do unto you, if ye forgive not every one his brother from your hearts" (verses 34, 35).[49] This passage is recorded in Matthew only.

Parable of the Drag Net. Matthew 13:47-50. "So shall it be in the end of the world: the angels shall come forth, and sever the wicked from among the righteous, and shall cast them into the furnace of fire: there shall be the weeping and the gnashing of teeth" (verses 49, 50). This parable is found only in Matthew.

The Unprofitable Servant (Parable of the Talents). Matthew 25:14-30; Luke 19:11-28. "And cast ye out the unprofitable servant into the outer darkness: there shall be the weeping and the gnashing of teeth" (verse 30).

---
49 Cf. Matt. 6:15.

PASSAGES APPARENTLY JUSTIFYING FORCE 117

In Luke, the unprofitable servant receives the same rebuke as in Matthew, and he is likewise deprived of his pound ("talent" in Matthew) but he is not ordered to be cast out. Luke concludes with this statement: "But these mine enemies, that would not that I should reign over them, bring hither, and slay them before me" (verse 27).

The nobleman who later becomes king in this Lucan story displays what appears to be an unreasonable, brutal type of justice which is difficult to reconcile with Jesus' general picture of God as a loving, forgiving, merciful Father. But it is probably quite unwarranted to draw so close a parallel between this nobleman king[50] in this parable and God as to make his action an exact characterization of God's own character and His attitude to the unfaithful and rebellious. Nevertheless, this parable desires to convey the idea that God deals severely with the unfaithful, defiant, lawless, and indifferent.

The Unfaithful Servant. Matthew 24:45-51; Luke 12:42-46. "The lord of that servant shall come in a day when he expecteth not, and in an hour when he knoweth not, and shall cut him asunder, and appoint his portion with the hypocrites: there shall be the weeping and the gnashing of teeth" (verses 50, 51).

Woes Against the Cities. Luke 10:13-15; Matthew 11:20-24. We quote here only the severest statement in the series. "And thou, Capernaum, shalt thou be exalted unto heaven? thou shalt be brought down unto Hades" (verse 15). This passage again emphasizes that God acts severely toward willful impenitence.

The Apocalyptic Coming of the Son of Man. Mark 13:24-27; Matthew 24:29-31; Luke 21:25-28. "But in those days, after that tribulation, the sun shall be darkened, and the moon shall not give her light, and the stars shall be falling from heaven, and the powers that are in the heavens shall be shaken. And then shall they see the Son of man coming in clouds with great power and glory" (verses 24-26).

---

[50] The word "lord" does not here refer to the "Lord God" or the "Lord Jesus Christ" but merely to "his lordship the king."

Matthew and Luke record various additional details descriptive of the judgment. While there is no definite suggestion that these different calamities are a punishment on evildoers, they nevertheless point to God's use of force in His attempt to bring them to penitence.

Are men to imitate God in this respect by dealing severely with evildoers in society? Is this picture of divine justice to serve as the norm for human justice? Are *all* relations of men to be patterned after God's relations to men?

It is very doubtful whether Jesus argued this question in this analytical way. His approach to the problem of life was not analytical but prophetic. He did not urge imitation of God as the result of a comprehensive analysis of the character of God's dealings with men or of the essential problems of human relationship. Neither did He urge imitation of God as an abstract principle. What He urged was emulation of certain aspects of the divine example. As a matter of fact, the imitation He solicited is confined to an imitation of the gentler side of God's dealings with men. Men were to love not only their friends but also their enemies in order that they might be sons of their Father in heaven, for He sent rain and sunshine alike on the good and the evil.[51] They were to be merciful as God was merciful.[52] And they were to be forgiving in their relations one to another even as God was forgiving in His relations to men.[53]

Nowhere did Jesus suggest that men were to think of themselves as agents of God visiting divine punitive justice on evildoers. Nowhere did He suggest imitation of God in His severer dealings with men. Paul likewise held that punishment was a prerogative of God which men did not share. "Vengeance is mine; I will repay, saith the Lord,"

---

51 Matt. 5:43-47.

52 Luke 6:36. Luke's reading is generally preferred to that of Matthew who writes: "Ye therefore shall be perfect . . ." (5:48). But "perfect" in Matthew can hardly be intended to mean perfect in the abstract sense. In its context, it can hardly mean more than "perfect" in love. In other words, men are to strive for the perfection of this gentler side of God's dealings with men.

53 Cf. Matt. 6:14, 15; Mark 11:25.

PASSAGES APPARENTLY JUSTIFYING FORCE

Paul writes in Romans 12:19.[54] This attitude, however, is neither affirmed nor denied in the Gospels, and so we are left without definite material to indicate whether Jesus did or did not approve imitation of God in His more severe dealings with men.

THE CLEANSING OF THE TEMPLE

Mark 11:15-19; Matthew 12:12-17; Luke 19:45-48

Mark 11:15, 16: And he entered into the temple, and began to cast out them that sold and them that bought in the temple, and overthrew the tables of the money-changers, and the seats of them that sold the doves; and he would not suffer that any man should carry a vessel through the temple.

The account of the cleansing in all four Gospels clearly suggests that compulsion of some sort was used in driving the traders from the temple. Jesus was here proceeding in no uncertain terms against a situation which He regarded as a gross violation of the sacred uses and purposes of the temple. Abrahams, while protesting that the temple trade as such was not an evil, but even a necessary convenience, nevertheless readily admits that "there might well have been occasions on which indignation such as that of Jesus would be justified."[55]

That Jesus in this instance used more than indignant protest is evident from the "whip of cords"[56] in His hand and from His "overthrow" of the tables of the money-changers and of the "seats of them that sold the doves." Whether He used physical violence against the traders themselves may well be doubted in view of the fact that such physical attack on the traders would have been self-defeating. His cleansing of the temple was a moral cleansing and it carried with it a moral appeal. To have launched into a physical attack against the persons of the traders would have lowered the plane of His attack to the level of physical combat. It

54 Cf. Deut. 32:35; Psalm 94:1.
55 Israel Abrahams, *Studies in Pharisaism*, I, p. 87.
56 John 2:15.

would have brought confusion into His appeal and would have served to dissipate its power.

One gets the impression from a reading of the records that the cleansing of the temple was an outburst of prophetic zeal. Coming to the temple, which stood for the very life of Jewish religion, seeing the confusion and hearing the noise and sensing intuitively the immeasurable harm it was doing to the religious life of the people, Jesus' indignation rises to fever heat. Instinctively His arm reaches for some object, some extension of itself, passionately needed to express unmistakably and with vigor the hot fury of His soul. Catching sight of a piece of rope, He seizes it,[57] hastily ties some knots into it, and strides forth into the midst of the traders voicing vehement and passionate protest against their demoralizing practice, swinging the scourge of cords, and punctuating His protests with irrepressible and spontaneous gestures of overturned tables and seats. There was violence of a sort in that procedure, but it was a violence called forth and controlled by a holy purpose. It did not consist in an abuse of persons and it was not called forth by hatred of the offenders or of the class to which they belonged. Its purpose was not to condemn and punish the offenders nor to arouse popular resentment against them or the class they represented. It was rather to arouse the conscience of the offenders to the enormity of their sin and to a sense of responsibility for the religious leadership of the nation.

This story of the cleansing of the temple and especially the reference to the scourge of cords has frequently been used to defend the war method and the Christians' participation in war and military training. But such use of this story is quite unwarranted. It is very doubtful whether Jesus used the scourge of cords on the temple traders. Hitting people over the head or lashing them on the back would at once have vitiated His deep moral-religious purpose. To that kind of physical attack, people would have responded in a physical way. They would have fought back, and by-

[57] Cf. John 2:15.

standers, even those inclined to be morally sympathetic to Jesus' action, would more than likely have rallied to protect them from physical abuse.

What the religious leaders and their subordinates needed most, was inner moral cleansing. Jesus knew that one could not cleanse the inside of a cup by merely washing the outside.[58] Jesus was just as keenly aware that one could not cleanse a man's inner life by merely flaying his outside or even by destroying his body. Frightening people might cow them temporarily, but it did not make them good. That could only be accomplished by the cleansing, transforming power of the Spirit of God. Jesus was not primarily interested in chasing these people out of the temple. He was more interested in challenging them to enter into such a relationship of surrender to God that they would help to make the temple a house of prayer for all nations, a place where it would be easy for men to find God.

It is likewise doubtful whether Jesus even used the whip on the cattle and the sheep. Why should Jesus vent the fury of His indignation on innocent animals? They were not to blame for being in the temple. Much rather they were innocent victims that were to give their life and blood as a sacrifice to atone for the sins of men. It does not seem reasonable that Jesus would brutally beat animals, especially victims about to be sacrificed, just to give vent to His anger. He might conceivably have used the whip sufficiently on the animals to get them to move, but even that is not necessarily required. Most every farm boy knows that animals generally start moving in response to an energetic "Shoo" or "Move on" supported by vigorous gestures of arm or stick. In any case, it appears quite out of character to portray Jesus as swinging the knotted scourge brutally over the backs of the animals.

Jesus' cleansing of the temple and His use of the scourge of cord is in no sense to be regarded as analogous to an act of war or to the war and military method. He did not use

[58] Matt. 23:25, 26.

a murderous weapon and He did not intend to kill anybody nor to disable or cripple. He had not trained for months or years with instruments of destruction trying to perfect His technique and efficiency so He could destroy temple traders and their like before they could destroy Him. He did not now carry a whip so He would be prepared for any such emergency. He did not here treat human life as being cheap. On the contrary, He treated it with sacred regard. That is why He appealed in such vigorous manner to their sense of moral-religious values. The temple traders were not hopelessly beyond redemption, incapable of moral appeal or appeal to reason and fit only to kill. They were worth saving.

This act of Jesus, therefore, cannot rightly be treated as a warlike act or as portraying a warlike spirit and as sanctioning the method of coercion, violence, and war. At most this incident indicates that Jesus had a place for physical force if it was under the control of the divine Spirit.

SUMMARY

Summarizing our findings in this study of passages that seem to imply that resistance of some sort is justified and perhaps even required under certain circumstances, we may point to the following conclusions:

1. Jesus evidently found a place for righteous indignation. But it was an indignation that had its roots not in personal resentments against wrong, but rather in love for one's fellow man. Sometimes the feeling of indignation sprang from His concern for the offenders themselves because of the immeasurable harm they were inflicting on themselves by their willful unbelief. Sometimes His indignation was aroused by the harm that was done to others by those who either stood in the way or actively misdirected them.

2. Jesus apparently thought that remonstrance and even public rebuke were perfectly consistent with the will and purpose of God. He did not hesitate to speak frankly and unmincingly when occasion and need seemed to demand it,

but His attack was never personal and never animated by personal feelings. Its purpose was not to punish, embarrass, or coerce, but rather to shake the spirit of complacency and to arouse the conscience with the hope of winning and saving. His remonstrance and public rebuke were not a gesture of impatience. They were not an evidence of loss of faith in the slower, gentler method of love. They were an expression of an active good will resorting to drastic measures in the attempt to save.

3. Jesus had a place for the use of physical force, but it was force motivated by, in control of, and in harmony with a holy purpose whose center was outgoing good will.

4. The larger question of the legitimacy of the use of force and of the method of war is not touched. Jesus' interest was personal and religious rather than social and ethical.

5. Jesus' exhortation for times of trouble, opposition, and war is not violent resistance and clever manipulation, but watchful waiting, steadfast loyalty, and patient endurance.

6. God's use of force in punishment is not held up to men for imitation. Men are urged to imitate God in His gentler dealings with His children, but nowhere is it suggested or implied that men are to imitate God in His severe dealings with mankind. And nowhere is it implied that men are to consider themselves as agents of divine punitive justice.

7. Obedience to government apparently is urged, but this obedience is constantly to be subject to and controlled and guided by the larger obedience to God.

6

Passages Emphasizing Love and Nonresistance

There remain now for examination a considerable number of passages that appear to be in harmony with the teaching on nonresistance. Space does not permit going into a detailed discussion of each of them. Some of them have only an indirect, incidental reference to the problem of nonresistance and will be discussed only from this incidental angle. No exhaustive listing of passages that have relevancy to the subject will be attempted, but rather a careful study of such representative passages as offer to throw light on the general problem involved in the teaching of Matthew 5:38-42 and its Lucan parallel.

JESUS REJECTED THE PRINCIPLE OF COMPROMISE WITH EVIL

Cf. The Story of the Temptation. Matthew 4:1-11; Luke 4:1-13; Mark 1:12 f.

What impresses one particularly in the reading of this story is the firm and uncompromising way in which Jesus rejects every suggestion of the devil. There is not the slightest hint of a disposition to bargain with evil for the accomplishment of recognized duty. Jesus refuses completely the use of compromising measures in the furtherance of His purpose. Having discovered what the will of God is, He trusts that will and way implicitly and follows it completely. He is determined to serve God only.

This utter refusal to compromise with evil is manifest on other occasions. Peter's suggestion of an easier course than that of rejection is firmly swept aside with a stern "Get thee behind me, Satan."[1] The request for a sign is rejected with

---

1 Mark 8:31-33 and parallels.

PASSAGES EMPHASIZING LOVE

an uncompromising "No sign [shall] be given . . . but the sign of Jonah."[2] The temptation suggested in the report that "All are seeking thee" is met with an unhesitating "Let us go elsewhere . . . that I may preach there also."[3] The prayer that the "cup" be removed if possible is concluded with the firm and unwavering "not my will, but thine, be done."[4]

It is well to consider here whether Jesus' rejection of the offer of the kingdoms of the world[5] signifies His definite rejection of the idea of political revolution as a method of furthering the cause of the kingdom. Whether this interpretation is permissible depends largely on whether or not the temptations center around the problem of His Messianic vocation. That Jesus should have been driven, by the experience of His divine call to mission, to a place of quiet where He might meditate and pray about its meaning and where He might try to discover, if possible, how this task was to be accomplished would seem inevitable. It would seem equally inevitable that in the course of this meditation and this attempt to discover the will of God there should flash into His mind various aspects of popular Messianic expectation, for instance, the popular picture of the Messiah coming in the clouds of heaven, overawing and winning men by signs and wonders and displays of power. Was the kingdom to come in that manner, and was He to play a role like that in His attempt to win men for the kingdom? He rejected the idea as untrue to the will of God. To attempt to overcome forcibly man's moral resistance to the will of God by dazzling and overawing him by "signs" and displays of power was not trusting, but tempting God.

Having rejected this popular Messianic expectation, there immediately flashed into His mind another picture, the picture of the Messiah coming as a conquering hero, freeing the nation from the hated and idolatrous foreign yoke,

2 Matt. 12:38 f. and parallels.
3 Mark 1:35-37; cf. Luke 4:42 f.
4 Luke 22:42 and parallels.
5 Third temptation according to Matthew.

slaying the wicked, and setting up in triumph His universal reign of righteousness. The offer of the kingdoms of the world was an offer of world rule; and world rule, according to the thought of the day, could be achieved and maintained only by military power.

This popular expectation He likewise rejected. The kingdom of God would embrace the world, but the method of political revolution and of military conquest was not the way to achieve it. That way was contrary to the will of God. Military power might achieve an outward, unwilling obedience and conformity, but it could never effect the free and willing obedience God desired. That could be produced only by the method of fellowship, friendship, and persuasion. To accept and to identify Himself with any of these various popular conceptions about the coming of the kingdom instead of trusting God to guide Him in His work was to betray a fatal lack of faith in God. He would trust God completely, and He would be guided in His work wholly by what God willed.

In the final analysis, however, the question as to whether Jesus actually faced these alternatives and deliberately rejected them as evil is comparatively insignificant in view of the fact that Jesus' ministry, its character and conduct, in itself constituted such a rejection of these types of Messiahship. The role He played and the kingdom He preached were both wholly nonmilitary and nonpolitical. Both were consistently free from the spirit and use of domination or coercion; their emphasis consistently lay in drawing men, not driving them. The kingdom of God, the kind of world that God intended, would not and could not come into being through the use of violence, military methods, and warfare.

JESUS PRAISED THE NONVIOLENT SPIRIT

Matthew 5:3-12: Blessed are the poor in spirit . . . they that mourn . . . the meek . . . they that hunger and thirst . . . the merciful . . . the pure in heart . . . the peacemakers . . . [the] persecuted. . . . (Cf. Luke 6:22 f.)

It should be noted that Jesus in these Beatitudes is not describing separate, unrelated virtues, nor is He picturing individuals with the particular virtues listed. He is describing the character of the kingdom citizen. He is describing the person who, knowing how dependent he is on God for every good, has made the great surrender, opening the door of his heart and mind to the rule of God. Having surrendered his life to the rule of God's Spirit, he also shares God's concern for people and their troubles.

He Mourns

"Blessed are they that mourn: for they shall be comforted" (verse 4). There is no human trouble, heartache, injustice, corruption, outrage, or strife that leaves him untouched, passive, indifferent. He is disturbed about them, disturbed with a godlike concern, so disturbed that he is challenged to do something God-pleasing about it. He does not sit back and worry himself sick over conditions, nursing his sense of futility and frustration. He does not allow such mournful situations to make him gloomy, pessimistic, bitter, and cynical. He is comforted, filled with strength, in the awareness of God's presence in his life, and in the assurance that God is greater than all man's trouble and His wisdom and strength available and sufficient for all such distressing situations in which he is called to act. Human troubles find the kingdom citizen with sufficient concern and needed spiritual reserves to be able to respond and act.

He Is Meek

"Blessed are the meek: for they shall inherit the earth (verse 5). This saying appears to be a quotation from Psalm 37:11. Meek in the sense in which it is used in Psalm 37:11 means *"sich (Jahve und seinem Willen) unterordnent, sich (ihm gegenueber) als Knecht fuehlend."*[6] The word used in

---

6 Gesenius, *Hebraeisches und Aramaeisches Handwoerterbuch*, p. 605. ("To subject yourself to Jahweh and His will, to feel toward Him as a servant.")

the Greek text means *"sanftmuetig, freundlich, milde."*[7] Perhaps the word partakes somewhat of the nature of both suggested meanings. The meek are those whose surrender to God and the rule of His Spirit makes them gentle, patient, self-controlled under provocation, friendly in their relations to their fellow men. They represent in every way the opposite of the spirit of aggression, self-assertion, self-confidence, self-conceit. They know how inadequate they are apart from God and their fellow men. They feel a sense of obligation to both God and man. So they do not deal with their fellow man in a spirit of proud aggression, self-sufficiency, or condescension, but in a spirit of gentle, regardful, understanding helpfulness. The meek are commonly regarded as the weak, but Jesus' saying expresses the conviction that in the end it will not be the dominating, aggressive, and combative, but the patient, the self-disciplined, and the gentle who will inherit the earth.

He Hungers and Thirsts After Righteousness

"Blessed are they that hunger and thirst after righteousness: for they shall be filled" (verse 6). The kingdom citizen hungers and thirsts for right relations between man and God and man and man. Having opened his heart to the rule of God's Spirit, he also shares God's concern about right relations of good will and mutual helpfulness between man and his neighbor. He not only mourns about wrong relations of ill will, greed, and selfishness anywhere, but he hungers so deeply for positive relations of good will and trust everywhere that he actively seeks to do something to realize them. Such an active godlike hunger, Jesus says, shall not go unfilled. God will see that it gets fulfillment.

He Is Merciful

"Blessed are the merciful: for they shall obtain mercy" (verse 7). The thought of this verse is a commonplace in rabbinical literature. Mercy in rabbinic circles, Moore de-

[7] Preuschen, *Woerterbuch* ("tenderhearted, friendly, mild"). Liddell and Scott concur in giving this Greek term the meaning of "mild, gentle, meek."

clares, is "an attribute which best describes His (i.e., God's) nature."[8] For this reason, we find passages like this: "He who has compassion upon men, upon him God has compassion. And upon him who has no compassion upon men, God has no compassion."[9] The same estimate of mercy is also common among Old Testament writers.[10] Such statements as "Go ye and learn what this meaneth, I desire mercy, and not sacrifice"[11] suggest that it also had an important place in Jesus' thought.

The mercy that is spoken of here is evidently the kind of mercy that moves God in His relation to the sinner. It is an attitude of compassion originating in a genuine consideration for and an intelligent, sympathetic understanding of the evildoer and representing the opposite of the spirit of revenge or of unfeeling justice. It expresses itself not in deeds of violence, but in generous gestures of understanding love.

He Is Pure in Heart

"Blessed are the pure in heart: for they shall see God" (verse 8). Since this Beatitude has only an indirect reference to our subject, it needs only a brief comment. "Pure in heart" in this saying means a "concentration of the whole personality on God, the exclusion of everything else."[12] It means, therefore, among other things, the exclusion of all attitudes which are contrary to the character and the will of God. The pure in heart are free from the spirit of hatred and ill will and coldheartedness and those other attitudes which issue in acts of violence and revenge and coercion. More than that, their whole being is focused on the attempt to emulate God in such positive elements of character as goodness, love, forgiveness.

---

8 Moore, *Judaism*, Vol. I, p. 535.
9 Sabbath 151b. Quoted by Montefiore, *Rabbinic Literature*, p. 23.
10 Cf. Psalm 103:8, 13; 145:8 f., 14-19; Ex. 33:19; 34:6 f.; Zech. 7:9 f.
11 Matt. 9:13 (quoted from Hos. 6:6).
12 Theodore H. Robinson, *The Gospel of Matthew*, 1928, p. 31. The meaning would appear to be very similar to the saying in Matt. 622: "If therefore thine eye be single, thy whole body shall be full of light."

He Is a Peacemaker

"Blessed are the peacemakers: for they shall be called sons of God" (verse 9). The Hebrew word for peace, *shalom,* had a much wider application than the English word "peace." It included in its meaning general prosperity and well-being. When used in reference to men's relations one to another, it meant "that harmony without which the welfare of the individual and the community [was] impossible."[13] It was the very opposite of aggression, enmity, and strife, forces destructive to human welfare. The promotion of harmonious relations between men was therefore repeatedly urged as one of the highest duties. The rabbis listed it as one of the four virtues which store up credit for a man in the world to come.[14] Hillel, the contemporary of Jesus, urged the men of his day: "Be disciples of Aaron, loving peace and pursuing peace, loving mankind and drawing them to the law (religion)."[15] These are but samples of numerous similar expressions.[16]

In this saying Jesus, therefore, ranks Himself with the best Jewish thought of His day. He not only praises the peacemaker in the highest terms, but He declares him to be morally akin to God, partaking of the very nature and character of God. ("Sons of God" clearly has reference to moral sonship.) The saying implies that one of the primary purposes of God is to establish a human society in which ill will, enmity, rivalry, aggression, and violence have disappeared and only harmony, good will, mutual concern, and general well-being prevail. To be actively engaged in building and upholding friendly relations between men and restoring harmonious relations where they had been marred by strife, that was to share the very purpose of God.

No statement is made in the saying to indicate what kind

---

[13] Moore, *Judaism,* Vol. II, p. 195.

[14] The list includes: "Honoring father and mother; deeds of loving-kindness; making peace between a man and his fellow; and the study of the law, which is equal to them all" (Moore, *op. cit.,* p. 196).

[15] Aboth 1:12. Quoted *ibid.*

[16] For Old Testament passages cf. Psalm 34:15; Zech. 8:16 f., 19; and others.

of peace efforts merit the words of praise or what motives are the spring and power of these efforts. Jesus would hardly describe peacemakers as "sons of God" unless a godlike concern for the good of man motivated their peace efforts. This would also imply that the ways and means employed in the promotion of peace conform with the will and purpose of God. In other words, the peacemakers are those who not only share God's great purpose to conciliate men and to promote their total well-being, but also are motivated and guided by that great purpose in their efforts to restore and maintain harmonious and constructive relations between them.

The question now arises whether this saying is confined to the promotion of peaceful relations between individuals or whether it includes also the promotion of international peace and well-being. The word "peacemakers" gives no clue unless the plural form implies an individual reference. The other Beatitudes would tend to support this view, for in all of them Jesus appears to address Himself primarily to questions of personal relationships. It is impossible to say just how large may have been the sweep of Jesus' mind as He made these penetrating observations. It certainly is unwarranted to assume that His mind might not have thought of any larger peace efforts than the purely personal. At least it is hardly fair to assume that Jesus would have excluded from His congratulation those whose efforts included the promotion of international peace and good will, provided, of course, their motives and methods were in harmony with the character and purpose of God. It is not right to picture Jesus as if He said: "Blessed are the peacemakers, but not if they strive to establish harmonious relations between social, economic, or political factions; if they are government officials, and seek to promote peaceful relations between nations in a God-pleasing manner and spirit." Can one rightly present Jesus as saying in effect: "You try to promote peace between man and God, but let men quarrel and fight it out as they will"; or "You try to promote peaceful relations between a man and his neighbor, but don't bother about peaceful relations between nations; leave that to pagan minds and spirits or just let them fight it out"? It is possible that Jesus, when He spoke this word, did not specifically think of the question of international peace, but it certainly appears wrong to conclude that the international peacemaker was not included provided he worked at it in a Christlike manner and spirit.

The word used here, "peacemaker," is not the "peace-loving" or the "peace-minded" or "those who keep out of trouble." It is not merely a something of which one thinks when strife and war have come. Peacemaking is an indispensable part of the spirit of the kingdom citizen. The one in whom the Spirit of God had become a ruling principle is a peacemaker always. He is never happy over strife and warfare whether on the personal, domestic, social, religious, or international plane. He mourns over friction, heat, misunderstanding, anywhere. He is forever pouring oil on troubled waters. He cannot add to the world's troubles. He is forever trying to reconcile men to God and to themselves and to their fellow men; forever at work ministering to man's well-being and preventing occasions for strife and warfare. "Peacemaker" is unqualified and includes all peacemaking done in this Christlike manner and spirit.

He Is Persecuted

"Blessed are they that have been persecuted for righteousness' sake: for theirs is the kingdom of heaven" (verse 10). "Blessed are ye when men shall reproach you, and persecute you, and say all manner of evil against you falsely, for my sake. Rejoice, and be exceeding glad: for great is your reward in heaven: for so persecuted they the prophets that were before you" (Matthew 5:11 f.; Luke 6:22 f.). In this passage it is assumed that the persecution has come upon them because of their loyalty to the cause of Jesus and has been borne with a spirit of patient, steadfast, and loyal endurance. The followers of Jesus have not only submitted

PASSAGES EMPHASIZING LOVE 133

to the persecution, but they have endured the ill will and hatred and violence in a manner and a spirit that is in harmony with the spirit of Him who is the object of their devotion. They are called blessed not merely because they have been harassed, hated, and maligned, but because, having been ill-treated for the sake of Christ, they have through it all maintained their loyalty, inwardly and outwardly, to Him. Their submission has not been one of expediency or resentment. Instead, it has been wholly free from the spirit of retaliation and devoid of all violent efforts at self-protection. Theirs has been a submission whose soul and strength have been derived from a steadfast loyalty to Christ and the cause He represented.

Jesus gives the kingdom citizen no assurance that he will always be saved from suffering and death. Much rather he is told to expect persecution.[17] That is what the world has always done to its prophets, its spokesmen for God. That is what the world will also do to Jesus and "if they persecuted me, they will also persecute you."[18] The kingdom citizen who unreservedly allows the Spirit of God to rule in him will in a world yielding to the rule of the spirit of evil experience misunderstanding, ridicule, abuse, and opposition.

But such suffering because of an uncompromising love for and loyalty to Christ is blessed because it serves the redemptive purposes of God. "Except a grain of wheat . . . die, it abideth by itself alone; but if it die, it beareth much fruit."[19]

JESUS EXHORTED MEN TO LIVE PEACEFUL LIVES

Matthew 10:16: Behold, I send you forth as sheep in the midst of wolves: be ye therefore wise as serpents, and harmless as doves. (Cf. Luke 10:3.)

It is worth noting (1) that Luke reports only the first half of this saying; (2) that in Matthew these words are

[17] He is not told to *seek* it.
[18] John 15:20.
[19] John 12:24.

part of Jesus' final instruction to the Twelve whom He is sending on their first missionary tour, while in Luke they are final instructions to the seventy; (3) that the parallels to the verses following in Matthew (verses 17-23) are found in the apocalyptic discourses of Mark 13 and Luke 21. It, therefore, does not appear possible to point to any *one* particularly grave situation as having called forth this specific saying. Perhaps it is not very essential in this instance to know the particular occasion for this word. The meaning of Jesus' counsel would be practically the same whether He anticipated trouble for His disciples in some immediate or some more remote situation. His counsel does not appear to have been conditioned by any one set of circumstances.

The point of emphasis in the saying apparently is: (1) on "wolves," i.e., on the hostile situation that will confront them, not necessarily on the immediate tour or in the immediate environment, but perhaps in the work that must soon be theirs in view of His expected rejection; and (2) on the good judgment with which they ought to meet these various acts of unfriendliness. Just how much of hostility and violence one is to read into the figure of the "wolves" is difficult to determine. It is doubtful whether anything more is intended by the figure than to suggest in a general picture the unscrupulous, unrelenting, and often fierce opposition which they would frequently meet.

There is less danger of reading too much into the phrase "wise as serpents" because it is qualified by the addition "and harmless as doves." The word "wise" means "practically wise," "clever," "resourceful," *einsichtsvoll* (i.e., judicious).[20] "Serpents" is a figure frequently used as a symbol of wisdom of this kind, though it is often used with a side reference to "cunning" and "trickery."[21] In the balancing clause, the word "harmless" means "pure," "unmixed";[22] and the word "doves," as in other passages of Scripture, is

[20] Preuschen, *Woerterbuch*.
[21] Cf. Gen. 3:1; Psalm 140:3; II Cor. 11:3; Rev. 12:9.
[22] Abbott-Smith, *Greek-English Lexicon*.

used as a symbol of sincerity, the absence of deceit.[23] Both figures, of the "serpents" and the "doves," are used in the above sense in rabbinical literature. The following saying is attributed to Rabbi Juda (A.D. 200): "God saith of the Israelites, Towards me they are sincere as doves, but towards the Gentiles they are prudent as serpents."[24]

Apparently, then, what Jesus wants to emphasize is that His followers ought to meet the hostility of men with prudence, understanding, and resourcefulness, but that in any case they must keep themselves free from the taint of compromise and evil.

The figure of the "sheep" (or lambs) in the previous statement apparently is intended to carry a larger meaning than that of mere contrast to "wolves." The simile is not merely an attempt to picture the contrast between the impotence and defenselessness of the disciples as compared with the number and strength of the "wolves" who will not hesitate to use all manner of weapons against them. The saying is more than a declaration of fact. It is an exhortation as well. It is intended to suggest the manner and the spirit with which they are to enter this work in which hostile men will be ready to prey on them. They are to go out with the gentleness of sheep who, when they are attacked, do not snarl and bite, but patiently bear the pains and rendings which fierce opponents may inflict. They are to meet the attack of the wolves with the gentle nonviolence and nonretaliation of sheep.

But does the figure of the sheep imply the use of such pacific virtues as loving one's enemies and doing good to those that hate you?[25] That would seem to be reading too much into the meaning of this simile. It appears rather doubtful whether anything more is intended than to suggest the gentle, patient, nonviolent, suffering, forbearing manner in which the disciples are to carry on their work in the midst of "wolves."

23 Cf. Song of Songs 1:15; 4:1; 5:12; also Gen. 8:7-11.
24 Canticles 2:14 (101a), quoted by McNeile in *Gospel According to St. Matthew*, p. 139. Also by Bultmann, *Gesch. der Syn. Tradit.*, p. 112.
25 Luke 6:27-29.

Something more positive is implied when in the course of these same instructions to the disciples Jesus charges them to approach each house with the friendly greeting and the spirit of peace.[26] Necessarily such a greeting presupposes the presence of the spirit of good will. Putting it negatively, this means that they are not to approach any house with the expectation of finding it inhabited by "wolves."

Matthew 10:23 suggests that one way of meeting persecution in a city is to flee to the next. Apparently this is regarded as a prudent way of meeting that particular hostile situation.[27] Rather than fight, they are to flee. They are to do what they can to avoid unnecessary clashes with unfriendly opponents. It is even possible that the saying is intended to discourage the seeking of martyrdom by advising against an unnecessary continuance in a hostile city.

Matthew 10:14[28] gives specific directions as to what the disciples are to do when men will neither receive nor hear them. In that case they are to "shake off the dust" from under their feet. This was a gesture that symbolized the shaking off of pollution. "The Jews considered that the soil under the feet of Gentiles, with its waters, its dwellings, and its ways, was polluted. Hence the gesture . . . may be a token that Israelites unfriendly to the kingdom are no better than the heathen."[29]

But this act was in no sense to be a gesture of scorn or disdain. It was a symbolic act intended to serve as a testimony—a final appeal, as it were—to the impenitent.[30] Its purpose was to make unmistakably clear to those concerned that the guilt of rejecting the messengers and their message

26 Luke 10:5 f.; Matt. 10:12 f.
27 The exhortation to flee from Jerusalem (Mark 13:14 and parallels) is not analogous. The latter is an exhortation to seek personal safety in a situation that has no specific relation to them as followers of Jesus. They are to flee because they would simply be crushed in a meaningless struggle between rival forces.
28 Both Matthew and Luke follow their Marcan source here. (Mark 6:11; Matt. 10:14; Luke 9:5; 10:10 f.)
29 Manson, *The Gospel of Luke*, p. 101.
30 Mark 6:11b.

rested at their own door. It was not a demonstration of despair or a symbolic way of consigning them to the fate of the Gentiles, but the strong gesture of a deep concern resorted to in an effort to penetrate their hard shell of indifference to the message of the kingdom.

MEN TO LOVE THEIR NEIGHBOR AS THEMSELVES

Mark 12:28-34; Matthew 22:34-40; Luke 10:25-37

Mark 12:30 f.: Thou shalt love the Lord thy God with all thy heart, and with all thy soul, and with all thy mind, and with all thy strength. The second is this, Thou shalt love thy neighbor as thyself.

Several things are worth noting:

1. Certain interesting variations occur in the accounts of the three Gospels. The setting, for instance, is different. In Matthew and Mark, the words are uttered during "Passion Week" in the course of a series of controversies with Jewish leaders. In Luke this teaching has its setting in the framework of the so-called Perean Ministry. Again, in Mark the questioner is a friendly scribe who at the close of the interview is complimented by Jesus as being "not far from the kingdom of God."[31] In Matthew and Luke, the questioner is pictured as "trying" Jesus. Finally, according to the Gospel of Luke, it is not Jesus who gives the summary of the law, as in Matthew and Mark, but rather the lawyer, and Jesus merely adds His word of approval. These variations in detail, however, do not change the essential meaning and significance of the principle announced. Its meaning and importance are not derived from its setting, but rather from its own independent worth and from its connection with the person of Jesus.

2. This summary of the law was not original with Jesus. The commandment to love God with one's whole heart, etc., was found in Deuteronomy 6:5[32] and the commandment to

[31] Mark 12:34.

[32] According to Mark and Luke, Jesus does make an original and significant contribution to this O.T. commandment by adding "with all thy

love one's neighbor as himself was found in Leviticus 19:18. The combination of the two into one is found in the "Testaments of the Twelve Patriarchs."[33] The Lucan version which credits the summary of the law to the lawyer would imply that his statement has been accepted in scribal circles as a summary of the law. Apparently we have here another instance where Jesus ranges Himself on the side of the best Jewish thought of His day and where He, either by His reemphasis or by His approval, adds to it the dynamic of His own personality. The principle announced was therefore not new but it acquired new meaning and vitality when Jesus breathed upon it the spirit of His own life and thought.

3. The word "neighbor" in this passage does not have a restricted meaning. It is not necessary here to go into a discussion as to whether the Jews in the time of Jesus limited the meaning of this term to "fellow Jew," or whether they thought of neighbor in the more liberal term of "fellow man."[34] It is sufficient to point out that the finer spirits among the Jews, at least on occasions, interpreted the word "neighbor" in the broader sense of fellow man.[35]

Just how broadly Jesus interpreted it in this specific passage is impossible to say. The word is unqualified. But in view of the whole broad emphasis of Jesus' life and message

---

strength." It is as if Jesus wanted to emphasize unmistakably that a man was to love God with *all* the resources of his being, mind, heart, soul, *and strength*.

33 Dan. 5:8: "Love the Lord through all your life, and one another with a true heart." Cf. also Issachar 5:2; 7:6. R. H. Charles dates the Hebrew original of this work at approximately 109-107 B.C. (R. H. Charles, *Testaments of the Twelve Patriarchs*, Introduction, p. 53.)

34 The question of the exact meaning of the word "neighbor" in the passage in Lev. 19:18 was felt to be a real problem by the Jews. Note the large number of quotations cited by Strack and Billerbeck in connection with the passage in Matt. 5:43, p. 354 ff.

35 Cf. Hillel: "Be of the disciples of Aaron, loving peace and pursuing peace, loving 'the creatures' and drawing them near to the law" (Aboth 1:12. Quoted in Montefiore, *Rabbinic Literature*, p. 73) or Hillel's summary of the law given to the Gentile: "What is hateful to thee, do not to thy neighbor: that is the whole law and the rest is commentary. Go and learn" (Sabb. 31a. See Strack and Billerbeck, p. 460); or Ben Assai's summary: "These are the generations of man." (Sifra, Kedoshim Perek 4. See Moore, *Judaism*, Vol. II, p. 85.)

PASSAGES EMPHASIZING LOVE

and, furthermore, in view of the story of the "Good Samaritan" that follows in the Lucan account, it does not appear possible to assign to the words any particularistic meaning. Whether Jesus consciously and deliberately intended to give it a universalistic meaning in contrast with current popular particularism may well be doubted,[36] for such a contrast is not clearly indicated. Moreover, it is very doubtful whether a distinction between a Jewish "neighbor" and a Gentile "neighbor" even occurred to Him. His mind did not seem to run in particularistic channels. When He spoke of "neighbor," He thought of the man, not of his nationality or his religion.

The summary statement of the law is followed in the Lucan account by the story of the "Good Samaritan." In this setting, this story undoubtedly is intended to answer the question: "Who is my neighbor?" and to prevent its being answered in any narrow terms. The story does not really give a definition of "neighbor," as the question of verse 29 leads one to expect. Instead, it gives a picture of neighborly conduct.

Nevertheless, by implication, the story does give an answer to the question: "Who is my neighbor?" There are certain deft touches that serve to bring this answer to the surface. First, the man who fell among the robbers is described in the most general terms as "a certain man." He is not specifically a Jew nor any other nationality. He is just a certain man, some fellow human being. Such a general term, of course, at once effectively excludes any particularistic reference. Its use does not appear to be a studied attempt to eliminate any narrow associations, but rather the general introduction to a story when one has no particular kind of individual in mind. The net result is the same in either case.

Second, the man who "proved neighbor" is pictured as a "Samaritan," i.e., as one who, in Jewish circles, was classed with the Gentiles. Abrahams commends this use of a "Sa-

---

36 Cf. Montefiore, *Rabbinic Literature,* p. 61 f.

maritan" in the story as a skillful "device of moral art. To castigate one's own community, it is sometimes effective to praise those outside it."[37]

The contrast is not so much between priest, Levite, and "Samaritan" as between the indifference of the former and the spontaneous neighborly response of the latter, not to a Jewish need, but to a *human* need. That is to say, the Samaritan as such is not pronounced a better man than the priest or the Levite, not even by implication. That question has no relevancy to the point of the story and receives no consideration. The specific mention of the priest, the Levite, and the Samaritan is made merely for the purpose of setting forth in as graphic a contrast as possible the neighborly man, who, seeing a man in need, immediately goes forth and allows his warm human sympathy and friendliness to assert itself in generous and thoughtful helpfulness. The neighborly spirit does not stop to argue and inquire whether the man in need is a Jew or a member of a hated race, an innocent victim of violence or a robber, etc. It sees a human being in need and, forgetting all other considerations, it freely gives itself in service not only to the need but to the person himself.

Third, the story at once raises the issue from the level of academic discussion and makes it a question of conscience and humanity. Neighborliness in this story is not an academic question to be discussed and defined. It is rather a facing of one's fellow man in need with an understanding sympathy and friendliness and with a sense of responsibility, and then allowing this spirit of friendliness and responsibility to assert itself in generous service. It is a spirit that cannot be confined or restrained by considerations of race, religion, prejudice, or ill feeling.

Thus, while the story does not directly answer the question: "Who is my neighbor?" its implications clearly indicate that my neighbor is anyone who needs my love and help. It leaves no room for a particularistic interpretation of the

[37] Israel Abrahams, *Studies in Pharisaism*, II, p. 36.

PASSAGES EMPHASIZING LOVE

term "neighbor." There is no one whom one can excusably exclude.

4. The love one is to bear to his neighbor is to be like that which one bears to himself. No explanatory word is added describing more fully the practical and spiritual implications of this statement or endeavoring in any way to safeguard it against narrow interpretations. Obviously the exhortation is not an attempt to formulate precise modes of conduct, but rather to sum up in a single concise statement the whole of man's moral obligations, to indicate in a sentence the basic principle from which will flow conduct approved not only by man but by God as well. The value of such a statement lies in its penetration and its power of suggestion. Brushing aside all attempts to solve the problems of human relations by prescribing rules of conduct, it boldly declares the solution to these problems to lie in the realm of attitudes and motives, and it kindles the imagination with the suggestion that happy, just, and God-pleasing relations between men will result when they are filled with a love and regard for one another so deep and far-reaching that the highest good of the other becomes a matter of equal concern to their own well-being.

This attitude of love derives its meaning and vital power from its relation to the previous commandment. The fact that the commandment to "love God with the whole heart . . ." is mentioned first in all three Gospels would in itself suggest that it was regarded not only as prior in importance, but as absolutely basic for the proper observance of the commandment to love one's neighbor as oneself. Its definite designation as "first" in Matthew and in Mark and the designation of the commandment on loving one's neighbor as "second"[38] greatly strengthens this viewpoint. The "first" commandment in the mind of Jesus unquestionably was to love God with all one's heart. . . . That was the very es-

---

38 Matthew's version, "a second like unto it," apparently attempts to point out the closeness of the relation between the two commandments and the great importance of the "second" commandment by comparing it with the one which admittedly was "first."

sence of His call to repentance and surrender. It meant to love and trust God and His cause to the point of surrender. Then out of this relationship of wholehearted love and surrender to the will of God, there flowed self-forgetful, self-giving love for one's fellow man. The opening of the heart to God meant the inflow of His spirit of self-giving love. This enabled men to love their neighbor as themselves.

The quality of this outgoing love, therefore, is determined by God's own love for man. This love Jesus revealed in His own life of self-giving and in His self-giving death on the cross. It causes men to lose themselves for Jesus' sake.[39] This ultimately means giving oneself to one's fellow man with the same spirit of self-giving love with which He gave Himself to men. It means doing unto others as we would have them do unto us; for the spirit required for the fulfillment of the "Golden Rule" is essentially the same as that required in loving one's neighbor as oneself.[40] The good a man desires for himself, he is to seek to achieve for others with the same generous good will with which he seeks it for himself.

The love one is to bear to his neighbor, therefore, is not to be determined by prevailing human standards of love. The nature of the good a man desires for himself, or the quality of the love he bears to himself is not to decide the nature or the quality of the love or service that he will give to his fellow man. That is determined by the character and will of God as it is discovered and experienced through the

39 Cf. Mark 8:34 f. and parallels.

40 Matt. 7:12; Luke 6:31. In Matthew the saying, like that on loving one's neighbor, is declared to be a summary of the "law and the prophets." This fact would tend to emphasize the essential similarity, at least in spirit, between the two sayings. (In Didache, A.D. 120-60, 1:2 the two summaries are combined into one statement: "The way of life, then, is this: First thou shalt love the God who made thee; secondly, thy neighbor as thyself; and all things whatsoever thou wouldst not have befall thee, thou, too, do not to another.") However, the similarity of spirit required in this saying and in that on loving one's neighbor would be apparent even apart from this Matthaean conclusion. Its observance in the spirit of the Master requires such a sympathetic understanding of the other's needs and such a large measure of good will, that a man would seek to do for his fellow man what he would desire for himself if he were in the other man's position.

PASSAGES EMPHASIZING LOVE

relationship of whole-souled love to Him. The reference to one's own love and desires for himself is intended, first, to suggest the high quality of love required of members of the kingdom, and, second, to furnish a concrete background against which to measure the depth and sincerity of one's regard for his fellow man.

The commandment to love one's neighbor as oneself or to do unto him as one would have him do in return is therefore removed at once from the realm of calculation and speculation. The love that has its source in God and that comes into being through loving Him with the whole heart does not stop to ask in a calculating spirit who the neighbor is whom one is under obligation to love as oneself, whether friend or foe, Jew or Gentile, or whether one has met the obligation to do unto him as one would desire him to do in return. The person in whom the divine love has become a burning flame will not see in the standard suggested merely a maximum to which he feels he ought to measure up as a matter of duty, but he will see in it rather a picture of a minimum that constantly serves to challenge the reality and sincerity of his regard for his fellow man. The question of the possibility and the practicability of obedience to these commandments does not greatly concern him. He is sure that if the love required has its source in God, then living up to its standard is not only possible, but is at the same time the most urgently practical course one could undertake.

In popular discussions of this demand to love one's neighbor as oneself, the trend of thought is frequently conditioned by the unexpressed worry that obedience to its request will require loving persons or groups whom we have no desire to love or feel incapable of loving. We apparently are more concerned about finding reasons why we can excusably exclude some persons or groups as falling outside the scope of our obligation to "neighbors" than about finding reasons why we may include them.

Popular discussion of this question also appears worried about the meaning of loving him *as ourselves*. The kind of questions raised about this would indicate that we are afraid this requires loving oneself less. But that is not what Jesus demanded. He did not ask men that they love themselves less, but that they love the other more. They are to have such a depth of concern for the other that they will actively seek for him the good they desire for themselves. The basic consideration now is not "Who is my neighbor?" "Must I love as myself the evildoer, or the member of a despised race?" but "Do I possess the neighborly spirit?"

"Love your enemies . . ."

That this love is to transcend all barriers of human life is suggested clearly in the saying: "Love your enemies, and pray for them that persecute you" (Matthew 5:44). Luke 6:27 f. reads: "Love your enemies, do good to them that hate you, bless them that curse you, pray for them that despitefully use you." The love that is enjoined here presupposes the possession of a quality of spirit that transcends all barriers of race, nation, prejudice, and hatred. It presupposes an attitude of good will so superior to the spirit of revenge and ill will that it cannot be interrupted by acts of hostility, but continues to seek actively the good of the offender. It presupposes a spirit of such sympathetic and penetrating understanding that it judges the enemy not in terms of the personal ill will he bears to you or your cause, but in terms of the being he represents in the sight of God and the being he, by the grace of God, may become. It is a spirit which hopes and believes that the continued manifestation of genuine, undiscouraged good will will ultimately prevail to save the man from his ugliness of spirit to a winsomeness of spirit such as that which marks true sons of the Father in heaven.

In other words, this passage pictures much more than mere proper and God-pleasing conduct toward the evildoer. It ultimately presents love as the supreme redemptive force in human life. That is clearly implied in the saying: "Love your enemies, and pray for them that persecute you." It is

PASSAGES EMPHASIZING LOVE

strongly reinforced by the words that follow in the immediate Matthaean context.[41] Men are to love their enemies because God is "kind toward the unthankful and evil" (Luke 6:35). He does not take revenge on those who flout His will nor deal with them according to their desert. With boundless, generous good will, He showers blessings upon the evil and the good alike, not because it makes no difference to Him whether or not men respond to the appeal of His love, but because the rebellious, the unloving, the unresponsive need His love as much as the thankful and the good, and because He hopes that His continued benevolence will ultimately win them to a wholehearted surrender to His role of love. The strongest power available is required if they are to be won back to their true selves and to a relationship of trust and love to God and their fellow men. And the great redemptive power God uses in His attempt to win and to save the unloving and rebellious is the appeal of unwearied, outgoing, self-giving love.[42] It is not the kind of love that pampers and spoils and saves men from the just consequences of their wrongdoing. It is that deep, discerning, adventurous, creative good will and self-giving love that approaches a man on the plane of his noblest self. It appeals to his sense of self-respect and to his intuitive appreciation of generous, understanding, regardful treatment by fellow human beings.

The attainment of this immeasurable, undiscouraged, self-giving, redemptive love Jesus holds up before men as their goal. They are to be perfect as God is perfect. Matthew 5:48. The possession of this love will set them apart from others and will stamp them as true sons of the Father in heaven, who does not deal with men on the basis of their love for Him, but on the basis of His love for them and their need of Him. For He is not a God of vengeance, but

---

41 Essentially the same thought is presented in briefer and less forceful manner in Luke 6:35b, "And ye shall be sons of the Most High: for he is kind toward the unthankful and evil."

42 "God so loved the world, that he gave his only begotten Son, that whosoever believeth on him should not perish, but have eternal life" (John 3:16).

a God of love, mercy, and forgiveness, and His method of dealing with men is not coercion, but inexhaustible good will.

The redemptive power of love is emphasized in such teachings as those about the lost sheep and the prodigal son. Luke 15. It is the persistent, undiscouraged love of the shepherd that causes him to leave the ninety-nine and go out to seek the lost sheep until he finds it. And when he finds it, he restores it to the fold and rejoices with a joy that knows no bounds. Again it is the love that "would not let him go" that restores the prodigal son to the place of sonship and self-respect and to all the filial relations with the father. Even the winning of Zacchaeus (Luke 19:1-10) is but a story of the conquest of understanding, outgoing good will. It is impossible to imagine a man like him being transformed by cynicism, condemnation, prosecution, or coercive measures of any sort. A spontaneous, understanding "I must abide at thy house" from the lips of Jesus wins from Zacchaeus at the end of the visit an equally spontaneous "Behold, Lord, the half of my goods I give to the poor; and if I have wrongfully exacted aught of any man, I restore fourfold."

The love that Jesus emphasizes here is not a vaporous *Allgemeine Menschenliebe* (love of mankind). He did not think in such abstract terms. The terms "neighbor" and "enemy" are used in an inclusive sense, but they are, nevertheless, in the mind of Jesus distinctly flesh and blood individuals. Men are to love the specific neighbor (or enemy) of the moment whoever he may happen to be.

Did Jesus have in mind any specific kind of enemy when He urged men to love their enemies? Did He think specifically of the political enemy of the Jews, perhaps with the aim of counteracting the fierce hatred preached by extreme nationalists? Would the picture of the Roman oppressor be the first one to flash into the minds of His Galilean audience as they listened to these words? Jackson and Lake give a few observations on this point.[43]

---

[43] Jackson and Lake, *Beginnings of Christianity*, Vol. I, p. 289 f.

PASSAGES EMPHASIZING LOVE

The immediate political situation does not appear to have been so acute nor the political feeling so intense that the exhortation to love one's "enemies" would necessarily and inevitably suggest the political enemy. Neither was the situation such that Jesus could not possibly avoid thinking of the political oppressor as He urged men to love their enemies. Neither was the situation so hopelessly poisoned with hate for the Romans as to make it imperative that He, by all means, try to remove this venom of political hatred. If such was the case, the saying itself certainly gives not the slightest indication that it was specifically or primarily the political adversary to whom He referred. The exhortation to "pray for them that persecute you" has no definite reference to political persecution, i.e., to political oppression of the Jews by the Romans.[44]

Luke's verb "despitefully use" (instead of Matthew's "persecute you"), meaning "to threaten abusively, to deal despitefully with or act despitefully toward, or to be insolent,"[45] is quite general and reflects that personal approach to problems of human relationship which is so common to the thought of Jesus.

What Jesus very probably had in mind was the "private life in the villages which Jesus knew, where life was often embittered by animosities and feuds of a personal kind— where the social life was exposed to bad temper and ill feeling, and permeated with love of scandal and the virulent, petty vendettas which often accompany narrow virtue

---

44 See Matt. 5:43 ff. The exact quotation, "Thou shalt love thy neighbor, and hate thine enemy," is not found in the Old Testament. The statement may have reflected the common attitude of the people of His day, but it did not correctly reflect the best thought either of the O.T. or of the apocryphal and the rabbinic writtings (note many illustrations in Strack and Billerbeck, p. 364 f., and in Montefiore, *Rabbinic Literature,* pp. 65, 74 f., 78 f.). Easton perhaps summarizes the situation fairly when he remarks: "Jesus would scarcely have quoted it (i.e., the citation in the antithesis) as a precept if it had not received some scribal support and some scribal support was inevitable." But Easton adds emphatically that "the later rabbis rejected resolutely any religious justification for hatred in any form" (*Christ in the Gospels,* p. 115).

45 Liddell and Scott, *Greek-English Lexicon.*

and rigid piety in local communities."[46] The "despitefully use you" "suggests the conduct of people who interfered with or thwarted the plans and wishes of others, even though they themselves gained nothing by it. The interference might take the form of abusive insults or spiteful acts or malicious injustices."[47] It is in these everyday personal relationships, where petty forms of friction, resentment, retaliation, and shunning are so common and so ruinous to relations of trust and love to God and fellow man, that Jesus urged men to emulate the Father's patience and love in order that they might prove their true kinship with Him.

To say this is not to suggest that Jesus may not in an incidental thought have included the political enemy as He uttered these words. Living, as He did, among a people where foreign domination was by many heartily resented (and that especially because the oppressor in this case was a Gentile and an idolater) it is not at all improbable that Jesus might have spoken these words with at least a side reference to the all-too-prevalent political animosities of the day.

It is not affirmed, therefore, that Jesus totally ignored the political situation of His day when He urged His hearers to love their enemies. It is affirmed, however: first, that it is very doubtful whether Jesus in any sense in this statement attempted to deal with the national political situation by urging a peaceful, nonviolent policy toward Rome;[48] second, that it is very doubtful whether Jesus had any specific intention of counteracting the incendiary propaganda of patriotic nationalists; third, that it can hardly be maintained that Jesus specifically excluded the political enemy in this exhortation. One would hardly be willing to assert that Jesus would have excused any Jewish listener from obeying

---

46 James Moffat, *Love in the New Testament*, p. 114.
47 *Ibid.*, p. 115.
48 Jesus Himself appears to have accepted Roman rule without much critical analysis. Cf. His answer to the question about the tribute money. Mark 12:17.

PASSAGES EMPHASIZING LOVE 149

this commandment if the enemy at the moment happened to be a Roman instead of a Jew, or if the cause of enmity happened to be political rather than, say, economical. Jesus apparently neither explicitly included nor explicitly excluded the political enemy in His exhortation to love one's enemies.

But in the last analysis, it is not the enemy on whom Jesus' interest centers, and so He does not particularize as to who the enemy might be. In His mind he is any person whose personal relations with or toward you are or appear unfriendly. Jesus' interest here, as in the passage on "non-resistance,"[49] centers wholly on "you" and "your" right response in the situation. "Your" right response to the enemy, whoever he may happen to be, is to love him as God loves those who are cold and hostile to His appeal and His rule.

The love demanded here is more than a mere emotional sentiment toward the offender. One's attitude toward his enemy is to be modeled after the attitude God shows toward the unthankful and the evil. That makes this love at once a most active and adventurous principle. It seeks to "do good to them that hate you, bless them that curse you, and pray for them that despitefully use you."[50] It leads a man to turn the other cheek and to do unto others as he would have them do unto him. It inspires him to varied acts and expressions of good will. He is led to pray for the wrongdoer not merely in order that he may cease his acts of hostility but in order that he may be restored to relations of friendly fellowship with God and his fellow men.

But what Jesus has in mind here is apparently something deeper and more far-reaching than a mere temporary attitude which men were to assume for the occasion when they were subject to the unfriendliness of enemies. It was apparently something more permanent, more constant. He urged the possession of a spirit so constant and so akin to the spirit of the Father in heaven that one would never "demit

---

[49] Matt. 5:38-42 and parallel in Luke.
[50] Luke 6:27 f.

under any circumstances the obligation to seek the good of men."[51] In other words, Jesus is here not merely prescribing a specific attitude for a more or less specific situation. He is pointing to an attitude that should be constantly present in all who would share in the coming kingdom, constantly leavening, directing, vitalizing all one's relations to one's "neighbor," no matter whether he be friend or foe, Jew or Gentile.

Other Sayings Presupposing This Spirit of Love

There are numerous other sayings dealing with tension situations which clearly presuppose the presence of this kind of spirit. They are difficult to explain except as the fruit of a spirit of genuine, outgoing, self-giving good will.

Sayings Emphasizing Unselfish Service

1. "I was hungry . . . thirsty . . . a stranger . . . naked . . . sick . . . in prison" and ye ministered unto me. Matthew 25:31-46.[52] In this parable "the kingdom prepared . . . from the foundation of the world" is promised to those who in giving to their fellow men in need have given themselves with a generous, active spirit of sympathy and love. Moreover, their service is declared to be as valid as if it had been offered directly to the "king." The reward of the kingdom

---

51 Manson, *Gospel of Luke*, p. 68.

52. This material is peculiar to Matthew. Bultmann points to strikingly similar sayings in Isa. 58:7; *Testaments of the Twelve Patriarchs*, Joseph 1:5 f.; Sotah 14a: "R. Hama ben Hania said: What does the Scripture mean when it says, After the Lord your God ye shall walk? Is it possible for a man to walk after the Presence (Shekinah)?—Nay, but to walk after the attributes of the Holy One (imitate His character). As He clothes the naked (Gen. 3:21), so do thou clothe the naked. He visits the sick (Gen. 18:1); do thou also visit the sick. He comforts mourners (Gen. 25:11); do thou also comfort mourners. He buries the dead (Deut. 34:6); do thou also bury the dead" (quoted in Moore, *Judaism*, Vol. II, p. 111). Joseph 1:5 f. reads: "I was sold into slavery, and the Lord of all made me free; I was taken into captivity, and His strong hand succored me. I was beset with hunger, and the Lord Himself nourished me. I was alone, and God comforted me: I was sick, and the Lord visited me: I was in prison, and my God showed favour unto me; in bonds, and He released me" (Charles, *Testaments of the Twelve Patriarchs*, p. 173).

is not promised merely on the basis of certain services, for those "on the left" assert they have not failed to minister aid whenever they saw him hungry or thirsty, etc. This detail would suggest that the primary distinction between those on the "right" and those on the "left" did not lie in whether they had or had not given aid, for apparently both had done so, but it lay rather in the spirit in which the service, whatever it was, had been performed. Those on the "right" apparently had been moved in their service by a spontaneous, self-forgetful spirit of sympathy and good will which had served to ease tensions, those within and those without.

2. "Whosoever would become great among you, shall be your minister; and whosoever would be first among you, shall be servant of all" (Mark 10:43 f.). A sufficient motive for making oneself the "servant of all" can be found only in a regard for men so deep that it overflows in acts of self-forgetfulness and good will. The mere promise of greatness certainly is not sufficient to lead a man to such self-denying service. In becoming the "servant of all" men are but emulating the example and spirit of the Master Himself, who "came not to be ministered unto, but to minister, and to give his life a ransom for many" (verse 45). This saying, therefore, is but an illustration of the generous, self-forgetful spirit which men ought constantly to bear toward their fellow men. This is Jesus' positive antidote to the tensions produced by pride and the overbearing attitude of men.

Passages Urging Self-denial for Jesus' Sake

1. "If any man would come after me, let him deny himself, and take up his cross, and follow me. For whosoever would save his life shall lose it; and whosoever shall lose his life for my sake and the gospel's shall save it" (Mark 8:34 f. Parallels in Matthew 16:24 f. and Luke 9:23 f. Cf. also Matthew 10:38 f.; Luke 14:27; 17:33).

This passage has been discussed previously.[53] We stop

---

[53] Page 142 f.

here only to reiterate that denying oneself for Jesus' sake ultimately means not merely to give up every selfish interest for the sake of one's love and loyalty to Jesus Himself, but for the sake of one's loyalty to the cause He represents, the cause for which He was willing to give up even life itself, for Jesus cannot be separated from His cause. Denying oneself for the sake of Jesus and His cause of the kingdom, therefore, means denying oneself for the sake of the highest good of fellow beings, and doing it with the same self-forgetful love with which Jesus gave Himself.[54] Self-denial for *Jesus'* sake, therefore, presupposes not only complete love and loyalty to Jesus as supreme, but wholehearted love and loyalty to one's fellow men. There is no self-denial for *Jesus' sake* that does not involve thoughtful, self-forgetful concern for the good of one's fellow man.[55]

2. "One thing thou lackest: go, sell whatsoever thou hast, and give to the poor, and thou shalt have treasure in heaven: and come, follow me" (story of the rich young ruler—Mark 10:17-31).[56]

This demand to sell whatsoever he had and give to the poor was a test not only of the completeness of this young man's loyalty to and love for Jesus and His cause, but also of his concern for the poor, for fellow men in need. The radical demand was undoubtedly intended to test the completeness of his devotion to the kingdom by confronting him with a clear-cut critical decision, God or mammon, but there is perhaps some significance in the fact that thought of "the poor" is introduced as an element in the decision. The young man is urged not merely to leave all he had, but to give it to the poor. It is almost as if Jesus were suggesting here that the reality of the young man's devotion to Him would manifest itself in a thoughtful, sacrificing concern for

---

54 The full meaning of words like these can be discovered only as we try to understand the spirit and motive that guided the life and conduct of the man who uttered them.

55 The sacrifice of hand or foot or eye (Mark 9:43-48; cf. Matt. 5:29 f.) is not apropos. It is a sacrifice undertaken for one's own sake.

56 Cf. Matt. 19:16-30 and Luke 18:18-30.

the underprivileged, and that a self-denying love for God demanded a concomitant self-denying concern for man. In any case, the young man's rejection of the demand of Jesus reflected unfavorably not only on the depth of his love for God and the kingdom, but also on the reality of his love for man.

At the close of the subsequent discourse on the dangers of riches, Jesus, drawn out by a question of the disciples, assures them that "no man . . . hath left house, or brethren, . . . or lands, for my sake, and for the gospel's sake, but he shall receive a hundredfold now in this time, houses, and brethren, . . . and lands, with persecutions; and in the world to come eternal life." This sacrifice of home and family and property *for Jesus sake*,[57] i.e., for the sake of one's unreserved faith in and loyalty to the cause he represents, presupposes the presence of a love that transcends all these other attachments, a love such as that which dwelt in Jesus. His love encompassed in its scope God, and man, for whom God's good news of the kingdom was intended. The sacrifice Jesus commended was not one undertaken from a sense of duty. It was a self-denial that flowed spontaneously from a spirit of warmhearted love for and loyalty to God which, in the mind of Jesus, was wholly inseparable from a warmhearted, active love for one's fellow man. This spirit which embraces in one great abandon of love both God and man Jesus commends in terms of highest praise and promise.

There is no indication in any of the sayings urging self-denial that Jesus definitely presupposed as motivation thoughtful, self-forgetful concern for fellow men, but we make no mistake in crediting Jesus with such a spirit and assuming that He spoke out of a life charged with a loving, self-forgetful concern for His fellow man.[58] This spirit was thoroughly a part of His life, ever-present, actuating, controlling. It formed the background and basis of His whole

---

57 Luke reads, "For the kingdom of God's sake." The ultimate meaning is not essentially different from that of Mark or Matthew.
58 Cf. I Cor. 8:11-13.

154   JESUS AND HUMAN CONFLICT

life and thought. He could not speak of loving God with all the resources of one's being without feeling His heart go out to His brother man with thoughts of love and sympathy and self-forgetful service.[59] His whole life of self-sacrificing devotion to the kingdom of God was in its very essence self-sacrificing devotion to the cause of man.

If this is so, must we not then assume that Jesus, in urging self-denial for the sake of the kingdom, presupposed in His hearers a measure of the same spirit of regard for and devotion to their fellow men? Self-denial for Jesus' sake appears to be inseparably linked with self-denial for the sake of man. What Jesus urges is not isolated acts of self-renunciation, but rather the constant possession of a spirit that thinks not first of self but first of God and His kingdom.[60]

Sayings Urging the Spirit of Forgiveness

1. The disciples are exhorted to forgive not "seven times" but "seventy times seven."[61] Luke's "seven times" in reality urges the same unlimited, undiscouraged forgiveness as is demanded in a somewhat different, and perhaps more unmistakable, way in Matthew. In Matthew the question: "Lord, how oft shall my brother sin against me, and I forgive him? until seven times?" (which apparently proposes an upper limit to a man's obligation to forgive) is opposed with a demand for unlimited forgiveness. In Luke the hearer is urged that even if a person "sin against thee seven times in the day, and seven times turn again to thee, saying, I repent; thou shalt forgive him." "Seven" in this saying is perhaps "merely a round expression for a moderately large number,"[62] but seven offenses *in a day* makes this a rather strong expression, even though the words do not necessarily

---

59 Cf. I John 4:20.
60 Cf. Matt. 6:33.
61 Matt. 18:21 f.; Luke 17:4.
62 Ed. Koenig in *Hastings' Dictionary of the Bible*, Vol. III, p. 562, "Numbers." On the following page, it is stated that "the same round character belongs to the expression . . . 'seventy times seven.'" (Cf. Gen. 4:24.)

imply that the same offense is repeated each time. Yet the very improbability of "seven" offenses being committed in one day, followed by "seven" requests for forgiveness, serves to make inescapable the conclusion that one ought always to be ready to forgive the offender.

The Lucan version with its repetition of "*if* he repent" "and *if* he . . . turn" (verses 3 and 4) appears to make one's forgiveness dependent on the offender's initiative in the matter. Actually, of course, forgiveness cannot achieve its full purpose until the offender acknowledges his wrong and desires reconciliation. That is perhaps what the Lucan version has in mind. It is doubtful, however, whether the saying means to suggest that one must wait until the offender takes the initiative, or that one needs to be forgiving only when the other is repentant. The willingness to forgive the same brother "seven" times in the course of a day in itself assumes the presence of a spirit of such generous, largehearted good will that it can forgive each offense gladly and from the heart. Any forgiveness that springs from a motive less than that is not forgiveness in the full sense in which Jesus meant it.

The Matthaean insistence on the willingness to forgive "seventy times seven" makes unavoidable the conclusion that the spirit of forgiveness, or better, the spirit of largehearted good will and sympathetic understanding, is to be an ever-present, controlling possession of the follower of Jesus. He is to be the possessor of such a constant and inexhaustible good will that he is ever ready to do his part in re-establishing relations of fellowship and trust broken by the offense of a brother.

The complete absence in Matthew[63] of any mention of repentance on the part of the offender would suggest that the spirit of forgiveness is to be present and active no matter

---

[63] Perhaps his repentance is taken for granted, but it is more likely that his part in the rebuilding of marred human relationships, as in other similar teachings, is not considered at all. The focus of attention is entirely on the person wronged and on the spirit he should manifest under the circumstances.

156   JESUS AND HUMAN CONFLICT

whether the offender is penitent or not, whether he seeks forgiveness or not.[64] The will and the desire to re-establish relations of fellowship and trust are to be present in any case even if the fulfillment of that desire is frustrated by the unresponsiveness, or perhaps the ill will, of the offender.

The term "forgive" by itself does not carry this larger meaning of forgiveness, i.e., the thought of the re-establishing of a relationship of trust and friendship between the offender and the offended. Dr. Burton declares the term "undoubtedly was taken from the legal vocabulary of the time and refers to remitting or forbearing to enforce a debt or penalty. . . . To forgive the sinner is to remit the penalty which would otherwise have been enforced."[65] But it is obvious that forgiveness in this passage looks far beyond a mere legal remitting of a debt or penalty. And Dr. Burton rightly continues:

> In the thought of Jesus, it is not the legal sense which is emphasized. In the Parable of the Prodigal Son the repentant sinner is not simply released from punishment, but positively received into fellowship and favor with his father. That this aspect of the matter is for Jesus the important, if not the only, element of forgiveness, is strongly favored by the fact that He names various moral conditions of forgiveness such as repentance, forgiveness of others, love, and faith, thus suggesting that forgiveness is essentially the assumption of an attitude of approval and favor toward one whose character was formerly disapproved but has now become such as calls for approval.[66]

In other words, the forgiveness Jesus had in mind looked for the re-establishment of conditions of true fellowship between persons whose relationship of trust and love had been marred by the wrongdoing of one or the other. And speaking to the person wronged, Jesus states that he ought to be possessed of such a spirit of forgiveness that he longs for and seeks to re-establish, perhaps on a higher plane, a

64 Cf. Jesus' prayer, "Father, forgive them; for they know not what they do" (Luke 23:34), and somewhat similar prayer by Stephen (Acts 7:60).
65 Burton, *New Testament Word Studies*, p. 5 f.
66 *Ibid.*, p. 6.

spontaneous, free, and loving fellowship with the one who has offended him.

2. The Parable of the Unforgiving Debtor[67] urges the all-importance of the spirit of forgiveness. The story draws an impressive contrast between God's free, full, and magnanimous remission of an enormous debt in response to the debtor's pleading and the hard, unrelenting attitude of the same debtor toward those who owed him insignificantly small sums. The unforgiving temper of the debtor provokes the king to wrath and causes him to recall the pardon and to reimpose the penalty. The latter detail, including the merciless collecting of the debt, plays a necessary part in the completion of the story for the hearers, but it must not be pressed too far as a picture of God's attitude toward the unforgiving. Nevertheless, it serves to make graphically clear that forgiveness is more than a mere legal transaction, a remission of a debt or a penalty, a forgetting of a wrong. It is a supralegal transaction in which the generous, understanding good will of the injured person reaches out to welcome back into a relationship of trust and of unhampered fellowship the penitent wrongdoer who desires not so much to escape the penalty of his wrongdoing as to be received back into fellowship with the one he has ill treated.

This restoration of conditions of true fellowship can be complete only when the wrongdoer has a genuine appreciation of the magnanimous, understanding spirit of good will that is willing to receive him back into fellowship and favor. The depth and sincerity of his appreciation will be measured by the quality of the spirit of good will with which he meets those who wrong him. Any subsequent ungenerous, hardhearted attitude toward others will cast doubt on the depth and sincerity of his previous protestations of repentance and of his desire to be received into relations of trust and love, with the result that the flow of fellowship is checked and the relationship of trust marred. That is why God's forgiveness flows out freely to the forgiving and is

[67] Matt. 18:23-35.

158   JESUS AND HUMAN CONFLICT

withheld from the unforgiving.[68] The withholding of forgiveness from the hardhearted is not a piece of vindictive justice. It is rather a situation that arises from the very nature of forgiveness itself; for the restoration of a spontaneous relation of trust and love between the injured party and the wrongdoer can take place only where magnanimous, understanding good will is met by a similar attitude of good will. Where hardness toward others proves a genuine spirit of good will to be lacking, there the restoration of complete trust and free fellowship lags and there forgiveness remains incomplete, for no one can shut the door of his heart against an evildoer without also to that extent closing the door against his friends, including God. Forgiving love may (and should) indeed reach out toward the wrongdoer with the hope of effecting a reconciliation, but its purpose remains unfulfilled until it meets forgiving love in the other. The continuing sense and experience of divine forgiveness, therefore, presupposes the continuous presence in man of a generous, understanding, forgiving love toward his fellow man.

3. Men are urged to pray: "Forgive us our debts, as we also have forgiven our debtors" (Matthew 6:12). Luke reads: "Forgive us our sins; for we ourselves also forgive every one that is indebted to us" (Luke 11:4).

The expression "as we forgive" is not a petition bargaining for God's forgiveness on the ground of one's own exercise of this virtue. It does not state the condition on which God is willing to grant forgiveness, but rather the condition on which men are able to receive it. If men would enjoy the continuing sense of God's forgiveness and favor, and the free flow of fellowship between God and themselves, they must themselves be possessed of the spirit of forgiveness. Divine forgiveness is theirs only as they carry with them a forgiving, self-forgetful love toward their fellow men.

---

68 This thought finds frequent expression. Cf. Matt. 18:35: "So shall also my heavenly Father do unto you, if ye forgive not every one his brother from your hearts"; Mark 11:25: "And whensoever ye stand praying, forgive, if ye have aught against any one; that your Father also who is in heaven may forgive you your trespasses"; Matt. 6:14 f.: "For if ye forgive men their tres-

The forgiveness Jesus emphasizes, therefore, clearly presupposes the presence of self-forgetful love as a motivating principle. No other motive is sufficient to induce free and full observance of the spirit of His sweeping demand. Forgiveness is love triumphing over injury, bearing no resentment, refusing to be provoked, suffering long and being kind, seeking not its own, bearing all things, hoping all things, enduring all things,[69] working no ill to its neighbor.[70] It is this spirit which was so constant and controlling in Jesus' own life and relations which He, consciously or unconsciously, assumes to be a constant and controlling principle in the lives and relations of His followers.

JESUS FORBADE WHAT WAS INCONSISTENT WITH THE PRINCIPLE OF LOVE

He Forbade the Spirit of Faultfinding

"Judge not, that ye be not judged. For with what judgment ye judge, ye shall be judged: and with what measure ye mete, it shall be measured unto you." The accompanying illustration of the "mote" and the "beam" reinforces and clarifies this saying. Matthew 7:1-5.

The word "judge" here means "to pass sentence upon, to condemn."[71] But apparently it is not criticism as such that is disallowed[72] but rather the spirit of faultfinding, the habitual severity with the mistakes, faults, and weaknesses of the other, the hasty, unjustifiable criticisms of one's fellow man which Jesus wants to discourage. He speaks of that disposition of mind which is quick to detect and to condemn defi-

---

passes, your heavenly Father will also forgive you. But if ye forgive not men their trespasses, neither will your Father forgive your trespasses." Matt. 5:23 f.
69 I Cor. 13:4-7.
70 Rom. 13:10.
71 Liddell and Scott, *Greek-English Lexicon*, p. 996. Preuschen, *Woerterbuch*, gives essentially the same meaning: "Ein Urteil faellen . . . besonders 'aburteilen,' 'kritisieren,' 'schlechtmachen,' 'verdammen' " (page 709). ("Pass sentence"—especially "condemn," "criticize," "run down," "damn.")
72 Cf. Jesus' sharp criticisms of the Pharisees and the scribes, for instance. Matt. 23 and parallels.

ciencies in others, but is uncritical and blind to the faults in its own life and relationships. He has in mind that unfeeling, unfair criticism of others which is devoid of the spirit of sympathetic understanding and of the spirit of respect and regard for the other person. This unfeeling, unloving criticism of others Jesus completely disapproves. Criticism of others is warranted only when it starts with self-criticism. In this insistence on self-criticism, Jesus seems to suggest an understanding, sympathetic approach to this problem similar in spirit to that of the so-called Golden Rule.

Why is one to refrain from judging others? The reason given is "that ye be not judged. For with what judgment ye judge, ye shall be judged. . . ."[73] Apparently a man is to refrain from judging for prudential reasons. If a person would not be judged, whether by God on the last day[74] or by his fellow men now, he had better refrain from harsh judgments of others. It is of course possible that Jesus might have used such an appeal to self-interest in His attempt to curb the spirit of censoriousness, but the motive of self-interest is hardly big enough to explain the full mind of Jesus in this instance. Jesus did not urge men to refrain from judging others simply because He would spare them unpleasant criticisms on the part of their fellows. He urged men not to pass sentence upon one another because He felt that "judging" was contrary to the will of God, likewise contrary to the kind of character God approved. God approved of men who love their neighbor as themselves, who did unto others as they would have others do unto them, who were patient, understanding, forgiving, and who lived in relations of trust and fellowship with their fellow men. Sitting in judgment on fellow men disturbed and disrupted the relationship of trust and love, the free fellowship between His

---

[73] The illustration of the mote and the beam suggests a rather close connection between a hypocritical blindness to one's own deficiencies and the habit of faultfinding, but it is not suggested as an additional reason for refraining from criticism. No causal connection between the two is suggested.

[74] So Manson, *Gospel of Luke*, p. 71.

children which God intended. His children were to be free from the spirit of faultfinding, from the hasty condemnations of their fellow men, from the spirit of vindictiveness and gloating which often accompanies the practice of "judging."

Jesus very likely urged men to refrain from judging others also because He felt that in doing so they were assuming a prerogative which belonged only to God.[75] He alone was able to pass on the demerits of men. Man's own imperfection and limited insight unfitted him for the role of judge of his fellow men.

Undoubtedly the unfriendly, unsympathetic nature of the act of judging was another reason why Jesus reacted so strongly against it. His sensitive and ever-present regard for the feelings and the welfare of His fellow man would make Him keenly aware of the injury this practice was inflicting on the person criticized. Concern for the victim is not mentioned nor suggested in the saying, for the focus of attention is not on him, but on the disastrous consequences of the practice on the person engaging in it. But such concern was not lacking in the one who uttered these words. It was a subconscious factor helping to shape His attitude toward the whole problem of "judging."

Jesus Disallowed the Taking of Human Life

Jesus put His seal of approval on the old commandment: "Do not kill"[76] (Mark 10:19; Matthew 19:18; Luke 18:20). The commandment is quoted in reply to the question of the rich young man: "What shall I do that I may inherit eternal life?"[77] No specific importance attaches to this quotation in the story (verses 17-22). The answer appears to be one of those ready replies which is made not for the purpose of giving a complete answer to the query, but for the purpose of soliciting further thought and inquiry. Such a reply usually states a truth which is so generally accepted that it

---

75 Cf. Deut. 32:35; Psalm 94:1; Rom. 12:19; Heb. 10:30.
76 Ex. 20:13.
77 Mark 10:17.

needs no argument and for that reason is unsatisfactory to the inquiring mind. That appears to be the case here. The answer of Jesus in this instance implies not only that the validity of the commandment cited was widely accepted, but that it was so accepted by Jesus. For this reason the commandment, "Do not kill," needed no special emphasis or argument. Having been reared in the belief that God had commanded men not to kill, Jesus found the murderous taking of human life simply unthinkable.[78]

This passage, of course, has reference only to the killing of one man by another. There is no evidence to indicate that Jesus generalized about this commandment and included in it such forms of manslaughter as capital punishment or war. Nowhere does He indicate specific disapproval of killing in war or in the performance of a judicial sentence. Whether He would have drawn any distinction cannot be determined. It is difficult, however, to imagine Him sanctioning any form of human slaughter.

No reason is suggested why one should not kill. Nothing is said here about the sacredness of human life or about destruction of human life being an utter denial of the principle of love, even though such destruction could not help being utterly repugnant to one who came to give His "life a ransom for many."[79] For Jesus "Do not kill" was a commandment of God, and as such it needed no further reason to secure obedience.

---

[78] There are several other instances where Jesus expresses His disapproval for the taking of human life. In Mark 7:21 f. and Matt. 15:18-20 He mentions "murder" as one of the evils which proceed out of the heart of man and defile the man. In Matt. 5:21, in the first of the antitheses of that chapter, the above commandment, "Thou shalt not kill," is quoted with approval. The words that follow penetrate beyond the literal commandment, but in no sense do they attempt to invalidate it. In fact, so completely does Jesus appear to accept it and so seriously does He regard its transgression that when He wants to indict the inner disposition from which the crime springs, He makes the hateful disposition equally culpable with the commission of the crime itself.

[79] Mark 10:45 and parallels.

Jesus Forbade Anger and Scorn

Jesus went beyond the commandment, "Do not kill"; He forbade the anger and scorn that lay back of it and prompted it.[80]

"But I say unto you, that every one who is angry with his brother shall be in danger of the judgment; and whosoever shall say to his brother, Raca, shall be in danger of the council; and whosoever shall say, Thou fool, shall be in danger of the hell of fire" (Matthew 5:22).

Being angry with one's brother was, in Jesus' mind, apparently as serious as the act of killing, for the same degree of guilt is applied to both.[81] The statement is unqualified,[82] just as many of Jesus' other sayings are.[83] Evidently, however, not every form of anger is excluded, for we read how Jesus "looked . . . on them with anger, being grieved at the hardening of their heart."[84] Evidently there was a place for righteous indignation in the thought of Jesus. The anger He condemned apparently was anger of a personal kind that had its root in personal animosities, resentment, prejudice, or ill will.

---

80 Matt. 5:21-26. Verses 25, 26 ("agree with thine adversary") have a parallel in Luke 12:58 f. in a somewhat different setting. In their setting in Matthew, they appear to be nothing more than an earnest admonition to be conciliatory toward the adversary lest he involve one in troublesome litigation. But the point of emphasis here as in the Lucan setting is on the urgent need of getting rid of the feeling of ill will at once and on the need for the immediate re-establishment of relations of friendship and good will.

81 The rabbis also denounced anger in strongest terms: "By the angry man even the shekina itself is not esteemed" (Nedarim 22b). "All the divisions of hell rule over the angry man" (Nedarim 22z). "The angry man loses his learning" (Pesachim 66b). (Quoted in Montefiore, *Rabbinic Literature*, p. 38.)

82 There is variation here in ancient New Testament manuscripts. The addition, "without cause" (see King James Version), is found in some important ancient manuscripts, but omitted in the oldest and most dependable Greek manuscripts. Many New Testament scholars therefore are inclined to believe the addition "without cause" was not part of the original saying of Jesus.

83 For example, Matt. 5:38 ff.; Luke 16:18 (on divorce), etc.

84 Mark 3:5. Cf. also the incident of the cleansing of the temple. Mark 11:15-19 and parallels.

It does not appear necessary to go into a detailed discussion of the following two clauses of verse 22, for instance, as to the exact difference between calling a man "Raca" and calling him "Thou fool," or as to the exact meaning of the punishments promised or the reason for the difference made. There is some obscurity as to the real meaning of "Raca" and of "Thou fool." Torrey translates the former as "worthless fool" and the latter as "outcast," "persistent rebel (against God)," "apostate."[85] There is, however, no uncertainty about the essential meaning of these sayings. They forbid in the strongest terms possible attitudes and expressions of contempt, scorn, and derision. Such acts make men subject not only to the punitive justice of the courts of men (the Sanhedrin) but also to the judgment of God. (The "judgment" of verse 22 certainly is not the local court, and the "hell of fire" has undoubted reference to the judgment of God.) That is to say, such acts are disapproved by God as much as by men, and more.

The words are directed not at the victim of anger, but at the wrongdoer. His attention is directed to the immeasurable harm he is doing to himself. So serious are the consequences of this spirit of anger and contempt that a man is to interrupt even so sacred and important a transaction as the offering of a gift at the altar in order to effect a reconciliation with his brother.[86] A man had better settle the difficulty at once and out of "court," for if he allows it to come to "court," the decision will unquestionably go against him.

No attempt is made to point out the inconsistency of the spirit of anger and scorn with the principle of love. No reference is made to the harm acts of anger and contempt may inflict on the victim psychologically, or to the fundamental disrespect for personality that they involve. These concepts may have been present in the mind of Jesus, but

---

[85] Torrey, *The Four Gospels,* p. 10; notes p. 290 f.

[86] The interruption of the sacrifice may be a suggestion that the offering was futile while the strained relations remained between the two. The saying would then serve to reinforce the teaching urging the necessity of the forgiving spirit if one would receive the forgiveness of God.

they are not brought to the surface. They are instinctively felt, sensed, rather than consciously reasoned. Jesus' insistence on an immediate restoration of relations of fellowship was not based on rational insight arrived at by a process of deduction from the principle of love, but on a prophetic insight into the kind of life God willed.

Numerous practical difficulties that might arise from a literal application of this principle[87] Jesus characteristically leaves unanswered. He was not interested in detailed legislation. He declared the will of God as it was revealed to Him and left the detailed application to the good judgment of men who were bent on doing God's will above everything else. But, in any case, the spirit of anger and scorn is completely ruled out.

Jesus speaks of being angry with one's "brother." In rabbinical literature, "brother" commonly referred to a brother Jew and did not include the non-Jew.[88] Whether Jesus thought of brother-Jew in this narrower sense or simply of brother-man it is impossible to say. It is probable that the mental picture which flashed into His mind as He uttered these words was that of a brother Jew, but the picture need not have carried any narrow, exclusive meaning. It seems much more probable that His mental picture reflected not nearly so much the Jew as the fellow man.

---

87 For instance, suppose the anger and scorn were induced by malicious acts of another. Would not a conciliatory attitude merely serve to strengthen the evil disposition in him?

88 So Strack and Billerbeck, Vol. I, p. 276. Sifre on Deut. 15:2 (17b) speaking of *neighbor* adds: "Ausgeschlossen sind die 'andern' (Nichtisraeliten)" ("Others," i.e., non-Israelites, are excluded), and speaking of *brother* adds: "Ausgeschlossen ist der Ger-Torschab . . ." (Excluded is the Gentile neighbor). Montefiore concedes this. *Rabbinical Literature*, p. 66, Dt. Rabba 6 (203c) quotes R. Jochanan (A.D. 297) as saying: "Wenn du deine Zunge daren gewoehnst deinen Bruder, der nicht ein Sohn deines Volkes ist (d.h. den Proselyten) zu bereden, so wirst du schlieszlich auf den Sohn deines Volkes (d.h. den Israeliten) Verderben bringen." (If you habituate your tongue to persuade your brother who is not a descendant of your race, i.e., a proselyte, you will finally bring ruin upon the descendant of your race, i.e., the Israelite.)

Jesus Forbade Attempted Killing of Another

"But a certain one of them that stood by drew his sword, and smote the servant of the high priest, and struck off his ear" (Mark 14:47).

"Then saith Jesus unto him, Put up again thy sword into its place: for all they that take the sword shall perish with the sword" (Matthew 26:52).

"But Jesus answered and said, Suffer ye . . . thus far. And he touched his ear, and healed him" (Luke 22:51).

According to Luke, the disciples generally ask whether they shall smite with the sword and then one of them takes the offensive without apparently waiting for an answer. The blow in this case is struck before the seizure of Jesus. In Mark and Matthew, the blow is struck after the seizure when resistance was already futile. The Greek word used here, "one certain one," would suggest that only one of Jesus' followers resorted to this act of resistance. John 18:10 states specifically that it was Simon Peter who struck the blow. It also identifies the wounded man as Malchus, a servant of the high priest.

That there should be such an attempt to defend Jesus on the part of the disciples, especially in view of the two swords among them, does not seem unexpected. It does, however, appear strange that Mark does not record any protest on the part of Jesus because some protest Jesus would certainly have made, if for no other reason than at least for the sake of the safety of His disciples.

Matthew and Luke record Jesus' reply somewhat differently. In Matthew Jesus' words, "Put up again thy sword into its place . . . ,"[89] are clear enough. They register unmistakable disapproval of the use of the sword on this occasion. Practically the same words are used in John 18:10 to check Peter's impulsive attack on Malchus.

The meaning of Jesus' reply as recorded in the Greek in Luke: "Suffer ye thus far," is obscure. Are the words addressed to the disciples? If so, they may mean, as Plum-

[89] Matt. 26:52 f.

PASSAGES EMPHASIZING LOVE

mer suggests: "Suffer my assailants to proceed these lengths against me."[90] Or are they addressed to those who have come to arrest Him? If so, they may mean: "Tolerate thus much violence on the part of my disciples."[91] Goodspeed renders this passage as follows: "Let me do this much,"[92] i.e., let me touch the wounded man. Moffatt gives the same interpretation. Preuschen, however, offers a translation that appears more plausible than any of those mentioned above. He thinks the expression was used here in an absolute sense, and he translates it as: *Lasst ab! Nicht Weiter!*[93] ("Hold! No more of this!") The Revised Standard Version reads: "No more of this!" The expression then becomes a rebuke of the violent resistance.

Luke offers no reason why the attacker is to desist from further use of the sword. The healing of the servant's ear, however, would suggest by implication that Jesus desired no bloodshed. Matthew, on the contrary, suggests two reasons why the sword should be put up: "All they that take the sword shall perish with the sword," and resistance was contrary to the will of God. It would tend to prevent the fulfillment of the Scriptures. If He (Jesus) had desired to offer resistance to arrest, He could have asked the Father and He would have sent Him "more than twelve legions of angels."

In the Gospel according to John, a somewhat similar reason is given: "The cup which the Father hath given me, shall I not drink it" (18:11)? This saying is reminiscent of Jesus' Gethsemane prayer as recorded in Mark 14:36 and parallels.

The thought of this saying in Matthew was not an unfamiliar one. It is expressed in Genesis 9:6: "Whoso sheddeth man's blood, by man shall his blood be shed." It is repeated again in essentially the same words as found in Matthew in Revelation 13:10. Jesus apparently used this thought of Old

---

90 Plummer, *Gospel According to St. Luke*, I.C.C., p. 512.
91 *Ibid.*
92 *The Bible, An American Translation.*
93 Preuschen, *Lexicon*, p. 330. The Herman Menge Bible concurs: "Lasst ab! Bis hierher und nicht weiter!" (Hold! Thus far; no farther!)

Testament Scripture on this occasion to drive home the solemn warning that violence begets violence.

The question now arises: Just how much meaning did Jesus put into these words? How much did He include? The answer is difficult and for that reason caution is necessary lest one read too much into the statement. However, it would seem that the following assertions can with some confidence be made:

Jesus did not here philosophize about war, or try to answer the question of the legitimacy of the use of the sword by the state in meting out punitive justice. Jesus was not here declaring Himself on a war situation. He was speaking to the particular situation that confronted Him and His disciples.

The saying offers no counsel on the ethics of the use of the sword in the protection of an innocent third party, or in behalf of a great cause. That thought was probably outside the range of His interest on this immediate occasion.

The words were called forth by a certain critical situation that threatened the personal safety of His disciples and that endangered in fact the possible success of His whole cause. These words were uttered with the intention of meeting that immediate critical situation. Whether it was concern for the personal safety of the disciples, and perhaps indirectly for the fate of His cause which depended for its continuance on the ability of the disciples to carry on, that caused Jesus to forbid the further use of the sword cannot be firmly established. These factors may easily have entered in. But it is more probable that His words were called forth by the conviction that the realization of God's purpose somehow required His suffering and rejection—a conviction which had gradually taken possession of Him and which had finally crystallized into an unshakable certainty in the Gethsemane struggle.[94]

Having discovered that His suffering formed an indis-

---

94 Cf. Jesus' prayer in Gethsemane. Such a prayer implies a certain puzzlement. Mark 14:35 f. and parallels in Matthew and Luke.

J. Lawrence
   Burkholder
I should like
to meet you
at the platform
at the close of
this morning
session.
   Paul Erb

90)190(
   2

Congregation:
1.
2.
3.
4.
5.
6.
7.

3,600,000

pensable part of the Father's plan of redemption,[95] He freely accepted this way of suffering and rejection with the wholehearted surrender and obedience that were characteristic of His whole life. He would work today and tomorrow[96] and be rejected when, in the wisdom of God, the critical hour had struck. To resist arrest now that the fateful hour had come, or to allow a blow to be struck in His behalf or in behalf of His cause, was to be disobedient to the recognized will of God and to frustrate His purpose. It was this conviction that caused Him to decline all efforts at resistance and led Him to go the way of the cross willingly and nonresistingly.

However, it can hardly be maintained that personal considerations played no part in His quick repression of the demonstrations of violence on this occasion. On the contrary, it is quite probable that His concern for both His friends and His enemies, lest there be bloodshed, furnished the immediate impetus to His protest against the use of violence. In view of the dangerous situation created by the rash act of one of the disciples, it appears almost inevitable that He would have added a word of warning to them to guard against a resort to weapons of violence. "They that take the sword shall perish with the sword." Their safety as His followers, therefore, lay not in an attempt to meet violence with violence, but rather in patient endurance and in submission to the will of God. By implication it also pointed out that the kingdom could never be established by resort to compulsion.

Nevertheless this utterance of Jesus reveals a wideness of reflection that goes far beyond the demands of the immediate situation. It reveals a mature judgment that can only be explained as the product of keen observation and sustained meditation on the methods and futility of the whole method of force. Here He states as His ripe judgment that

[95] Cf. Mark 8:31 f.; 9:30-32; 10:32, 34, 45 and parallels. Also Luke 9:22; 17:25.
[96] Luke 13:32.

violence only begets more violence. It does not settle but rather aggravates a difficulty.

While it is true that Jesus in this instance does not go out of His way to deliver a pronouncement on war and the military method, His statement nevertheless constitutes such an indictment because it comes out of a background of mature judgment and reflection.

Jesus Disallowed Reprisals. Luke 9:51-56

In this story the disciples, James and John, indignant that the Samaritan villagers would not receive their Master, exclaim: "Lord, wilt thou that we bid fire to come down from heaven, and consume them?"[97] But he turned, and rebuked them."[98]

This passage needs little explanation. It is a story in which Jesus, confronted with a concrete situation, firmly rebukes the spirit of retaliation. He had on other occasions urged His disciples to live above the level of vindictiveness, to love their enemies, and to be forgiving toward those wronging them. Their uncharitable, vengeful temper in this instance, therefore, brings forth a new reproof of this spirit.

Jesus Warned Against Covetousness

Jesus insistently warned men against covetousness, that fertile breeder of all kinds of discord, resentment, and revenge; inciter of exploitation, ruthlessness, violence, murder, and war; instigator of a spirit of selfishness utterly contrary to the self-giving love which Jesus exemplified and which He persistently commended to others as the answer to the problem of human conflict.

Jesus in His warning against covetousness appealed to men from different angles. On some occasions He cautioned against an excessive devotion to the pursuit of material wealth, "treasures upon the earth,"[99] because where their

---

[97] Some manuscripts add: "Even as Elijah did?"
[98] Some manuscripts add: "And said, Ye know not what manner of spirit ye are."
[99] Matt. 6:19-24. Cf. Luke 12:33 f. Note also the Parable of the Rich Farmer. Luke 12: 16-21.

PASSAGES EMPHASIZING LOVE

treasure was their heart would be also. He saw clearly how the desire for gain tended to become the dominant motive of life. He saw how "mammon" was constantly usurping the place of God, crowding out interest in the kingdom and in unselfish concerns for man. Men were depending on wealth to save them and sought it first instead of seeking first the rule of God and the righteousness valid before Him.[100] Their worship of mammon was futile and the God whose power and love could save they neglected.

On other occasions He emphasized the harmful effects of covetousness on the spiritual life of men. "What doth it profit a man, to gain the whole world, and forfeit his life?"[101] In the Parable of the Rich Fool[102] the rich man is told that his preoccupation with the accumulation of wealth and his greed for gain have destroyed his own best self. "But God said unto him, Thou foolish one, this night is thy soul required of thee; and the things which thou hast prepared, whose shall they be?"[103] Covetousness in these passages is disallowed, not specifically because of its social mischief and harm, but because of its disastrous results on the higher spiritual relations of men to God.

However, the verses just preceding this parable (13-15) also picture some of the social consequences of covetousness.

"And one out of the multitude said unto him, Teacher, bid my brother divide the inheritance with me. But he said unto him, Man, who made me a judge or a divider over you? And he said unto them, Take heed, and keep yourselves from all covetousness: for a man's life consisteth not in the abundance of the things which he possesseth."

This parable does not state whether the questioner made a just claim or not. But in either case covetousness, whether that of the questioner, of the brother, or of both, was the basic cause of the difficulty between the brothers, stirring up the strife and the hard feelings and destroying the cordial

---
100 Matt. 6:33.
101 Mark 8:36 f. and parallels.
102 Luke 12:16-21.
103 Luke 12:20.

brotherly relations of trust and love that should exist between them.

The situation pictured is not an uncommon one. Two brothers disagree about the disposition of the inheritance. One of them, sure in his own mind of the justice of his claim, brings the matter to Jesus with the request that He use His influence and authority to force his brother to divide the inheritance, presumably on the basis of his own judgment in the matter. Obviously there was some injustice involved in the situation, although we are not sure where to place the blame; but Jesus refused to intervene. With a touch of indignation He turns the questioner back: "Man, who made me a judge or a divider over you?"

The somewhat brusque answer of Jesus may designate either strong disapproval or a determined desire to remain aloof. But neither appears a satisfactory explanation. Even a refusal to arbitrate appears unsatisfactory. The situation demands a statement that will be broadly corrective of that which is basically wrong in the relationship. This we find in Jesus' warning to keep free from all covetousness. But even Jesus' refusal to arbitrate the case in itself constitutes a rebuke of the unbrotherly spirit of covetousness. Mere settling of the external inequities in the situation would not solve the fundamental problem, and Jesus firmly refused to gratify the greed and the vengefulness of either or of both of the brothers.

An additional problem arises out of Jesus' example in the situation. Did Jesus intend to teach the disciples by example how they were to deal with such cases of social injustice? Jesus in this instance was confronted with a plain and simple case of social injustice. Did He intend to suggest by His example that His followers should not concern themselves with the righting of social wrong?

Just to what extent Jesus, on this occasion, was conscious of the influence of His example on the conduct of His followers cannot be determined. The account does not reveal Him as having been overly self-conscious in the situation.

PASSAGES EMPHASIZING LOVE

It seems very doubtful whether He would have been willing to have His disciples make such sweeping deductions from His example that they would refuse every appeal to help in the solving of social wrongs.[104] We can be quite certain He would have insisted that the solution of the problem did not lie in the adjusting of the external inequities but rather in the removal of the wrong disposition from which social conflict sprang. He would have insisted that the root of the trouble lay in the inner disposition and that this wrong attitude must be displaced by a spirit that was in harmony with the will and character of God before the difficulty could be said to have been solved. For this reason, Jesus refused to settle the strife between the brothers and instead rebuked the disposition that caused the unbrotherly conduct and the bitterness and strife.

It is obvious, however, from Jesus' frequent reference to wealth, His criticism of the rich, and His strong sympathy for the poor that He was keenly aware of and greatly disturbed by the suffering and the deep social cleavages produced by covetousness. Some of His sayings and parables were doubtless motivated by the desire to produce such a change of heart in the rich and privileged that they would do something about the social injustices and the suffering caused by their greed.

Note His reference to those who "devour widows' houses"[105] or to the rich man who feasted sumptuously every day but whose selfish, covetous, and complacent spirit kept him from offering the underprivileged at his very gate a self-respecting job and living. All he gave were the crumbs of niggardly charity. The problem of social injustice apparently never bothered him, neither did the healing of the breach between poor and rich. This issue at least never became clear to him until in the life beyond he realized how deeply God was concerned about the active functioning of brother-

---

104 Cf. Jesus' breaking up of the temple trade which in its more unworthy aspects was both a religious and a social abuse. Mark 11:15-19 and parallels.

105 Mark 12:40. Cf. also Matt. 23:23.

ly relations of love and sharing between man and man. Now he discovered how, by his own covetous spirit and unbrotherly action, he had worked himself gulfs apart from God. He suddenly became anxiously concerned that his brothers repeat not his tragic mistake of perpetuating or adding to the world's trouble and strife by continuing in their covetous ways.

While it is of course clear that Jesus on this specific occasion did not stop to reason in the exact manner suggested above, it is nevertheless plain that Jesus' purpose, in this and similar teachings referring to relationships between rich and poor, includes more than a mere exhortation to be charitable to the needy. He desires the establishment of such relations of good will, brotherly love, and conciliation as will prevent the occasion for social and economic injustice with resultant resentment, strife, violence, and even war. This larger and deeper purpose He portrays in His message of the kingdom in which He challenges men to let the spirit and power of God transform and rule in their lives and relationships.

JESUS CALLED FOR CONCILIATION IN DISPUTES

The passage in which Jesus urges the interruption of the sacrifice at the altar[106] in order to effect a reconciliation between a man and his brother has already been discussed.[107] The person who suddenly discovers that his brother has something against him is to go at once and seek out that person and attempt a reconciliation.

Conciliation is also demanded in Matthew 18:15-17. This teaching suggests an approved method of re-establishing amity.[108] One is to approach the wrongdoer, first, privately and confidentially and discuss the question at issue. An understanding, sympathetic approach is presupposed, hav-

106 Matt. 5:23 f.
107 Cf. pp. 197-200.
108 Strack and Billerbeck, *op. cit.*, offer numerous illustrations of rabbinic teaching on this subject. The rabbis repeatedly urge the need for reproof and reconciliation, but they also point out the extreme difficulty of administering it properly. Vol. I, pp. 787-90.

PASSAGES EMPHASIZING LOVE

ing as its primary purpose the restoring of fellowship. If the wrongdoer responds to this approach with penitence, the reconciliation is regarded as complete. "Thou hast gained thy brother." But if he shows himself impenitent and unwilling to admit his share of guilt, one is to make a second visit, taking one or two persons as witnesses to the attempted reconciliation and to his impenitence. Presumably these witnesses are also to assist in the endeavors, though that fact is not stated. If this second attempt fails to move the wrongdoer to penitence, the matter is to be presented to the Christian fellowship, the church. This is the final appeal. Presumably the church also is to use its full power of appeal in an attempt to bring about the penitence of the wrongdoer and the reconciliation of the estranged brethren. If this final appeal fails, "let him be unto thee as the Gentile and the publican."[109] The impenitent brother is henceforth to be regarded as no true member of the church. Is his company to be shunned as unwholesome? Very probably Jesus meant to suggest nothing more than that one temporarily cease efforts at reconciliation lest repeated attempts, before the brother was ready, aggravate the difficulty rather than alleviate it.

It is hardly warranted to assume that he is to be treated with contempt. Jesus would hardly suggest that one could ever treat a Gentile or a publican with cold indifference, hard unbrotherliness, or scornful disdain. He who had insisted that men forgive seventy times seven, love their neighbor as themselves, and love even their enemies, would still insist that they treat the impenitent brother with concern, hoping and praying and fully believing that an unwearied, active good will like that of the Father would ultimately prevail to restore him to a better state of mind and a re-established fellowship.

The significant thing, however, in this whole suggested procedure is its sensitive regard for the feeling of the wrongdoer and the extent to which one is to go in the attempt to

[109] Matt. 18:17.

win him back to a relationship of trust and love. The efforts at reconcilement are here presented in the form of a definite scheme, but the scheme involves considerable effort in behalf of reconciliation before one is justified in giving up further attempts.

JESUS' OWN EXAMPLE OFFERS REINFORCEMENT

He Disregarded the Barriers of Racial and National Prejudice

Jesus' healing of the daughter of the Canaanitish woman[110] and of the servant of the Roman centurion[111] ultimately helped to break down racial and national prejudices, those fertile breeders of discord and strife. It is doubtful, however, whether in these instances Jesus had the specific intention of breaking down such prejudices. In fact, both stories take pains to point out that there were special reasons —an unusual faith or special excellence[112]—why Jesus should have honored the appeal of these "strangers." In the Synoptic Gospels the healing of non-Jews is always treated as noteworthy even though exceptional. Nevertheless, the fact that Jesus, in response to the cry of distress and faith, did overstep the bounds of racial and national prejudice, had as its ultimate, if not its immediate, effect the breaking down of those barriers. It showed that Jesus thought in terms of human beings and human need rather than in terms of race and nation.

He Treated Outcast Groups with Respect and Regard

Jesus disregarded the principle of "tit for tat" in His treatment of outcast groups, "publicans" and "sinners." The "publicans" were engaged in the very unpopular and un-

110 Mark 7:24-30 and parallel in Matthew.
111 Matt. 8:5-10; Luke 7:1-9.
112 In the Lucan story of the healing of the ten lepers, there is no mention of unusual merit as the basis for the healing of the Samaritan leper. But he is praised for the sincerity and depth of his appreciation. The repeated praise of Samaritans in Luke appears to emphasize Jesus' appreciation of "strangers."

PASSAGES EMPHASIZING LOVE

patriotic business of collecting taxes for a foreign occupying power, Rome. The public generally retaliated against them by treating them with scorn and contempt.

There is some uncertainty as to the identity of those who in our Gospels are referred to as "sinners," but undoubtedly the term had reference to people who failed in living up to the many religious obligations of the day. Very probably they belonged to the peasant and more ignorant class of people, sometimes identified as the "people of the land" (the *am ha aretz*). The attitude of the more learned and pious groups to these defections was contempt and scorn. They shunned them as they did the publicans.

Jesus, on the contrary, ate with them,[113] befriended them,[114] and believed in them.[115] He invited one of them, Levi, to follow Him as a member of the inner circle of His friends.[116] He pictured them as being more willing than the Pharisees to give heed to God's call to repentance.[117]

The response of these outcast groups to His sympathetic understanding, His faith in them, and His generous, outgoing good will was a corresponding trust in and love for Him. They crowded around Him[118] and they surrendered themselves to Him and to His leadership.[119]

Nowhere do we find more clearly pictured Jesus' genuine, self-forgetful interest in these groups, and His regard for them, than in the story of the anointing in the house of the Pharisee.[120] Here His attitude is seen against the background of that of His host. The Pharisee would have had nothing to do with the woman; he would not even have

---

113 Mark 2:15 f. and parallels.
114 Cf. the accusations of His enemies (Matt. 11:19; Luke 7:34), and the visit with Zacchaeus (Luke 19:2-10).
115 Publicans and harlots would enter the kingdom sooner than the priests and elders. Matt. 21:31.
116 Mark 2:14 and parallels.
117 Luke 18:9-14 (the Pharisee and the publican).
118 Luke 15:1; Mark 2:15; Matt. 11:19.
119 Instances: Zacchaeus (Luke 19:2-10), the woman who was a "sinner" (Luke 7:36-50).
120 Luke 7:36-50.

178   JESUS AND HUMAN CONFLICT

allowed her to touch him because she was a "sinner."[121] Jesus, on the contrary, allowed her to shower the full wealth of her penitence and gratitude on Him. He met her approach with a rare, understanding sympathy that was free from all distrust and suspicion, ready to believe in her sincerity, and glad to welcome her into relations of free, full fellowship. With sensitive regard He avoids giving her any occasion for embarrassment. And in the end He restores her to the full confidence and friendship of God's children by assuring her that her sins are forgiven.[122]

It is difficult to imagine Zacchaeus or the woman who was a "sinner" or these groups generally being won by the method of condemnation. The appeal of sympathetic understanding and friendly good will won them to a life of surrender.

His Triumphal Entry into Jerusalem Was a Peaceful Gesture[123]

Without going into a discussion of various problems connected with this narrative, we may point out the following pertinent facts as significant for our study.

This procession was a Messianic demonstration which was either deliberately planned by Jesus or else permitted by Him. Certainty in regard to the matter is impossible. One can easily discover reasons why Jesus might have wanted to stage some such dramatic appeal as this in the nation's capital.

Such a procession was not without political danger. It might easily have aroused false hopes in the minds of excitable revolutionary groups and caused riots and bloodshed.[124] Jesus could not have been unaware of this danger, which would have been particularly acute during great festival seasons like the Passover.[125]

---

121 Luke 7:39.
122 Luke 7:48.
123 Mark 11:1-11 and parallels.
124 The rioting in which Barabbas was apprehended was but a recent instance demonstrating how easily riots got started.
125 His ministry in Galilee would have taught Him something about

The triumphal procession was entirely free from military symbols or revolutionary gestures. The crowd, instead of carrying weapons of violence, "spread their garments in the way; and others cut branches from the trees, and spread them in the way."[126] Instead of riding on a prancing steed, the animal commonly used in military campaigns and processions, Jesus rode on the lowly donkey, the beast of peaceful labor.[127] The shouts of the multitude were not cries of war and aggression, but of peace and blessing.[128] And the procession ended in a manner wholly peaceful and undemonstrative: "And he entered into Jerusalem, into the temple; and when he had looked round about upon all things, it being now eventide, he went out unto Bethany with the twelve."[129]

That this Messianic procession was staged in such a wholly nonmilitary manner and that the demonstration ran its course without even a trace of political excitement, without even arousing the suspicion of the Roman authorities,[130] can hardly be regarded as entirely without significance. It meant by implication, if not by intention, that Jesus had definitely rejected a military Messiahship. He was to be a Prince of peace and His kingdom was to be a kingdom not of might and war and coercion, but of peace and good will. The kingdom God came to establish would not come by human intervention or military aggression. To go beyond this and see in the peaceful demonstration, and specifically

the excitability of Galilean crowds. John 6:15 claims that the crowd on one occasion wanted to "take him by force, to make him king." Note the ease with which men like Simon and Athronges, Messianic pretenders, came to be honored as "kings." Josephus, "Antiquities" XVIII, 10:6, 7.

126 Matt. 21:8.
127 One can make too much of Jesus' choice of a donkey instead of a horse, but the point cannot be wholly denied.
128 Mark 11:9 f.
129 Mark 11:11.
130 It can be argued, of course, that this element was suppressed by the evangelists, but that explanation does not account for all the facts. Why should Luke, for instance, suppress the charge that he had stirred up political excitement when he does not hesitate to include the accusation that he forbade giving tribute to Caesar, which was plainly an attempt to brand Jesus as a political agitator? Luke 23:2.

in the selection of the peaceful donkey instead of the horse of military processions, an intended protest against the method of war or against the use of military force is scarcely warranted.

Jesus Went to the Cross Nonresistant

Jesus made no attempt to resist arrest[131] and He would not allow others to strike a blow in His behalf.[132] He would not even pray for divine intervention.[133] This decision not to offer any resistance to the authorities seeking His arrest and destruction was not due to an acceptance of and loyalty to an abstract principle of nonresistance. It had a more fundamental basis. It was based on the conviction that God's purpose to save man and to establish the kingdom in some way required His suffering and death. Having arrived at this conviction, He walked with steadfast and unwavering courage the path it prescribed for Him. He maintained a nonresistant attitude through all the ill-treatment of the trial and even to the very end. He made no attempt to defend Himself against the false charges of His accusers,[134] or the physical abuse of the bystanders;[135] or against the mocking of the soldiers[136] or of Herod.[137] He did not answer either the high priest[138] or Pilate,[139] except where the question was a direct inquiry about the truth of His claim to Messiahship. Then He answered with an unequivocal: "I am"[140] or "Thou sayest."[141] The silence of Jesus was not the silence of proud disdain or of stoic calm. It was the silence of a regal spirit which, having discovered and having accepted the divine will with complete surrender, remained serene and confident in the assurance that God's great purpose to bring in the kingdom was even now being fulfilled. It was the silence of one whose life and ministry had been an open book[142]

[131] Mark 14:43-52.
[132] Matt. 26:53.
[133] Matt. 26:52.
[134] Mark 14:60 f.; cf. also Luke 23:9 f.
[135] Mark 14:65.
[136] Mark 15:16-20.
[137] Luke 23:11.
[138] Mark 14:60 ff.
[139] Mark 15:2, 5.
[140] Mark 14:62.
[141] Mark 15:2.
[142] Mark 14:49.

known to all. If the charges against Him were false, His life and ministry were the only answer. His accusers would well know, and Pilate could easily see whether or not the charges against Him were false. In this sense it may be said that Jesus' silence was an implied rebuke of His accusers, and also of His questioners for listening to false charges.

However, it is also quite possible that Jesus' conduct during His arrest and trial may have been influenced by the ideal of the Suffering Servant.[143] With the cross looming up as a certainty before Him and with the conviction that it was so willed in the divine purpose, the picture of the Suffering Servant of Jahweh would almost inevitably flash into His mind. And now in the hour of His affliction, He found Himself guided by that vision of Isaiah: "He was oppressed, yet when he was afflicted he opened not his mouth; as a lamb that is led to the slaughter, and as a sheep that before its shearers is dumb, so he opened not his mouth.[144]

Whatever may have been the specific and immediate reasons for Jesus' refusal to offer resistance to the arrest or defense against His accusers, the ultimate reason for His going the way of the cross lay in the conviction that God's great and loving purpose to bring in the kingdom for the salvation of men in some way required it. And it is significant that Jesus conceived of God as saving men not by coercion and aggression, but by self-giving, suffering love.

Jesus Accepted the Cross from Choice

The Gospels consistently picture Jesus as having accepted the cross not from necessity but from choice. It was not an unavoidable fate that overtook Him or that He was forced to accept. It was a way which He deliberately chose to walk because He recognized it as the will and way of God. This is evident in such a passage as Mark 8:31-33.[145] Jesus had just heard Peter's great confession and now He followed it

[143] Isa. 52:13—53:12.
[144] Isa. 53:7.
[145] Cf. also Matt. 16:21-28.

up with the explanation that the kind of Messiahship to which He was called involved suffering and death. Peter at once began to rebuke Him impetuously: "Be it far from thee, Lord: this shall never be unto thee."[146] The vehemence of Jesus' reply, "Get thee behind me, Satan: . . . for thou mindest not the things of God, but the things of men," would imply that Peter's suggestion had been a real temptation to Him. It had suggested less painful and less tragic ways of trying to achieve God's redemptive purpose. The temptation in Peter's rebuke may not have been greatly dissimilar to the temptation in the wilderness[147] when Jesus had faced various alternative ways of fulfilling His divine mission. But He resolutely rejected Peter's suggestion and chose instead the way of suffering as God's way of achieving His purpose.

The Gethsemane prayer, "Remove this cup from me; howbeit not what I will, but what thou wilt,"[148] also implies that Jesus weighed other alternatives before finally accepting the way of the cross. The Father's will, however, was determinative for Him and He deliberately chose to walk that way. Though the way of escape remained open to Him almost to the moment of arrest, He resolutely refused to take advantage of it. When finally His captors were approaching, He not only calmly and nonresistantly waited for them, but He apparently went out to meet them: "Arise, let us be going: behold, he that betrayeth me is at hand."[149] He willingly gave His life for the sake of furthering God's gracious purpose to save men.

This willingness to give Himself for the good of men was no new intrusion into the life and thought of Jesus. It had been at the heart of His whole ministry. Through the intimacy and reality of His experience of God He had come to share God's spirit of self-giving love so that He could say that He had come not to be ministered unto but to minister

[146] Matt. 16:22.
[147] Matt. 4:1-11.
[148] Mark 14:36 and parallels.
[149] Mark 14:42; Matt. 26:46.

and to give His life a ransom for many.[150] Walking the way of the cross, therefore, meant for Jesus simply walking to the very end the road on which He had been traveling, the road of complete surrender to the will of God and of utter devotion to the good of man. The cross was self-giving love facing triumphantly and bringing to nought the power of sin and the violence of man. It was making unmistakably and graphically clear for all the world to see God's saving answer to the violence and wickedness of man. The cross was the *way* of salvation and the *power* unto salvation, "the *wisdom of God*" (I Corinthians 1:24) upon man's predicament.

Jesus Forgave His Enemies

Luke reports Jesus praying for His enemies on the cross: "Father, forgive them; for they know not what they do."[151] This prayer is in complete harmony with the spirit of His own teaching: "Bless them that curse you, pray for them that despitefully use you."[152] Such magnanimity in the hour of death, as this prayer reveals, does not appear at all surprising in a life like His. It appears rather as the full ripe fruit of the life He had commended and lived. But even without the evidence of this prayer it is clearly manifest from the Gospel record that Jesus went to the cross without bitterness or resentment. He remained consistent to the last.

JESUS' CONCEPTION OF GOD AS FATHER THE ULTIMATE BASIS FOR HIS TEACHING ON LOVE AND NONRESISTANCE

God is the center of all of Jesus' life and thought. To reveal God, His will and way, was His primary concern. From Him He derived the whole of His ethic. The heavenly Father was the pattern and standard by which all human attitudes, conduct, and relationships were and are to be measured.[153] The teaching on "nonresistance" and love is no detached saying of Jesus; neither is it merely a virtue nor a

---

150 Mark 10:45.
151 Luke 23:34. This prayer is peculiar to Luke.
152 Luke 6:28.
153 Cf. Matt. 5:43-48; Luke 6:32-36.

rule of ethics which one may take or leave. It has its roots in the very character of God and is an inseparable part of the character He desires in man. It therefore also derives its meaning and validity from the character and will of God.

Jesus' conception of God, however, was based not on a process of reasoning, but rather on experience. And Jesus' experience of God had revealed Him supremely as a good and loving Father.[154] But God's goodness and love was never merely an abstract value. It was always an active, creative goodness forever reaching out toward men in acts of unmerited favor. Jesus' God was a Father who cared. He clothed the grass of the field and "shall he not much more clothe you?"[155] He fed the birds of the heaven and "are not ye of much more value than they?"[156] He cared for the lowly sparrow and "ye are of more value than many sparrows."[157] "The very hairs of your head are all numbered."[158] Man was of more value to God than even the Sabbath, one of the most sacred of human institutions, for "The sabbath was made for man, and not man for the sabbath."[159] And if men, "being evil," cared enough to give good gifts to their children, how much more would the Father in heaven give good things to them that asked Him.[160]

A love like that was something more than an abstract, general benevolence toward mankind. It was more than love for men in the mass. The God of Jesus loved and cared for each individual. He was like the shepherd who, though having a hundred sheep, yet failed not to notice when one of them went astray. Having discovered the loss he hurried out into the night and rested not until he recovered it.[161]

---

154 No attempt will be made to discuss the full meaning of Jesus' conception of God as Father. We are concerned here only with those aspects of His thought which throw light on the problem of one's relation to the evildoer.
155 Matt. 6:30; cf. Luke 12:28.
156 Matt. 6:26; cf. Luke 12:24.
157 Matt. 10:29 ff.; cf. Luke 12:6 f.
158 Matt. 10:30; cf. Luke 12:7.
159 Mark 2:27.
160 Matt. 7:11; cf. Luke 11:13.
161 Luke 15:3-6; cf. John 10:3, 14, where Jesus compares Himself to the

PASSAGES EMPHASIZING LOVE

And when he had found it he rejoiced over it "more than over the ninety and nine which . . . [had] not gone astray."[162] Luke reports this saying somewhat differently: "There shall be joy in heaven over one sinner that repenteth, more than over ninety and nine righteous persons, who need no repentance."[163] "Even so," Matthew continues, "it is not the will of your Father . . . that one of these little ones should perish."[164] So valuable was each individual in the sight of God that it were better a man be "thrown into the sea . . . than that he should cause one of these little ones to stumble."[165] Inversely, the least service of love to one's fellow man was honored by God as service to Himself.[166] So simple a service as a cup of cold water given "unto one of these little ones" would "in no wise" fail of a reward.[167] "Whosoever shall receive one of such little children in my name, receiveth me: and whosoever receiveth me, receiveth not me, but him that sent me."[168]

The God of Jesus bestowed His gifts on His children not grudgingly and sparingly, but freely and generously. Repeatedly Jesus drove this thought home. "Ask, and it shall be given you . . . for every one that asketh receiveth."[169] "If ye then, being evil, know how to give good gifts . . . how much more shall your Father . . . give good things to them that ask him?"[170] God did not have to be importuned with pertinacious, wearisome petitions in order to prevail on Him to be merciful and gracious. His blessings did not have to be earned through the offering of a multitude of sacrifices or through the storing up of a large credit of good deeds. His blessings could be had for the asking, "for it is your Father's good pleasure to give you the kingdom."[171]

---

good shepherd who knows "his own sheep by name" (verse 3). "I know mine own," He says, "and mine own know me" (verse 14).

162 Matt. 18:13.
163 Luke 15:7; cf. also verse 10.
164 Matt. 18:14.
165 Luke 17:2; cf. Mark 9:43; Matt. 18:6.
166 Matt. 25:31-46.
167 Matt. 10:42; cf. Mark 9:41.
168 Mark 9:37.
169 Matt. 7:7f.
170 Matt. 7:11.
171 Luke 12:32.

These blessings were bestowed no less freely or generously on enemies. God's fatherly love and care were not conditioned by the response He received. God made "his sun to rise on the evil and the good"[172] and He was "kind toward the unthankful and evil."[173] His fatherly love and care were extended freely and equally to the undeserving and the deserving. His beneficence was not conditioned or called forth by the desert of men but rather by their human need and by the goodness and generosity of His own spirit.[174]

Obviously such an attitude of fatherly concern for the enemy as well as the friend demanded a boundless spirit of forgiveness. Jesus pictured God as wistfully longing to forgive and to welcome back the penitent sinner into a relationship of trust and love. He was not like the "elder brother"[175] who closed the door against the return of his wastrel brother, but He was like the "father" whose waiting compassion discovered the penitent son "while he was yet afar off," and he "ran, and fell on his neck, and kissed him."[176] To the son's penitent cry, "Father, I have sinned . . . ," he replied with the command to the servants: "Bring forth quickly the best robe . . . a ring . . . shoes . . . the fatted calf . . . and let us eat, and make merry: for this my son was dead, and is alive again; he was lost, and is found" (verse 23 f.). With never a word of reproof the father welcomed back the wayward son, not on a lower plane of trust and fellowship, as servant, but on the full plane of restored sonship. There was nothing but glad, joyous welcome for the penitent son, for there was "more joy in heaven over one sinner who . . . [repented] than over ninety-nine righteous persons who . . . [needed] no repentance."[177]

Jesus pictured God as responding at once to the simplest cry for forgiveness. The publican, who could point to no

[172] Matt. 5:45.
[173] Luke 6:35.
[174] Cf. Parable of the Vineyard and the Husbandmen. Matt. 20:1-16.
[175] Parable of the Prodigal Son. Luke 15:11-32.
[176] Luke 15:20. The Greek word means to "kiss fervently" (Abbott-Smith, *Lexicon*).
[177] Luke 15:7.

PASSAGES EMPHASIZING LOVE 187

record of good deeds like the Pharisee and who could find no words in which to clothe his petition except to cry, "God be merciful to me a sinner,"[178] yet "went . . . to his house justified rather than the other."[179] Jesus assured men that the simple petition, "Forgive us our debts,"[180] would be granted by the Father, provided the sincerity of the petition was evidenced by the presence of a spirit of forgiveness toward others—that is to say, provided the simple and indispensable conditions for the experience of divine forgiveness had been met.[181]

How boundless Jesus viewed God's forgiveness to be is seen in the fact that He exhorted Peter not to forgive seven times, but to forgive "seventy times seven."[182] Jesus would hardly have urged Peter to a standard of compassion to which He felt God Himself did not measure up. He urged Peter to such unlimited forgiveness because God's forgiveness was utterly without limit.

God's fatherly love and care, in Jesus' mind, were not restricted to the Jews. Jesus believed that God would heed the cry of the Roman centurion who appealed for help for his servant,[183] and the cry of the Syrophenician woman who was pleading for her daughter,[184] and of the Samaritan leper who cried to Jesus out of his own distress,[185] and so He did not hesitate to speak the word that was to bring help and healing. God's compassion and help were not conditioned by race or nationality. He helped men because they were His children and needed His help whether they be like the "elder brother" or the "lost son."[186] And when God's fatherly ministry was extended to Jews, Jesus never indicated or even implied that help was granted because they belonged to the "chosen" race. The help was granted on the basis of their human need and their readiness to receive the help available. Weinel, after a detailed survey of Jesus' teaching

178 Luke 18:10-14.
179 *Ibid.*
180 Matt. 6:12, 14; cf. Luke 11:4.
181 See above pp. 187-93.
182 Matt. 18:22.
183 Matt. 8:5-13.
184 Mark 7:24-30.
185 Luke 17:11-19.
186 Luke 15:11-32.

about God as Father, draws this conclusion: "From all this it is quite clear that Jesus did really think of God as the Father of *all men*, i.e., really the Father of the Jews with whom He is speaking; but He didn't think in this of their Jewishness but of their human need and their human responsibility."[187]

God's purpose in all this fatherly activity in behalf of men was to give them the kingdom.[188] He wanted to save them from their sin and from themselves and help them to surrender to the will of God and become sharers in the blessings of the kingdom.[189] He forgave men their sins and showered them with blessings in order that He might win them to sonship and to membership in the kingdom.

This inexhaustible, outgoing, forgiving, saving love of the Father, Jesus held up before men as their standard of conduct one to another. They were to be merciful even as the Father was merciful,[190] i.e., they were to be magnanimous, loving, forgiving, forbearing as God was magnanimous, loving, forgiving, forbearing. They were to be sons of their Father who was in heaven,[191] i.e., they were to be morally akin to Him. And Jesus pointed out that they would establish their true kinship to the Father most fully by their imitation of Him in His boundless love for His children, including His enemies.

Specifically all this meant:

1. The love men were to possess was not to be a vague, abstract *allgemeine Menschenliebe* (a general love of mankind), but it was to be an active, creative good will that was forever reaching out toward men in acts of generous, understanding helpfulness.

2. Men were to share God's boundless love for each man individually. They were to regard human life and person-

---

187 H. Weinel, *Biblische Theologie des Neuen Testaments*, p. 126. "Es ist aus alledem ganz deutlich, dass Jesus wirklich Gott als den Vater *aller Menschen* gedacht hat, d.h. eigentlich als den Vater der *Juden*, mit denen er spricht: aber er hat dabei nicht ihr Judentum im Auge, sondern ihre menschliche Beduerftigkeit und ihre menschliche Pflicht."

188 Luke 12:32.   190 Luke 6:36.
189 Mark 1:15.   191 Matt. 5:45.

ality the most precious thing in the world. No person was to be treated as without value or even as inferior in value. If any man went astray, they were to do all they could to find him and to restore him to the fellowship of the children of God. And they were not to count the cost involved. Even the most sacred institutions and the most time-honored customs were to be made to serve the good of men. Their welfare was to be a primary consideration in the solution of every problem. Men were to think so highly of their fellow men, even the least among them, that they would avoid putting any temptation or hindrance in their way. They would never treat any person with disrespect or disdain, not even a child.[192] On the contrary, they would, as far as they were able, take advantage of every opportunity to minister to the needs of their fellow men. With such a high regard for the value of human life and personality there was obviously no place for a willful, hasty, or careless destruction of human life. It was wholly unthinkable.

3. Men were to give themselves to their fellow men, even their enemies, freely, generously, and spontaneously and not grudgingly or as a matter of duty. Their love was to be quick to discover and quick to respond to the appeal of human need.

4. Men were to share God's inexhaustible spirit of forgiveness. It was to be a constant possession, independent of the response of the wrongdoer and always ready and eager to assert itself in the effort to restore marred relationships of trust and love.

5. This unselfish, self-giving love was to transcend all barriers of race or nation. There was to be no person anywhere whose welfare could be a matter of unconcern, or who could be treated with contempt or used as a mere tool. All men were of infinite worth in the sight of God and they were to be treated with such respect and regard as became those whom God regarded as His children.

6. The cross, God's supreme revelation of Himself and

---

[192] Cf. Matt. 18:10, "Despise not one of these little ones. . . ."

His way of salvation in Christ Jesus, also describes the way, the spirit, and the power by which men can, by the grace of God, work redemptively in any conflict situation. That is the way God in His infinite wisdom found necessary to use if He would save men from their wickedness and violence and make them to become sons of God, brothers one of another, men of peace and good will.

"God so loved . . . that he gave his only begotten Son. . . ."[193] That describes both the character of God and also His way of redemption. Love was His answer to sin and the violence of man. That is still His answer. This love He commends to men as also their answer to the same problem. They are to love one another as God loves them[194] or as Christ loved them.[195] That demands a spirit and a life of self-giving and self-sacrifice even unto death. That is the way to share in God's saving purpose.

If men would work redemptively in conflict situations in a world full of friction and violence, they must yield themselves in the spirit of Christ and His cross to become channels for God's saving love and power. Only thus do they truly follow in His trail.[196] The cross, not the sword, is God's way of redemption, and that is also the way for man.

193 John 3:16.
194 Matt. 5:43-48; cf. Luke 6:35, 36.
195 John 13:34.
196 Mark 8:34; Luke 14:27; cf. also Matt. 10:38; 16:24.

7

Summary and Conclusion

In this study it has been necessary to examine a large variety of Scripture passages, particularly from the Gospels, for whatever light they might throw on Jesus' answer to the problem of human conflict. Now it is imperative that we gather together and state in brief the conclusions reached in the preceding chapters in order to present, if possible, a complete picture of the whole of Jesus' teaching on the subject of our study. With this purpose in mind we present for your consideration the following propositions:

THE "NONRESISTANCE" PASSAGE

Matthew 5:38–42; Luke 6:29, 30

1. Its primary purpose is religious rather than ethical. That is to say, Jesus' primary purpose is *right relations* to God resulting in right attitudes to fellow men rather than in *correct conduct* toward fellow men. For this reason He seeks to make known the will of God in order to win men to a wholehearted allegiance to that will. He describes the kind of character which God approves, the kind of spirit that prevails in the kingdom. This passage therefore does not aim to give a carefully balanced and well-rounded code of conduct which takes account of every eventuality and of all the best interests of every individual concerned or of society as such; neither does it seek to set up an ethical system which men generally ought to adopt as their standard of conduct in conflict situations. He does not even intend this to be a code for His own followers.

The concrete situations cited are chosen, not for the purpose of prescribing precise modes of behavior for specific kinds of provocation, but rather for the purpose of making graphic and real the spirit that should possess would-be members of the kingdom. Jesus wanted to teach men how to conform their lives to the will of God, not to prescribe methods of reducing friction or of solving particular difficulties. The individual remedies proposed in this saying must, therefore, be understood not as precepts of ethics but as descriptions of the spirit of true religion. The injunctions to resist not, but turn the other cheek, go the second mile, etc., were probably meant more or less literally, i.e., they were meant to be more than mere figures of speech, but they were not intended as mandatory legislation to be followed invariably, indiscriminately, and slavishly. They were illustrations of a godlike spirit and a godlike approach to the given situations.

2. Its advice is personal rather than political. Though the illustrations are taken from real life, the focus of attention is not centered on the life situations, but on the person wronged and on his personal response to the situation. These life situations are chosen not because they represent acute and pressing problems of the day which need specific attention, but because they have illustrative value. Not one of the instances cited has an unmistakable military or political reference, not even the one on impressment. The latter instance apparently refers quite generally to any kind of impressment, and, hence, may include political and military coercion, but the figure as such does not carry an unmistakable and necessary reference to political or military compulsion. It is possible that the crowds on hearing these words may have thought first of all of impressment into service by their foreign overlords, but the saying itself gives no evidence that it had reference to any particular kind of aggressor or was intended to ease a tense political situation.

The historical evidence available does not show the political situation in Jesus's time to have been so acute, the national feeling so bitter, or the revolutionary spirit so tense, aggressive, and widespread that the facing of national-political issues by Jesus was imperative and unavoidable. On the contrary, the evidence, and the lack of it, points to the fact that the period A.D. 6-44, i.e., the period that would exercise the most direct influence on the thought and teaching of Jesus, was a time of comparative peace and progress. After the strong measures undertaken against Judas the Gaulonite and his followers in their attempted revolt of A.D. 6, there appear to have been no major political disturbances of sufficient strength to embroil the nation and upset the general tranquillity. The feeling of resentment against Roman domination and the spirit of revolt was strong and tense, but apparently not as a self-conscious organized movement so widespread and menacing as to make violence and insurrection a constant threat.

3. It completely repudiates the law of revenge and forbids all use of violence and all efforts at retaliation. It goes further in that it forbids the spirit of retaliation as well. Not a mere passive submission to injury is demanded, but a resourceful, creative way of meeting the wrong. However, the saying as such does not specifically intend to give a general condemnation of the method of force or of the use of the sword or of the bearing of arms generally. That is outside the range of this saying. It deals entirely with the personal reaction to the kind of annoyances, insults, spoliation, and acts of revenge to which people commonly are exposed. All such offenses against personality are to be met wholly without efforts at resistance or retaliation and with a spirit wholly free from the feeling of resentment and revenge.

4. The saying demands not merely the absence of a wrong attitude, but also the presence of a positive, creative spirit. It enjoins more than the stoic endurance of wrong, more even than the practice of nonviolence and non-co-operation. It demands more of the injured person than that he suffer wrong rather than do wrong; more also than that he maintain his inner purity and keep himself free from all taint of hatred and all traces of resentment and ill will. It demands of him a spirit so superior to the feeling of resentment and

revenge—demands also reserves of such inner strength and poise that he can meet provocations like those pictured in ways as resourceful and creative as turning the other cheek, going the second mile, etc.

5. The passage suggests no reason why the person wronged is to act in the way indicated. It does not suggest that its purpose is to convert the wrongdoer to a better state of mind and restore him to relations of trust and fellowship. The point of concern apparently is exclusively on the person wronged and on his right attitude in the situation. And his attention is focused not on the other but on himself. Presumably he is to turn the other cheek to the smiter because that expresses the will of God for him in the situation. But mere obedience to the will of God in so radical a demand does not present a satisfactory answer to the question why a man is to act in the way suggested.

6. A satisfactory explanation of the radical course of action suggested in the saying demands as a contributory motive a genuine concern for the evildoer because:

Jesus was never satisfied with a mere literal and mechanical obedience to the expressed will of God.

The one who had proclaimed God as more concerned over those who were sick than over those who were well, more concerned over one sheep that went astray than over ninety-nine which had not strayed away, could not possibly proclaim as God's will a course that showed no interest whatever in the person who had committed the wrong.

It is impossible to isolate one person in a difficulty that involves two and prescribe for him an ethically right attitude or course without including, at least in the background of one's mind, a thought for the welfare of the other.

No one could possibly follow the radical demands of this teaching, i.e., turn the other cheek, go the second mile, etc., without thinking of its possible effect on the wrongdoer and on the solution of the disturbed relation between the offender and his victim.

Obedience to the demand of God, in the mind of Jesus,

SUMMARY AND CONCLUSION 195

always meant obeying it in a manner and with a spirit that was in accord with God's own spirit and character. Obedience to the divine demand to turn the other cheek, therefore, assumed that one would do it with a spirit akin to that which controls God in His relations to the evildoer. God sends sunshine and rain and fruitful seasons on the ungrateful and the evil (He turns the other cheek, as it were) from motives no less than love, love reaching out toward the offender with the hope that his undeserved patience and beneficence may convert the evildoer to a better state of heart and mind. It would seem that true obedience to this demand of God would require the presence of a similar spirit in the performance of the demand.

The best Jewish thought of the day in its attempt to solve similar cases of provocation expressed a genuine concern for the welfare of the evildoer and urged conduct, the purpose of which was the conversion of the wrongdoer and his restoration to normal relations of trust and fellowship. It does not seem probable that Jesus would fall below this contemporary standard of thought and conduct.

Jesus, when confronted with situations similar to those pictured here, shows a thoughtful and generous concern for the evildoer. He prays for His enemies; He restores the ear of one of His captors; He refuses to take vengeance on the inhospitable Samaritan villagers.

7. It seems, finally, that this passage builds on certain presuppositions not expressed but taken for granted, presuppositions necessary for a satisfactory explanation of the radical demand it makes. The facing of particularly distasteful forms of coercion and insult, not only without retaliation and without a trace of resentment but also with positive resourcefulness, assumes the unbroken presence of a spirit of good will and understanding that cannot be caught off guard. It assumes the presence of a spirit that makes a man love his neighbor as himself, makes him love even his enemies, so that he seeks to do unto his enemy sympathetically and understandingly what he would have the other do unto him.

It assumes the possession of such a spirit of forgiveness that a man can instantly overlook the injury and face the critical situation with selfpossession and resourcefulness, eagerly searching for ways that may open the door to restored relations of trust and friendly fellowship. It presupposes a spirit that is not indifferent to the other's wrong attitude, but instead would gladly lose itself in the effort to change and transform the other's ill will into good will.

It is inconceivable that Jesus, who had emphasized so insistently love and forgiveness equal to that manifested by the Father in heaven, a spirit apparently never absent from His own life, would now in critical situations like those pictured in Matthew 5:38-42 suggest a course in which this attitude was either absent or quiescent and in which only selfish considerations, and the maintenance of one's own inner purity and integrity, were in control. One is, therefore, driven to conclude that Jesus assumed the presence of a godlike spirit of love and forgiveness in the person wronged which would impel him to resourceful and creative ways of meeting various provocations.

TEACHINGS SUPPLEMENTING THE PASSAGE

1. Jesus allowed no bargaining with evil in the interest of expediency or practicability. Men were to give their complete and wholehearted obedience to the recognized will of God. They were not at liberty to amend the will of God in ways that appeared less difficult and less hazardous.

2. Jesus deliberately chose a nonmilitary, noncoercive, and nonpolitical form of Messiahship. He believed that God would achieve His gracious purposes for men not by coercion, but by suffering, forgiving, self-giving love. His choice was not determined primarily by a reaction against the method of militarism and coercion, but by a recognition of the true character and will of God. His rejection of a political Messiahship was in effect, therefore, an expression of His lack of confidence in the power of force and violence and revolution to achieve ultimate social good. God's great

purposes for men could not be accomplished in that way. There was no salvation, either personal or social, except through the power and spirit of God.

3. Jesus consistently praised nonviolent and conciliatory attitudes. He lauded in highest terms the patient and gentle, the self-controlled and pure-minded, the peaceful, understanding, and considerate, and those who could bear malignity and persecution without resentment and in complete loyalty to the cause of Christ. By embodying these conciliatory and friendly attitudes men would show themselves spiritually children of God.

4. He insistently urged men to be self-renouncing and yielding in their relations to one another. But Jesus did not advocate self-renunciation for its own sake, but a self-denial rooted in sincere love and obedience to God and complete devotion to the good of men.

5. Jesus summoned men to a love that transcended all the urgencies and barriers of life, unconditioned by the response, merit, race, or nationality of the other. He demanded a love that valued a man for his own sake and for the sake of his value in the sight of God and that always stood ready to respond to the appeal of human need whether of friend or foe. He urged a spirit that would lead men to place themselves sympathetically and understandingly in the position of the other and give gladly and self-forgetfully the service and help they would desire for themselves. He challenged men to a love whose source, power, and pattern was the inexhaustible, self-giving, redemptive love of the Father, for He was forever reaching out in forgiving, self-forgetful love toward the offender in order to save him and win him back to relations of trust and fellowship with Himself. This love Jesus urged men to emulate and possess.

6. Jesus criticized the hard, unrelenting, unforgiving attitude toward one's fellow man. It was inconsistent with the spirit of God and effectively shut one off from a fellowship of love and forgiveness with God.

7. He forbade attitudes inconsistent with the principle of

love which often cause or perpetuate friction and wrongdoing. He therefore repudiated the spirit of faultfinding and of unloving, unsympathetic criticism, the hasty and prejudiced judging of others. Men are to judge the wrongdoing of others with the consideration with which they would wish others to judge them.

8. Jesus sanctioned the old law prohibiting the murderous taking of human life, but He went beyond it and forbade attempted killing as well. He cautioned against resort to the sword and the method of violence as merely engendering more violence and perpetuating and aggravating a difficulty rather than solving it.

9. He even forbade the anger and scorn that lay back of murder and violence.

10. He urged avoidance of unnecessary clashes with unfriendly people and the removal of the causes of friction and strife.

Jesus withdrew from scenes of anticipated trouble and He urged His disciples on occasion to do likewise. Men were not to flee from fear of a possible enemy, but they were not to seek martyrdom either. When opposition came, they were to meet it with equanimity, steadfastness, patient endurance, and good will.

He warned His followers against the spirit of covetousness, partly because it so frequently stood in the way of a man's highest good, his complete surrender to the rule of God, but partly also because it was such a frequent and fertile cause of bitterness and strife and unbrotherly conduct.

Jesus, by His own example, helped to break down another fertile source of discord and strife, namely, racial and national prejudices. Much ill-treatment and ill will has its source in racial and national feeling, but Jesus personally demonstrated that God honored the request of people of other races and nations and had regard for their human need even as He did for members of the "chosen" race. Disrespectful treatment of those whom God thus honored and

SUMMARY AND CONCLUSION 199

loved consequently became difficult, fellowship of love and respect became easier, and causes for friction and strife became correspondingly fewer.

11. Jesus dealt with outcast groups not on the basis of the principle of retaliation, but on a plane of respect, trust, and love; hence, instead of estranging them further, He succeeded in winning their friendship and allegiance.

12. Jesus went to the cross nonresistant, without bitterness, and with a prayer of solicitude and forgiveness for His enemies.

13. Jesus' conception of God as a Father, who cared for each individual with a boundless love, who met men with an inexhaustible spirit of forgiveness, and who gave Himself freely and without measure to both friend and foe, furnished the broad standard by which men were to gauge their conduct toward the evildoer. God's high estimate of the worth of each individual made disrespectful treatment of and harmful conduct toward the wrongdoer unthinkable and it made respectful and regardful treatment of him not only obligatory but easy.

TEACHING QUALIFYING THE PASSAGE

1. Jesus nowhere condemns Roman domination or Herodian rule. Our Gospel records do not report that He ever protested against their use of the sword, their rule by force,[1] or their standards of justice. The silence of the Gospels in this regard does not necessarily indicate that Jesus never expressed Himself on these issues. It is possible that the Gospel writers, composing the record of Jesus' life and teaching in a time when the early church increasingly had to defend itself against the accusation that this new religion

---

[1] Unless Mark 10:42 f. ("Ye know that they which are accounted to rule over the Gentiles lord it over them; and their great ones exercise authority over them. But it is not so among you: but whosoever would become great among you, shall be your minister") is meant to be an indirect criticism of the method of and rule by force. But even then the criticism is implied and general rather than direct and specific, and it is ethical rather than political disapproval.

was an "illicit religion"[2] and was "[turning] the world upside down"[3] (i.e., it was a religion that was politically dangerous), might have felt led not to embody in the written records such protests of Jesus (if there were such) because they could be too easily misunderstood or misinterpreted by those who were looking for an occasion. It appears, however, more probable that Jesus actually did not express Himself pointedly on policies and practices of government. He was not a social and political reformer and He did not think of government in these terms. Correcting wrong policies and practices at best was dealing only with the surface of things. The cure for mistaken and sinful measures of government did not lie in changing the outward form or manner of government but in changing the character of persons in government and no less of the people being governed. Such disapproval of prevailing governments as we find therefore is not political, but ethical and moral. Jesus disapproved of Herod's character, but said nothing about his rule.

2. Jesus points out that men owe certain obligations to the government whose rule they accept, but He does not urge unquestioning obedience to its every command. The duties men owe to their government are decidedly secondary and

---

[2] The Roman government was generally very tolerant of legally recognized religions of which Judaism was one. In the early days of Christianity, the Christian movement was apparently accepted by the government as simply another Jewish sect like the Pharisees and Sadducees. In time the differentiation between the Christian movement and Judaism became more and more apparent and serious tensions between the two arose (clearly reflected in Paul's letter to the Galatians), resulting in active and increasing Jewish opposition to the activity of the Christian Church. Vigorously and even vehemently the Jews disavowed the new movement as a Jewish sect (Paul and others, though for different reasons, had likewise emphasized this point). The Christian faith, being disowned by the Jews, became an "illicit religion." This together with charges that it advocated "customs which it is not lawful for us Romans to accept or practice" (Acts 16:21) caused the Roman government to watch with suspicion this new movement, for any dangerous political activities. The Christian community was therefore on the defensive and Christian writers had to be careful about statements that could easily be distorted.

[3] Acts 17:6. See similar charges implied or expressed in Acts 16:20 f.; 18:12-16; 19:35-40.

must be subject to the duties they owe to God. Obviously this emphasis on the primacy of a man's obligations to God limits his duties to his government to those acts which do not conflict with the recognized will and purpose of God. The question of the extent and nature of one's obligations to government is, therefore, not to be decided on the basis of prejudices of religious-national feeling, but on the basis of the larger loyalty owed to God and to the higher interests of one's fellow men.

3. The thought of Jesus permits a real place for the use of remonstrance and rebuke, provided it is free from all personal hatred and all desire to embarrass, provided it is called forth by a high sense of social responsibility, and provided further that its real purpose is not to condemn and coerce but to help and to save. On these conditions evidently even public rebuke has a place. Jesus' example, therefore, appears to give a relative justification to righteous indignation and to the use of moral force in dealing with the wrongdoer.

4. Jesus' advice for times of war and persecution, as He forewarns His followers, is steadfast loyalty to Him, with inner preparation for and patient endurance of the suffering that may come.

5. Jesus demands self-sacrifice, even to the point of death, in behalf of values more important than life. This sacrifice is not one paid on some field of battle but one offered freely on some Calvary. It is a sacrifice in which the aim is not to punish or to kill the wrongdoer, but rather to save him, if possible, from himself and from his wrongdoing. The values for which one is to be willing to give his life are those which conform with the ideal of the kingdom, God's supreme gift to men and man's highest good. The nature of the sacrifice must necessarily be in harmony with that ideal. In the final analysis, however, it is not so much self-sacrifice Jesus requires as such a complete devotion to the highest good of man, the kingdom, that all selfish interests and even life itself will be gladly sacrificed for its promotion and possession.

6. God uses force in punishing the recalcitrant, but Jesus, while bidding men to imitate God in His gentler dealings with men, never urges them to emulate Him in His severe dealings with them. Evidently Jesus thought punishment was a prerogative of God not shared by men.

7. Jesus' example seems to give a relative justification to the use of physical force, provided it is motivated by, in control of, and in harmony with a holy purpose whose vital principle is redemptive love, and provided it is free from the spirit of revenge and ill will.

8. Jesus apparently tests the rightness of any course of action in any specific case, first and foremost, by its accord with the will and character of God, and second, by its fruits in human life and relationships. That necessarily and inevitably involves consideration of the effect of the contemplated action on the other person or persons concerned. Since the final course of action adopted must necessarily vary in detail with varying circumstances, no fixed, unchanging procedure could be prescribed even though the basic attitude and approach should remain the same. The course adopted must validate itself by its accord with the will and character of God and by its effect on those concerned.

THE PLACE OF THE PRINCIPLE OF NONRESISTANCE IN THE TEACHING OF JESUS

1. The principle of nonresistance as seen in the perspective of the Gospel record is obviously not a fixed rule intended for literal legalistic application, allowing no variation, and specifically forbidding all use of force. It is rather a principle whose purpose is to point out a godlike spirit that can meet all kinds of provocation and aggression, not only without resentment and without resort to violence and retaliation, but also with a constructive, triumphant resourcefulness. It is a spirit that cannot be restricted to certain stereotyped methods of response. It will assert itself in ways most adapted to the situation, but its ultimate pur-

SUMMARY AND CONCLUSION

pose invariably is redemptive, the restoration of relations of trust, love, and fellowship. Such a spirit might find a place for the use of force, but it would inevitably find compulsion generally, and war and the military method invariably, inconsistent with its purpose and a negation and defeat of its aim.

2. That this principle is no mere principle of negation is obvious also. It is not so much nonresistance and nonretaliation that is urged as positive, outgoing, resourceful good will.

3. That the principle of nonresistance is not a separate and independent doctrine in the teaching of Jesus is likewise apparent. It is not the center and key to His ethic.[4] It is derived from and is the fruit of the principle of love, which in turn has its source in and acquires its meaning from the character and spirit of God as seen in Jesus.

4. The character of this teaching was not determined ultimately by the shortness of time until the present world order should come to a close and be replaced by the kingdom, but it was determined by the character and will of God. The advice He gave was indeed intended for conditions as they existed in Jesus' day; but it was the character of God and fundamental human need that determined the nature of the advice, not the shortness of the "interim" before the coming of the kingdom.

5. The principle of nonresistance derives its validity and meaning not so much from isolated sayings and incidents in the teaching of Jesus as from the whole tenor of His life and thought. His emphasis on love, forgiveness, conciliation, losing oneself for others, greatness through service, respect for personality, imitation of the Father, etc., is not only utterly opposed to the use of violence, coercion, the taking of human life, war, retaliation, resentment, anger, and ill will, but it is wholly on the side of a respectful, understanding, nonviolent, loving, reconciling, redemptive treatment of the evildoer. The primary passage in Matthew

---

[4] Cf. Count Leo Tolstoi, *My Religion*, pp. 10, 16.

and in Luke merely serves to bring to a sharp focus an emphasis that is inherent in the whole of Jesus' life and thought.

6. The principle of nonresistance is inherent in the very character and way and will of God. God is love, and He deals with men on that basis whether good or evil. With unwearied good will, utterly free from resentment, impatience, ill will, vindictiveness, and a desire to coerce or overawe, He seeks the vile, willful, and rebellious in order to win them to true sonship and restore them to relationships of trust, love, and fellowship. This attitude and method of the Father is the ultimate pattern for human life and conduct and the final standard by which to gauge human relationships.

7. The principle of nonresistance is also inherent in the cross. The cross is not merely going the second mile, but going clear to the end of the road, and giving *all*, even self, in order to redeem the evildoer. The cross is not only God's supreme redemptive act in history; it is also a picture of the self-giving, outgoing love with which God from all eternity has sought to fulfill His redemptive purpose to reconcile men to their heavenly Father and to their earthly brother. This way of the cross, Jesus urges, is also inevitable for His followers if they would work redemptively in human life and relationships, and in conflict situations.

8. "Nonresistance," in the sense in which Jesus meant it, is God's way (revealed in Christ Jesus and in the cross) of meeting the wrongdoer not merely with nonviolence and nonretaliation, passively, but with love so deep, strong, and ever-present (and resourceful because deep, strong, and ever-present) that it "never ends"[5] and never can be interrupted or defeated by acts of hostility. Instead, it actively, ceaselessly, and creatively seeks the good of the evildoer, hoping to change his ill will to good will and thus restore him to relations of full fellowship.

9. The principle of nonresistance, therefore, does not rest primarily on certain "proof texts"[6] which one might as-

[5] I Cor. 13:8.
[6] There are many if one desires to use this method.

semble and build up into an argument that one person might accept, another reject, and a third refute with other proof texts. Instead, it is so inseparably bound up with the character and will of God as revealed in Christ Jesus and supremely in His way of the cross that no one can well deny its claim without repudiating to that extent his faith in God and His way for man. Once a person has unreservedly and uncompromisingly accepted the God of Jesus, he is also inwardly driven to acknowledge His way and will as valid in relations of human conflict.

10. This principle is not merely an idea which a person may call into play when war or military training is imminent. It is an inherent and inescapable part of the everyday character and attitude of the person in whom the rule of God has become a living, working reality.

11. Finally "nonresistance" is not a principle of negation, passivity, acquiescence, and non-co-operation. Its negative and positive aspects are perhaps best expressed in Romans 12:17-21:

"Render to no man evil for evil. Take thought for things honorable in the sight of all men. If it be possible, as much as in you lieth, be at peace with all men. Avenge not yourselves, beloved, but give place unto the wrath of God: for it is written, Vengeance belongeth unto me; I will recompense, saith the Lord. But if thine enemy hunger, feed him; if he thirst, give him to drink: for in so doing thou shalt heap coals of fire upon his head. Be not overcome of evil, but overcome evil with good."

This passage disallows the spirit of retaliation, rendering "evil for evil," and instead urges that it be replaced by an attitude "noble in the sight of all." It exhorts people to make every effort to live "peaceably with all men." Vengeance is never permissible. That is a right which only God in His infinite wisdom, holiness, and love can be trusted to exercise with perfect justice. Meting out just deserts on evildoers must be left to God. There are truly positive, redemptive, and effective measures the kingdom citizen can and should use, namely, acts of unwearied, generous, and thoughtful concern. That will ultimately prevail to produce a burning sense of shame and repentance in the wrongdoer and will lead to reconciliation and restored relations of friendship and fellowship. The way to overcome evil is not to fight it with a greater evil, but to melt the ill will by a good will that has its source in God and wins by enlisting inner consent in the wrongdoer, by allowing the deep in you to appeal to the deep in him.[7]

Ultimately, however, Jesus' answer to this question does not lie in a few specific or general utterances on the subject. It is rooted in the very character of God. God and His will and way determine the whole character of His life, teaching, and ministry. That also leads to His self-giving death on the cross. This self-giving death is Jesus' ultimate answer to the problem of human conflict. The cross reveals the very heart of God and likewise His answer to man's violence and sin, namely, unwearied, outgoing, self-giving, saving, reconciling love.

[7] Cf. Psalm 42:7.

Bibliography

Abbott-Smith, G., *A Manual Greek Lexicon of the New Testament*, Scribners, 1922.
Abrahams, Israel, *Studies in Pharisaism and the Gospels*, Cambridge University Press. First Series, 1917; Second Series, 1924.
Albertz, Martin, *Die Synoptischen Streitgespraeche*, 1921.
Belden, Albert D., *Pax Christi*, Brethren Publishing House, 1947.
Branscomb, B. Harvie, *Jesus and the Law of Moses*, 1930.
———. *The Teachings of Jesus*, Abingdon-Cokesbury Press, 1931.
Bultmann, Rudolf, *Die Erforschung der Synoptischen Evangelium*, 1925.
———. *Jesus*, 1929.
Bundy, Walter E., *The Religion of Jesus*, 1928.
Burton. E. D., *New Testament Word Studies*, University of Chicago Press, 1927.
———. *A Source Book for the Study of the Teaching of Jesus in Its Historical Relationships*, 1923.
Butterfield, Herbert, *Christianity, Diplomacy and War*, Abingdon, 1953.
Cadbury, H. J., "Jesus and John the Baptist," *Jewish Quarterly Review* (Vol. 23), 1932-33.
Cadoux, C. J., *Early Christian Attitude to War*, 1919.
———. *The Guidance of Jesus for Today*, 1920.
———. *The Early Church and the World*, 1925.
Case, C. M., *Non-violent Coercion*, 1923.
Case, S. J., *Jesus, A New Biography*, 1927.
———. "Jesus and Sepphoris," *Journal of Biblical Literature* (Vol. XLV), 1926.
Charles, R. H., *The Apocrypha and Pseudepigrapha of the Old Testament in English*, Clarendon Press, Oxford (Vols. I, II), 1913.
———. *Religious Development Between the Old and the New Testaments*, Oxford, 1914.
———. *The Testaments of the Twelve Patriarchs*, Macmillan, 1908.
Deissmann, Adolf, *Bibelstudien*, 1895.
———. *Light from the Ancient East* (translated by L. R. M. Strachan), Harper, 1927.
Dibelius, Martin, *Das Soziale Motiv im Neuen Testament*, Berlin, Furche Verlag, 1933.
Dickey, Samuel, *The Constructive Revolution of Jesus*, 1923.
Easton, B. S., *Christ in the Gospels*, 1930.
———. *The Gospel According to Luke*, 1926.
Eisler, Robert, *The Messiah Jesus and John the Baptist* (translated by Alex. H. Krappe), 1931.
Fiebig, Paul, *Jesu Bergpredigt*, Goettingen, 1924.
Foakes-Jackson, F. J., *Josephus and the Jews*, Macmillan, 1930.
Foakes-Jackson, F. J., and Lake, Kirsopp, *The Beginnings of Christianity*, Macmillan (Vol. I), 1901.
Gesenius, Wilhelm, *Hebraeisches und Aramaeisches Handwoerterbuch ueber das Alte Testament* (16th ed.), 1915.

Glover, T. R., *The Jesus of History*, Harper, 1917.
Goguel, Maurice, *Life of Jesus* (translated by Olive Wyon), Macmillan, 1933.
Gore, Charles, *The Sermon on the Mount*, 1912.
Gould, E. P., *A Critical and Exegetical Commentary on the Gospel According to St. Mark*, International Critical Commentary, Scribners, 1907.
Gregg, Richard B., *The Power of Non-Violence*, Fellowship of Reconciliation, 1934.
Guignebert, Charles, *Jesus* (translated by S. H. Hooke), Knopf, 1935.
Harnack, Adolf, *Militia Christi*, 1905.
———. *The Sayings of Jesus* (translated by J. R. Wilkinson), 1908.
Hastings, James, *A Dictionary of the Bible*, Scribners, 1894-1904.
Herford, R. Travers, *The Pharisees*, 1926.
Hershberger, Guy F., *War, Peace, and Nonresistance*, Herald Press, 1944.
Holmes, John Haynes, *New Wars for Old*, 1916.
Hoyland, John S., *Simon the Zealot*, 1930.
Interpreter's Bible, The, Abingdon (Vols. VII, VIII).
Josephus, Flavius, *The Life and Works of Flavius Josephus* (translated by William Whiston). The contents consist of two sections: "Antiquities of the Jews" (XX parts) and "Wars of the Jews" (VII parts).
Kittell, Gerhard, *Die Probleme des Palaestinischen Spaetjudentums und das Urchristentum*, 1926.
Klausner, Joseph, *Jesus of Nazareth* Macmillan, (translated by Herbert Danby), Macmillan, 1929.
Krehbiel, H. P., *War, Peace, and Amity*, Newton Kans., 1937.
Lenski, R. C. H., *The Interpretation of St. Luke's Gospel*, Wartburg, 1946.
———. *The Interpretation of St. Matthew's Gospel*, Wartburg, 1943.
Liddell, L. H. and Scott, Robert, *Greek-English Lexicon*, Oxford, 1934.
Macgregor, G. H. C., *The New Testament Basis of Pacifism*, Fellowship of Reconciliation, 1936.
Manson, T. W., *The Teaching of Jesus*, Cambridge University Press, 1931.
Manson, William, *The Gospel of Luke*, London, 1930.
McNeile, A. H., *Gospel According to St. Matthew*, Macmillan, 1915.
Moffatt, James, *Love in the New Testament*, 1930.
Montefiore, Claude G., *Rabbinic Literature and the Gospel Teachings*, Macmillan, 1910.
———. *Some Elements of the Religion of Jesus According to the Synoptic Gospels*, 1910.
———. *The Synoptic Gospels* (Vols. I, II), 2d ed., 1929.
Moore, George Foot, *Judaism* (Vols. I, II), Harvard University Press, 1927-30.
Muste, A. J., *Rabbinic Literature and Gospel Teachings*, 1930.
———. *Not by Might*, Harper, 1947.
Oesterley, W. W. E., *The Book of Proverbs* (Westminster Commentary), London, 1929.
Page, Kirby, *The Sword or the Cross*, 1921.
———. *War, Its Causes, Consequences, and Cure*, 1923.
Peabody, Francis G., *Jesus Christ and the Social Question*, 1902.
Plummer, Alfred, *Commentary on the Gospel According to St. Matthew*, Scribners, 1909.
Preuschen, Erwin, *Griechisch-Deutsches Woerterbuch zu den Schriften des Neuen Testaments* (2d ed. by Walter Bauer), 1928.
Rall, H. F., *The Teachings of Jesus*, Abingdon-Cokesbury, 1918.

BIBLIOGRAPHY

Riddle, D. W., *Jesus and the Pharisees*, University of Chicago Press, 1928.
Robertson, A. T., *Grammar of the Greek New Testament in the Light of Historical Research*, Broadman.
Robinson, Benjamin W., *Sayings of Jesus*, 1930.
Robinson, N. L., *Christian Justice*, 1922.
Robinson, Theodore H., *The Gospel of Matthew*, Doubleday Doran, 1928.
Schechter, S., *Some Aspects of Rabbinic Theology*, Macmillan, 1930.
Schuerer, Emil, *Geschichte des Juedischen Volkes* (3d & 4th ed.), 1901.
Schweitzer, Albert, *The Quest of the Historical Jesus* (translated by W. Montgomery), 2d ed., Macmillan, 1911.
Scott, C. A. Anderson, *New Testament Ethics*, 1930.
Scott, E. F., *The Kingdom and the Messiah*, 1911.
———. *The Ethical Teaching of Jesus*, Macmillan, 1924.
———. *The Kingdom of God in the New Testament*, 1931.
Simkhovitch, V. G., *Toward the Understanding of Jesus*, Macmillan, 1925.
Stevens, G. B., *The Teaching of Jesus*, 1913.
———. *The Theology of the New Testament*, 1914.
Strack, H. L. and Billerbeck, Paul, *Kommentar zum Neuen Testament aus Talmud und Midrasch* (Vol. I), *Das Evangelium nach Matthaeus*, 1922.
Streeter, B. H., *The Four Gospels*, 1925.
Taylor, Charles, *Sayings of the Jewish Fathers*, 1897.
Tolstoi, Count Leo, *My Religion* (translated by Huntington Smith), 1885.
Torrey, Charles C., *The Four Gospels, A New Translation*, Harper, 1933.
Weinel, H., *Biblische Theologie des Neuen Testaments*, 1828.
Weiss, Johannes, *Predigt Jesu vom Reich Gottes*, 1900.
Wendt, H. H., *Der Inhalt der Lehre Jesu*, 1890. (Also English translation by J. Wilson, *The Teaching of Jesus*, 1892.)
Whiston, William, *The Works of Josephus* (Vols. I-III), 1893.
"Words of Christ Commonly Quoted for or Against War, The," Commission on the Church and Social Service of the Federal Council of Churches, 1929.